THIRD EDITION

PROGRAMMED PROOFREADING

H. FRANCES DANIELS
PROFESSOR
EAST CAROLINA UNIVERSITY

THADYS JOHNSON DEWAR
PROFESSOR EMERITUS
EAST CAROLINA UNIVERSITY

CAROL W. HENSON, Ed.D.
ASSISTANT PROFESSOR
CLAYTON STATE COLLEGE

POSTSECONDARY
MODEL CURRICULUM
FOR OFFICE CAREERS

ENDORSEMENT: THIS BOOK HAS BEEN REVIEWED AND AWARDED THE EXCLUSIVE ENDORSEMENT OF PROFESSIONAL SECRETARIES INTERNATIONAL FOR THE FUNDAMENTALS OF BUSINESS COMMUNICATIONS COURSE IN THE PSI POSTSECONDARY MODEL CURRICULUM FOR OFFICE CAREERS.

WC40CB
PUBLISHED BY
SOUTH-WESTERN PUBLISHING CO.
CINCINNATI, OH   DALLAS, TX   LIVERMORE, CA

Copyright © 1992

by SOUTH-WESTERN PUBLISHING CO.

Cincinnati, Ohio

ALL RIGHTS RESERVED

The text of this publication, or any part thereof, may not be reproduced or transmitted in any form or by any means, electronic or mechanical, including photocopying, recording, storage in an information retrieval system, or otherwise, without the prior written permission of the publisher.

ISBN: 0-538-70392-X

1 2 3 4 5 6 7 8 H 8 7 6 5 4 3 2 1

Printed in the United States of America

Library of Congress Cataloging-in-Publication Data

Daniels, H. Frances
    Programmed proofreading / H. Frances Daniels. Thadys Johnson Dewar, Carol W. Henson. -- 3rd ed.
      p. cm.
    ISBN 0-538-70392-X
    1. Proofreading--Self-instruction.   I. Dewar, Thadys Johnson.
II. Henson, Carol.   III. Title.
Z254.D35   1992
686.2'255--dc20   90-23313
                                                                       CIP

Acquisitions Editor: Randy R. Sims
Developmental Editor: Jane Phelan
Production Editor: Karen Roberts
Designer: Jim DeSollar
Marketing Manager: Shelly Battenfield

PREFACE

Business ranks communication skills high on the list of desirable qualities needed for success on the job. A person who is an effective communicator must possess good proofreading ability. *Programmed Proofreading*, Third Edition, provides business-related exercises that can improve proofreading ability for business or personal use. This text may be used in a traditional classroom setting, for one-on-one tutoring, or for individualized instruction.

Programmed Proofreading provides a comprehensive review of rules for effective written communication. Rules and proofreading exercises are presented in order of increasing difficulty, from simple keyboarding errors to errors in grammar, punctuation, format, and sentence construction. The final three chapters cover editing for errors in content, conciseness, and clarity.

SPECIAL FEATURES

Programmed Proofreading, Third Edition, offers the following special features:

1. Pretest and posttest for students to measure their achievement
2. Simple-to-complex approach to recognizing and correcting errors
3. Immediate reinforcement of learning
4. Realistic business-related practice exercises
5. Emphasis on using appropriate proofreading symbols
6. Application of frequently misspelled words
7. Tips to help develop effective proofreading skills
8. Computerized proofreading applications
9. Special aids in the Appendix

Each chapter concentrates on a specific type of error. Frequently misspelled words are applied in end-of-chapter exercises. Tips for strengthening proofreading skills also appear at the end of each chapter.

Four types of proofreading activities reinforce rules covered in each chapter:

1. Short proofreading exercises within the lesson frames immediately apply a rule or series of rules.
2. *Proofreading Applications*, consisting of four paragraphs or three mini-documents, apply all of the rules in the chapter.
3. *Progressive Proofreading*, consisting of three or four realistic business documents, apply the rules covered in the chapter and selected rules from previous chapters.
4. An optional *Computerized Proofreading* exercise provides practice in proofreading, editing, formatting, and printing documents prerecorded on a template disk.

NEW CHAPTERS

Three new chapters have been added to the third edition of *Programmed Proofreading*. Errors in abbreviation are now emphasized in a separate chapter, allowing two entire chapters to be devoted to keyboarding errors. Two chapters, on editing for conciseness and editing for clarity, provide opportunities to edit writing style. The new mini-documents and computerized proofreading exercises provide additional opportunities for proofreading realistic business documents.

TEMPLATE DISKS

Document files for the Computerized Applications are available for WordPerfect® and WordStar® programs. The template disks must be used in conjunction with these commercial word processing programs. Disks are available in either 5 1/4" or 3 1/2" for use with the IBM® Personal Computer, the Personal System/2®, and the Tandy® 1000.

MANUAL

The instructor's manual contains suggestions for evaluation, chapter quizzes, and five major tests.

WordPerfect is a registered trademark of WordPerfect Corporation.
WordStar is a registered trademark of WordStar International Corporation.
IBM and Personal System/2 are registered trademarks of International Business Machines Corporation.
Tandy 1000 is a registered trademark of Tandy Corporation.

Contents

	Preface	iii
	Pretest	1
1	Proofreading for Quality Control	3
2	Keyboarding Errors, Part 1	7
3	Keyboarding Errors, Part 2	19
4	Abbreviation Errors	33
5	Word Division Errors	47
6	Number Expression Errors	61
7	Format Errors	77
8	Grammar Errors: Subject and Verb Agreement	103
9	Grammar Errors: Pronoun Agreement and Selection	119
10	Errors in Confusing Words	133
11	Punctuation Errors, Part 1	149
12	Punctuation Errors, Part 2	163
13	Other Internal Punctuation Errors	179
14	Capitalization Errors	199
15	Editing for Content	215
16	Editing for Conciseness	227
17	Editing for Clarity	239
	Posttest	253
	Solutions	256
	Appendix	281

PRETEST

Proofread each of the following sentences for mechanical errors (spelling, abbreviation, word division, number expression, grammar, punctuation, capitalization), content errors, conciseness, and clarity. Write in your corrections. Sentences often contain more than one correction. Indicate a correct sentence by writing C after it. Each sentence is worth two points. Solutions to the Pretest are on page 257.

1. While waiting for the plane, my baggage was stolen.
2. Everyone except Barry Johnson and he joined the organization.
3. The governor of Georgia traveled to Europe to seek industry for the state.
4. 15 class members participated in the rally; thats more than one half of the class.
5. The clerk was insistant that those 3 sweaters I bought during the Fall sale could not be returned for any reason.
6. I would like to hire Susan Jackson, who all ready has had three year's experience.
7. If you move to Washington, please give me a call.
8. The board voted it's approval of the preformance of the company's officers.
9. Neither Enjou nor Tai are enrolled in Accounting 411, a graduation requirement.
10. I plan to take a cruise before the cruise company's special expires; however, circumstances prevent my going at this time.
11. Janice assured me that the idea to go rafting was her's.
12. The administrative assistant, as well as the office manager, is attending the time management seminar.
13. The State of Florida is also known as the Sunshine State.
14. Frank and Doris's car cost $20,000, and they obtained a loan with 7.5% interest.
15. In Chapter 4, page 14, the following rule appears—Do not divide a word containing 5 or fewer letters.
16. A number of responses has been recieved from the Febuary 5th mailing.
17. The employment survey which traced thirty three types of information in secretarial ads, revealed several key findings.
18. On June 1, 19-- I will travel to Hawaii to spend a three-week vacation.
19. You should select a paralegal program created, taught and graded by experienced attorneys.
20. Sam, Julie, and Bob has gone to the hardware store to get five gals. of paint.
21. Installing a computer in our records management department, will increase its efficiency.
22. The sign read, "Keep the Place Neat," but children's toys were scattered everywhere.
23. Of all the communication books you sent me, there was only one I liked—*Improving Business Writing*.

24. Here is the brochure and the check that was omitted from your letter.
25. Ham and eggs is a traditional breakfast dish in the South.
26. Isn't this where your twin brother, Don, lives?
27. Molly, I found three quarters, one dime, and twelve pennies—a total of 92 cents.
28. A County prosecutor appeared in a case before the California supreme court.
29. The news bullentin reported that Gen. Arnold's plane would arrive at Kennedy International Airport at 10:15 a.m.
30. There will, of course, be a charge for maintainance after the warranty expires.
31. She is a legal secretary in a Chicago law firm, and wants to join a professional association.
32. If you enjoy running check with your local runner's association about referral services in other cities.
33. Andy exclaimed, "Stop. The drawbridge is open!
34. The spelling test included these words: similar, accomodate, decision, and proceedure.
35. The old, dilapidated house will be replaced by a lovely two-story house.
36. The word "telecommuting" has now become a part of the office worker's everyday vocabulary and should be a familar term to all involved in the business world.
37. Before the consultant arrives find out why shes coming.
38. Interior folders come in the same colors as hanging folders, but there just a bit shorter.
39. Today's manager has to juggle dozen's of tasks.
40. A Mid-August survey revealed that many Americans declared French fries to be they're favorite food.
41. The travel agent said, "Your final payment for the November 1 cruise is due on October 1, which is sixty days before departure."
42. In Math 465, 49 percent of the class fialed the final exam.
43. Answering the telephone and filing is considered a routine office task.
44. Ms. Dorene Randal, a Yale alumnus, received her m.a. from Duke university and was recommmended for a doctoral fellowship by Dr. D. R. Brandon.
45. If your voice tends to drop as you utter the expression, then the expression is nonessential, if your voice tends to rise, the expression is essential.
46. Andy's job was to supervise a force of 6 salespeople in the southwest.
47. Scanning her schedule once more, Abilene decided to eat lunch at her desk.
48. We work for a small ten employees, relatively new advertising agency.
49. My guess is that all of you—president and creative professionals alike are younger than your counterparts at Franklin and Associates.
50. The immediate task for mangers is to get family issues on the company agenda.

CHAPTER 1

PROOFREADING FOR QUALITY CONTROL

Objectives: *After completing this chapter, you should be able to*
- Define proofreading and editing.
- Understand the importance of proofreading.
- Explain the various methods of proofreading.
- Understand how to use this textbook.

WHAT IS PROOFREADING?

Proofreading is the art of finding and correcting errors in written communication. Proofreading demands concentration, patience, and attention to detail. It requires reading the document for the deliberate purpose of finding errors. The proofreader may be the originator, a keyboarding specialist, a secretary, an administrative assistant, or a person designated as a proofreader.

Proofreaders use special symbols called **proofreaders' marks** to highlight errors. Because proofreaders' marks both identify the error and indicate how it should be corrected, they should be used by everyone who works with the printed document. Proofreaders' marks save the originator the time of writing lengthy instructions, and they enable anyone who is processing the document (keying or proofing it) to recognize the correction immediately.

To become proficient in proofreading, you must be able to recognize errors in mechanics, format, and content. To assure that the document is easy to read, you must also be sure that the message is concise and clear.

Proofreading for mechanical errors requires diligence in locating keyboarding errors and skill in recognizing errors in spelling, abbreviations, grammar, capitalization, punctuation, number expression, and word usage.

Document format influences the overall appearance of the document. The format should be attractive and easy to follow. Margins, spacing, and placement of document parts affect format.

Content errors occur in facts and meaning. When proofreading for content, you must ask yourself, "Does this copy make sense? Do I understand the message?" Sentence structure, word choice, and punctuation all affect the meaning. Checking addresses, dates, and figures is part of proofreading for content.

In addition to being correct, an effective message should be concise and easy to understand. **Editing** is the process of locating clichés, overused words and expressions, use of passive voice, and redundant phrases that cause the message to be wordy or unclear. Editing involves changing words or sentences or even rewriting a passage.

IMPORTANCE OF PROOFREADING AND EDITING

Proofreading and editing are extremely important to anyone whose daily activities involve working with written communication. Students, managers, professional persons, executives, and office support persons all strive for excellence in their communication. Why? Because a written message represents the person or firm who sends it. The sender will be judged as being either intelligent and competent or careless and uneducated. A document that is easy to understand, attractive, and correct creates a good impression.

Conversely, carelessness can cause a firm's reputation to suffer. The following apology appeared in a daily newspaper: "We very much regret our error in yesterday's edition in which we most unfortunately referred to the defective branch of the police force. We meant, of course, the detective branch of the police farce." Carelessness that causes a decision to be based on inaccurate figures can have far-reaching effects on any business. For example, in one instance a board of directors meeting had to be canceled when the chairperson noticed a typographical error in the financial report the board was to discuss.

Today's computers, as well as high-speed laser printers and telecommunication devices, have made creating, producing, and transmitting information easier and faster than ever before. Salespersons transmit information from the field, professionals create and combine words, and managers forward drafts to support persons for polishing or rearranging. If this information is to have value, it must be correct.

Although the originator (creator) of the message has the ultimate responsibility for the correctness of the document, in reality this responsibility is shared. Originators are responsible for the document's content. Keyboarders and proofreaders strive to perfect the mechanics and appearance. Alert proofreaders often detect errors in content as well.

PROOFREADING TECHNIQUES

Proofreading a document usually takes less time than rekeying it. Therefore, take the time to become a good proofreader.

To achieve a high degree of accuracy, a good proofreader will read the copy at least twice—once for mechanical errors and once for content and format errors. If the document contains statistical information, amounts of money, or technical terms, you may need to proofread it a third time. Likewise, if the document has several pages with different headings, proofread it once just for format.

Use the following methods of proofreading to improve your proofreading skill.

Comparative Proofreading

Comparative proofreading involves comparing the final document to the original document to be sure that the information has been keyed correctly and that copy has not been omitted. This method is especially important when proofreading statistical copy or tables. To use the comparative method, place a printed copy of the final document next to the original document and compare word for word and line for line. Use a card or your index finger to point to each word.

Team Proofreading

If the copy to be proofread is long, complicated, or especially important, the team method is an effective way of proofreading. Using this method, one person reads from the original copy and the other person checks the final copy. Because the time of two persons is involved, team proofreading is a more costly method.

Computer Screen Proofreading

Proofreading from a computer screen is especially demanding. Follow these tips to assure accuracy.

1. Use the spell checker if it is available to check for misspelled words or keyboarding errors. A spell checker compares each word in the document to its dictionary. Words that do not match the dictionary are highlighted in some way. Although a spell checker will highlight spelling errors such as *thier* or *accomodate*, it will not recognize errors in usage such as *there advise* (their advice). Be sure that the cursor is at the beginning of the document when you use the spell checker.

2. Proofread the document on the screen for errors that the spell checker will not detect: incorrect words (*as* for *is*), omitted words, or words used incorrectly. Check especially for extra words that may not have been deleted when text was edited.

3. Check line endings for large gaps or for words that have been incorrectly divided. Words are frequently divided in odd places if the automatic hyphenation feature was on when the document was keyed (explained in Chapter 5).

4. Print the document.

5. Proofread the printed copy in the usual manner.

6. If you find additional errors, revise the document and reprint it.

USE OF THIS SELF-INSTRUCTIONAL TEXT

You will develop proofreading skill more rapidly and productively if you complete each chapter in proper sequence, working each exercise and verifying your answer before proceeding.

Beginning with Chapter 2, various rules are reviewed within frames, each of which is numbered. Follow these steps to complete each frame:

1. Place a piece of paper over the page so only the first frame is exposed.
2. Read the rule and complete each exercise.
3. Slide the piece of paper down, and compare your answer with the correct response given in the right-hand column.
4. If your response is correct, continue with the next frame. If your response is incorrect, reread the frame to determine where you made a mistake.

In addition to numbered frames, each chapter contains a list of approximately ten spelling words taken from the Frequently Misspelled Words list that appears in the Appendix. To help you master these words, they will appear in the end-of-chapter activities and in subsequent end-of-chapter activities.

Strengthen your proofreading skills by reviewing the Proofreading Tips section in each chapter. These tips are summarized in the Appendix.

End-of-chapter activities will enable you to check understanding of the rules covered in various ways:

- *Proofreading Applications* provides short exercises that apply the rules within the chapter.
- *Progressive Proofreading* consists of several documents that apply the rules in the chapter as well as others from previous chapters.
- *Computerized Proofreading* is designed for computer users who are using the template disk that accompanies this text. (See your instructor.) Using your computer, you will retrieve a document from the template and then proofread, format, and edit one document for each chapter. Instructions will be given within each chapter.

PROOFREADING TIPS

1. Develop a critical attitude toward all written communication.
2. Develop your ability to spell. Use a dictionary whenever you are unsure of the spelling of a word. Review the list of frequently misspelled words given in the Appendix.
3. Be familiar with the principles of word division, capitalization, and number expression.
4. Review the principles of punctuation and grammar.
5. Proofread the copy after it is cold—come back to the document after you have worked on something else for a while.
6. Always practice proofreading for meaning.

Remember, proofreading, like keyboarding, requires concentration and practice.

CHAPTER 2

KEYBOARDING ERRORS, PART 1

Objectives: *After completing this chapter, you should be able to*
- ▶ Recognize keyboarding errors such as omissions, additions, or misstrokes.
- ▶ Use the appropriate proofreading symbols to indicate changes in text.
- ▶ Spell correctly a list of commonly misspelled words.

OMISSIONS, ADDITIONS, AND MISSTROKES

Every word in the English language can be distorted by a keyboarding error, or typo. A typo results when a keyboard operator sees the correct form in the copy but keys it incorrectly. A misspelled word in the original copy is not a typo. Regardless of whether errors are caused by keyboarding or spelling, it is the proofreader's responsibility to find the errors.

Keyboarding errors are usually one-letter or one-digit errors. They are often in the form of omissions, additions, or misstrokes. Entire words or sentences may also be omitted, added, or replaced. Chapter 2 will give you practice in identifying each of these types of errors.

2-1   A letter, character, or space left out of a word is an omission. Use these proofreading symbols to mark errors of omission:

    ∧   Insert copy.   Ms. Shackleford is late for the me͜eting.

    #   Insert space.   Joel and Katie talked to/Mickey Mouse at the fair.

Use the appropriate proofreading symbols to mark errors of omission in the following paragraph:

Proofreading is one of the most valuble skills you can aquire. Like keyboarding, however,proofreading requires patience and practice. It also requires intense concentration, attentin to detail, and mastery of Enlish skills.

7

2-2 Entire words or sentences may not be keyed. These, too, are omissions.

2-3 Errors of omission frequently involve single letters or closing parentheses or closing quotation marks. In order to locate such omissions, read each symbol or word carefully. Note the difference the omission of one letter makes in these words:

bridge, bride
debit, debt
exist, exit
them, then, they, the
your, you

 Use the appropriate proofreading symbols to mark errors of omission in the following paragraph:

After much discussion, the committee members approved the followin slogan for the new Keeter-Harris Grocery Store: When the slogan was presented the board members, the majority indicated strong approval. The new billboard will carry the new slogan along wit an appropriate ilustration.

2-4 Adding extra letters, digits, words, or spaces in text is another common keyboarding error. An extra letter may result in a word that *looks* correct but is not. Give special attention to such words as

country   county
envelope   envelop
interstate   intestate

Also check for words, phrases, or lines that may have been repeated when the text was keyed.
Use the following proofreading symbols to mark errors of addition:

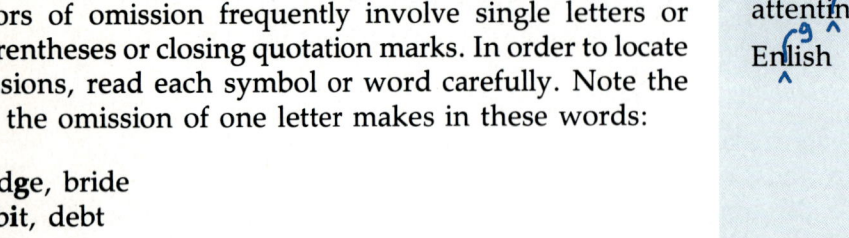

⌒   Close up the space.   I can̑ not go to school today.

⋠   Delete copy.   There are two er̸r̸ors in ~~this~~ this sentence.

2-1

val*a*uble
*c*aquire
however*#*proofreading
attentí*o*n
En*g*lish

2-2, 2-3

followin**g**
Slogan was omitted.
presented **to** the
wit**h**
illustration

8   Chapter 2—Keyboarding Errors, Part 1

Use the appropriate proofreading symbols to mark errors of addition in the following paragraph:

With the advent of the computer, the task of changing and correctting copy has become much easier, but the responsibility for prooofreading copy accurately has be come much more important. So ;many far-reaching decisions are made on the bassis of written communication. Dire consequences can result if the informration on which a decision is made is inaccurate.

2-5 Another common error is keying incorrectly, or making a misstroke. Careful proofreading is required in order to find misstrokes in short words such as those listed below:

of, on, or
not, now
than, that, then

Use the symbol below for marking misstrokes:

/   Change copy as shown.   The applicant's perseverence paid off.

 Use the appropriate proofreading symbols for marking errors in the paragraph below:

It iw very inefficient to print a document and then decide to proofread if carefully. When errors are discovered at this stage, the work processing specialist must recall the document to the screen, scroll to the proper line and space, correct the error, and them reprint the document. Time and supplies have been wasted.

SPELLING REVIEW

Spelling—it's basic; for the proofreader, it's critical. If you have trouble spelling, remember these tips:

1. Develop the *habit* of always spelling correctly.
2. Check a dictionary whenever you are not positive a word is spelled correctly.
3. Pronounce words slowly to be sure you are not missing any syllables (it's *mathematics*, not *mathmatics*.)

Chapter 2—Keyboarding Errors, Part 1

Refer to the list of frequently misspelled words in the Appendix, page 281, as necessary. Approximately ten words for you to master from this list will be given at the end of each chapter. The words in the list below are frequently misspelled as a result of omissions, deletions, or misstrokes. Watch for them in the exercises that follow and in succeeding chapters.

accommodate	consensus
analyze	familiar
brochure	integral
changeable	knowledgeable
commitment	persuade
congratulations	procedure

PROOFREADING TIPS

Suggestions for strengthening your proofreading skills will be included at the end of each chapter. Study these tips and apply them as you proofread. Check closely for the following kinds of keyboarding errors:

1. Omission of letters in long words
2. Repetition of short words, such as *the*, *and*, *you*, and *if*, at the beginning of a line
3. Omission of closing parentheses, brackets, or quotation marks
4. Omission of words in titles and headings
5. Addition of characters, words, or spaces
6. Addition of phrases or repetition of sentences

Proofreading Applications

Proofread the following exercises for keyboarding and spelling errors. To aid you, the number of errors is indicated in parentheses at the end of Exercises P-1 and P-2. You must find the errors on your own in Exercise P-3.

P-1 Is the ability to sell a knack that one is born with, or is it a skill that is learned as a result as a result of committment and practice? Steven Taback, president of T. E. M. Associates, says, "Selling is basically a series of strategies that turn leads in to prospects and prospects into customers. That may sound easy, but selling effectively is a matter of learning these strategies and than having the confidence to put them to use. (5 errors)

P-2 People are persuaded to buy a product becuse they feel a real or perceived need for it. This need is often linked to achievement, recognition, or money. To persade, therefore, the seller must anlyze the buyer to become knowledgeable or familar with person's primary need. For example, is the person concerned about prestige, comfort, convenience, or savings? Having identified the buyer's primary need, the seller can convert the features of the product into benefits. (5 errors)

P-1
1. **as a result**
2. commitment
3. leads into
4. and then
5. use."

P-3 Proofread the printed memo by comparing it to the original handwritten copy. Assume that the handwritten copy is correct.

TO: Nursing Staff
FROM: Ann Barnes, Superviser
DATE: January 6, 19--
SUBJECT: Managing Stress Lecture

The third lecture in our Fitness, Health, and Nutrition series will be held on Tuesday, Febuary 14, at 2 pm. Dr. Donald B. Fowlkes will be the speaker. The subject of his lecture will Manageing Stress. Dr. Fowles will include a question-and-answer session at the end of his his discussion.

Memo to the Nursing Staff, Jan. 6
The third lecture in our Fitness, Health, and Nutrition series will be held on Tuesday, February 14, at 2 p.m. Dr. Donald B. Fowlkes will be the speaker. The subject of his lecture will be Managing Stress. Dr. Fowlkes will include a question-and-answer session at the end of his discussion.
    Anne Barnes, Supervisor

P-2
1. because
2. persuade
3. analyze
4. familiar
5. **the** person's

P-3
1. Anne
2. Supervisor
3. February 14,
4. 2 p.m.
5. lecture will **be**
6. Mana**gi**ng Stress
7. Dr. Fowlkes
8. **his** discussion

PROGRESSIVE PROOFREADING

Job 1 Use the appropriate proofreading symbols to mark errors of omission, addition, or misstroke in the following letter.

 **Minneapolis Financial Corp.**
928 Irving Avenue S
Minneapolis, MN 55403-7640
(612) 555-5521

January 16, 19--

Dear Friend and Insured Member

We heard quite lot about "outpatient" surgery from members while attending the Kappa Phi regional meetings this summer. What we learned was that members want coverage for <u>outpatient</u> serviceces just as much as, if not more than,for hospitalizations!

Outpatient Surgery Covered

So, here you are. A Surgical Plan than pays for outpatient surgery as well as for surgeries performed in the hospital. Simple proceedures are covered as well as as complicated ones. You need not undergo major surgery in order to realize beneffits from this plan.

Pays ;Up to $2,000 for Each Surgical Procedure

After you've had surgery, you will receive a check for a specified amount--regardless of the actual cost of the operation! Easy, quick claim-payment procedures help keep costs down and premiums low.

The enclosed broshure provides information that will help you analize the benefits of this plan. Please fill out and mail the Surgical Assistance Enrollment Form a long with you check today. As soon as we receive your Enrollment Form and check, we will mail your Certificate, ID Card, and Claim Form by return mail.

Sincerely

Maurice Fulghum

fb

Enclosure

Job 2 In an effort to update our records, Minneapolis Financial Corp. sent an information sheet to each of our clients requesting certain information. Feedback from six clients has been entered into the computer. Proofread the information on the screen by comparing it to the information sheets.

```
Blackwood, D. D. {Mr.}              Quinton, Elbert
100 Pope Street                     306 Mill Road
Boykkins, VA  23827-1460            Jacksonville, NC  28540-4010
322-45-6601                         246-81-6621
Mechanic                            Attorney
Esther Blackwood                    Cletis Quinton

Butler, Ralph                       Sheppard, Paige {Ms.}
154 Anderson Avenue                 209 Gum Road
Merry Hill, N.C.  27957-3641        Raleigh, NC  27605-9142
238-88-6624                         233-44-2212
Teacher                             Computer Programmer
Kay Tice                            Mary Sheppard

Cox, James                          Wallace, Michael
116 Catawba Road                    201 Berkeley Street
Nashville, NC  27856-1468           Suffolk, VA  23444-2100
266-88-8811                         201-33-3444
Former                              Veterinarian
None                                Susan Wallace
```

Name **Mr. D. P. Blackwood**
Address **100 Pope Street**
City **Boykins**   State **VA**   Zip **23827-1460**
Social Security Number **322-45-6601**
Occupation **Mechanic**
Beneficiary **Esther Blackwood**

Name **Ralph Butler**
Address **154 Anderson Avenue**
City **Merry Hill**   State **NC**   Zip **27957-3641**
Social Security Number **238-88-6624**
Occupation **Teacher**
Beneficiary **Kay Tice**

```
Name      James Cox
Address   116 Catawba Road
City      Nashville              State NC  Zip 27856-1468
Social Security Number  266-89-8811
Occupation  Farmer
Beneficiary  None
```

```
Name      Elbert Quinton
Address   306 Mill Road
City      Jacksonville           State NC  Zip 28540-4010
Social Security Number  246-81-6621
Occupation  Attorney
Beneficiary  Cletis Quinton
```

```
Name      Ms. Paige Sheppard
Address   209 Gum Road
City      Raleigh                State NC  Zip 27605-9142
Social Security Number  233-44-2212
Occupation  Computer Programmer
Beneficiary  Mary Sheppard
```

```
Name      Michael Wallace
Address   201 Berkley Street
City      Suffolk                State VA  Zip 23434-2100
Social Security Number  201-33-4444
Occupation  Veterinarian
Beneficiary  Susan Wallace
```

Chapter 2—Keyboarding Errors, Part 1

Job 3 Use the appropriate proofreading symbols to mark errors of omission, addition, or misstroke in the following memo.

INTEROFFICE MEMORANDUM

TO: Judy Forrest, Medical Group Manager

FROM: Leo Thomas, Regional Sales Manager

DATE: January 16, 19--

SUBJECT: Kappa Phi Outpatient Surgery Campaign

Congradulations on a job well done in in organizing the Outpatient Surgery Campaign for the Kappa Phi educational group. As you know, sales have exceeded our goal by 21 percent.

The concensus among the membersof Kappa Phi was that this insurance plan met the needs of the group, made up primarily if women. Many of the members were not familier with our organization before you introduced this plan. Now we find that they are interested in other types of insurance, including life and automobile.

I look foward to recognizing individual members of you team at the annual awards banquet. Their efforts have been an integral part of our success.

fb

COMPUTERIZED PROOFREADING

Job 4 Proofread and Edit Letter

1. Load the file C2JOB4 from the template.

2. Proofread the letter on the template, making all corrections. Use the spell checker if it is available. Check the letter address to be sure that it agrees with the address card shown below.

```
Abernathy Lucas Mr

Mr. Lucas Abernathy
911 St. Andrews Drive
Fredericksburg, VA   22401-9110
```

3. Format the letter using block style. See page 84. Use 1" side margins, and begin the date on line 14. Save the letter as C2JOB4R.

4. Print the letter.

5. Proofread the printed document. If you find additional mistakes, revise, save, and reprint the letter.

CHAPTER 3

KEYBOARDING ERRORS, PART 2

Objectives: *After completing this chapter, you should be able to*
- ▶ Identify errors in enumerations.
- ▶ Identify transposition errors.
- ▶ Use the appropriate proofreading symbols to indicate changes in text.
- ▶ Spell correctly a list of commonly misspelled words.

ERRORS IN FIGURES, ENUMERATIONS, AND TABLES

Accuracy of figures is extremely important because important decisions are frequently based on figures. Amounts of money, dates, percentages, social security numbers, and telephone numbers are just a few examples of important numbers. Errors in such numbers could result in serious consequences.

Never assume that a number is correct. Always check the original document to be sure that a number has been copied correctly. Verify extensions and totals. Proofread numbers digit by digit.

3-1 When proofreading copy containing figures, always compare the printed copy digit by digit to the original copy or the source document.

Mark any errors in the printed list by comparing it to the correct handwritten copy.

```
① Invoice 3478      $28.20
② Invoice 3693      $363.20
③ Invoice 3649      $82.02
④ Invoice 3700      $19.20
```

Invoices unpaid as of April 30:
1. Invoice 3478 $28.20
2. Invoice 3693 $363.20
3. Invoice 3695 $82.20
4. Invoice 3900 $19.10

3-2 Errors frequently occur in the sequence of enumerations (listed items), especially when items are added to or deleted from the list or the list is rearranged. Check to be sure enumerated items are in the correct sequence.

 Use the appropriate proofreading symbols to mark any errors in the following paragraph:

The oldest federal constitution in existence was framed in Philadelphia in May 1787 by a convention of delegates from 12 of the 13 original states. (Rhode Island failed to send a delegate.) The states ratified the constitution in the following order:

1. Delaware — December 7, 1787
2. New Jersey — December 18, 1787
3. Pennsylvania — December 12, 1787
4. Georgia — January 2, 1788
5. Connecticut — January 9, 1788
5. Massachusetts — February 6, 1788
6. Maryland — April 28, 1788

TRANSPOSITION ERRORS

One of the most common keyboarding errors is the transposition error. Letters, numbers, words, or sentences keyed in the wrong sequence are called transpositions. Use the following symbol to mark transposition errors:

∽ Transpose letters, numbers, or words.

These letters must be transpsoed.

The speaker began to rapidly talk.

3-3 Short words (*hte*), word endings (*medcial*), and vowels (*thier*) are especially susceptible to transposition. Transpositions can be difficult to detect when proofreading, since a transposition

---

3-1

3. Invoice 3649 $82.02
4. Invoice 3700 $19.20

3-2

2. Pennsylvania
3. New Jersey
6. Massachusetts
7. Maryland

2. December 12, 1787
3. December 18, 1787

error can result in a word that is familiar but does not make sense when used in place of the original term. Can you locate the error in each of these sentences?

Geometry is the study of points, lines, angels, surfaces, and solids.

Larry received a letter form Fujio.

Karate, judo, and jujitsu are examples of marital arts.

 Proofread the following paragraph for transposition errors. Use the symbol given above to mark your corrections.

Continued use of electronic workstations can induce eyestrain, stress, and mucsular pain. Consideration must be to given purchasing adjustable furnitrue and to providing workstations with movable keyboards and adjustable displays. Employee productivity, health, nad job satisfaction are at stake.

ROUGH DRAFT APPLICATIONS

The originator may use certain proofreading symbols to revise text. Keyboard operators should learn to recognize and understand the following symbols in order to key and proofread text accurately.

Symbol	Meaning	Example
♂	Move copy as indicated.	Paul designed the new office with several ergonomic features in Kenwood Plaza.
stet or	Ignore correction; let it stand.	$15 for the preparation of 100 letters
—	Change copy as indicated.	advance notice *before* prior to the public sale.

3-4 Note the use of these symbols in the following paragraph and the manner in which the revisions were made in the second paragraph.

3-3

angles
from
martial

mucsular pain
be to given
furnitrue
nad job

Chapter 3—Keyboarding Errors, Part 2

21

Correspondence can be expensive ~~even without counting the originator's time~~ *stet*. Fast Copy Service charged us $15 for the preparation of 100 letters and envelopes. Additionally, a part-time employee was paid $3 an hour for folding the letters and stuffing the envelopes. They charged us $16.25 for the stationery and the envelopes. By the time we had paid $22 for postage, ~~one~~ *this* mailing had cost us $56.25.

Correspondence can be expensive even without counting the originator's time. Fast Copy Service charged us $15 for the preparation of 100 letters and envelopes. They charged us $16.25 for the stationery and the envelopes. Additionally, a part-time employee was paid $3 an hour for folding the letters and stuffing the envelopes. By the time we had paid $22 for postage, this mailing had cost us $56.25.

 Did the typist make all the necessary changes? _____

SPELLING REVIEW

3-4

To improve your ability to detect spelling errors, master the words below. Watch for them in the exercises that follow and in succeeding chapters.

Yes

believe	environment
committee	February
decision	guarantee
definitely	maintenance
eligible	ninety

PROOFREADING TIPS

Study these tips and apply them as you proofread:
1. Watch for repetition of numbers or letters in a list.
2. Watch for omission of numbers or letters in a list.

22   Chapter 3—Keyboarding Errors, Part 2

3. When proofreading the work of others, do not assume the original draft is error free. Originators often concentrate more on the content of the document than they do on its mechanics.

4. Compare the final copy word for word with the draft copy and note any differences. Often a word or phrase may be deleted unintentionally as the final copy is keyed.

PROOFREADING APPLICATIONS

P-1 Proofread the purchase order by comparing it to the partial price list. Verify all prices on the order, the total, and the following information: To **SUPERIOR ELECTRONICS INC, 411 MAIN STREET, WASHINGTON DC 20007-9800**; Date **3/31/**—; Purchase Order No. **4PS285710**; Terms **2/10, n/30**; Shipped Via **CNC Lines**; Date Shipped **3/31/**—.

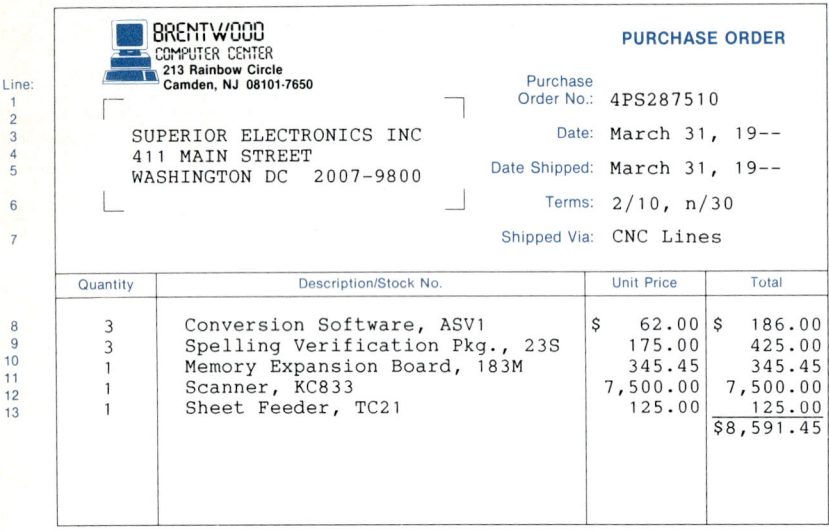

P-2 Proofread the printed Schedule of Accounts Receivable by comparing it to the computer printout. Assume the printout is correct.

```
                        THE FLOWER BASKET
                   Schedule of Accounts Recievable
                           March 31, 19--
    ─────────────────────────────────────────────────────────────
    Jo Ann Brown . . . . . . . . . . . . . . . . . . $    75.80
    Carrie Corey . . . . . . . . . . . . . . . . . .     125.30
    Mabel Fox   . . . . . . . . . . . . . . . . . .       26.50
    Louis Gurganus . . . . . . . . . . . . . . . . .      25.00
    Genevra Holden . . . . . . . . . . . . . . . . .      97.85
    Sam Johnson  . . . . . . . . . . . . . . . . . .     110.18
    Sid Kinsington . . . . . . . . . . . . . . . . .      32.50
    Alice Longmeadow . . . . . . . . . . . . . . . .      31.00
    Norris Noble . . . . . . . . . . . . . . . . . .     250.00
    Paulette Pullen  . . . . . . . . . . . . . . . .     495.00
    Ferell Quixote . . . . . . . . . . . . . . . . .     320.00
                                                       ─────────
    Total Accounts Receivable . . . . . . . . . . . $  1,625.93
                                                       =========
```

```
RUN DATE 03/31                       FLOWER BASKET
                        SCHEDULE OF ACCOUNTS RECEIVABLE
    ─────────────────────────────────────────────────────────────
    CUSTOMER              CUSTOMER
    NUMBER                NAME                AMOUNT

    1101                  BROWN, JO ANN        75.80
    1105                  COREY, CARRIE       125.30
    1200                  FOX, MABEL           62.50
    1201                  GURGANUS, LOIS       25.00
    1210                  HOLDEN, GENEVA       97.85
    1215                  JOHNSON, SAM        110.08
    1216                  KINSINGTON, SID      32.50
    1217                  LONGMEADOW, ALICE    31.00
    1305                  NOBL, NORRIS        250.00
    1400                  PULLEN, PAULETTE    495.00
    1410                  QUIXOTE, FERRELL    320.00
                                            ────────
                          TOTAL              1,625.93
                                             ========
```

P-1

1. 4PS285710
4. 20007-9800
8. ASC1
9. 525.00
10. 345.65   345.65
11. KC830
12. Sheetfeeder
13. $8,681.65

P-2

Mabel Fox   **62.50**
Lois Gurganus
Geneva Holden
Sam Johnson   **110.08**
Norris **Nobl**
Ferrell Quixote

Chapter 3—Keyboarding Errors, Part 2

Progressive Proofreading

As a proofreader for CP Word Processing Services, you must proofread a variety of documents. Carefully check the following items by comparing them to the original documents.

Job 1 Proofread the file cards on the following page by comparing them to the information contained in the printout below. Using the appropriate proofreading symbols, mark any errors you find on the cards. Check the social security numbers and the telephone numbers carefully.

NAME/SOCIAL SECURITY	STREET ADDRESS	CITY, STATE, ZIP	TELEPHONE
MRS DOROTHY BRANDON 255-58-6624	102 FLETCHER PLACE	GREENVILLE NC 27834-5645	919-756-3465
MS GRACE L MORAN 277-76-8283	106 BRINKLEY ROAD	DRY FORKS VA 24549-5492	703-766-2131
MISS BRENDA D ACEVEZ 245-34-5868	PO BOX 3066	DAVENPORT VA 24239-4392	703-311-4565
MR JERRIE BIDDINGER 246-66-7790	308 CIRCLE DRIVE	CRYSTAL HILL VA 24539-4308	703-456-8121
MR JOHN C ASLAKSON 266-87-9963	93 QUAIL RIDGE DRIVE	BRISTOL VA 24201-4019	703-222-9564
MR PAT STALLINGS 244-76-8888	PO BOX 1901	PINETOPS NC 27864-0381	919-674-9111
MR HENRY STINDT 258-68-8987	ROUTE 2 BOX 301	FRANKLIN VA 23851-7787	804-330-4565

Chapter 3—Keyboarding Errors, Part 2

```
Stindt Henry Mr


Mr. Henry Stindt
Route 2, Box 301
Franklin, VA  23851-7787
Tel. 804-3304565

(258-68-8987
```

```
Stallings Pat Mr


Mr. Pat Stallings
P.O. Box 1901
Pinetops, NC  27864-0381
Tel.919-674-9111

(224-76-8888)
```

```
Moran Grace L Ms


Ms. Grace L. Moran
106 Brinkly Road
Dry Forks, VA  24549-5492
Tel. 703-766-2131

(277-76-8823)
```

```
Brandon Dorothy Mrs


Mrs. Dorothy Brandon
102 Fletcher Place
Greeneville, NC  27834-5645
Tel. 919-756-3465

(255-58-6624)
```

```
Biddinger Jerrie Mr


Mr. Jerrie Biddinger
308 Circle Drive
Crystal Hill, VA  24539-4308
Tel. 703-456-8121)

(246-7790)
```

```
Aslakson John C Mr


Mr. John C. Aslakson
93 Quail Ridge Drive
Bristol, VA  24211-4019
Tel. 703-222-9564

(266-87-9963)
```

```
Acevez Brenda D Miss


Miss Brenda D. Acevez
P.O. Box 3066
Davenport, VA  24239-4392
Tel. 703-311-4565

(245-34-5868)
```

Chapter 3—Keyboarding Errors, Part 2

Job 2 The following form letter is to be sent to delinquent customers of Woody's Computer Service. Proofread the three completed letters by comparing them to the form letter, COLLECTION, and the variables list.

```
Document Name: COLLECTION

Current Date


    1
_____

Dear   2   :

Have you overlooked your   3   payment on your account,   2  ?
Your last payment of   4   for the   5   that you  purchased was
made over a month ago.  Please put a check in the mail to us by
   6  .  We believe you want to continue to be eligible for
credit.

If you have any questions about your account, please call    7
at 919-331-4211.

                                     Sincerely,
```

Variables List

FORM LETTER	Collection
1	Mrs. Abbie Nelson
	16 Sandcastle Drive
	Tallahassee, FL 32308-9000
2	Mrs. Nelson
3	February
4	$75
5	computer
6	April 15
7	Rosa

FORM LETTER	Collection
1	Dr. Lawrence Mayo
	673 Anderson Drive
	Rochester, NY 14626-8765
2	Dr. Mayo
3	February
4	$92
5	printer
6	April 15
7	Mary

FORM LETTER	Collection
1	Mr. James Holden
	200 Tenth Street
	Jacksonville, FL 32333-4182
2	Mr. Holden
3	February
4	$57
5	software
6	April 15
7	Mary

April 1, 19--

Mrs. Abbie Nelson
16 Sandcastle Drive
Talahassee, FL 32308-9000

Dear Mrs. Nelson:

Have you overlooked your February payment on your account, Mrs. Nelson? Your last payment of $75 for the computer that you purchased was made over a month ago. Please put a check in the mail to us by Apirl 15. We beleive you want to continue to be eligible for credit.

If you have any questions about your account, please call Rosa at 919-331-4211.

                                  Sincerely,

April 1, 19--

Dr. Lawrence Mayo
673 Andersen Drive
Rochester, NY 14626-8765

Dear Dr. Mayo:

Have you overlooked your February payment on your account, Dr. Mayo? Your last payment of $92 for the printer that you purchased was made over a month ago. Please put a check in the mail to us by April 15. We believe you want to continue to be eligible for credit with us.

If you have any questions about your account, please call Mary at 919-321-4211.

                                  Sincerely,

April 1, 19--

Mr. James Holden
200 Tenth Street
Jacksonville, FL 32333-4182

Dear Mr. Holden:

Have you overlooked your February payment on your account, Mr. Holden? Your last payment of $75 for the software that you purchased was made over a month ago. Please put a check in the mail by April 15.

If you have any questions about your account, please call Mary at 919-331-4211.

                                  Sincerely,

Job 3 Proofread the printed copy of the balance sheet by comparing it to the rough draft copy.

```
                    RIVERSIDE PAINT COMPANY

                         Balance Sheet
                         March 1, 19--

ASSETS

Cash . . . . . . . . . . . . . . . . . . . .              $10,250.20
Petty Cash . . . . . . . . . . . . . . .                      520.00
Accounts Recievable . . . . . . . . . .           895.55
    Less Allowance for Bad Debts . . . .          100.00      759.55
Merchandise Inventory . . . . . . . . .                    50,225.00
Supplies - Office . . . . . . . . . . .                     3,250.00
Supplies - Store . . . . . . . . . . .                      2,500.00
                                                           ─────────
Total Current Assetts . . . . . . . . .                    67,540.75

Plant Assets:
Office Equipment. . . . . . . . . . . . .      5,000.00
    Less Accumulated Depreciation . . .        1,200.00    3,800.00
Store Equipment . . . . . . . . . . . .        9,000.00
    Less Acummulated Depreciation . . .        2,000.00    7,000.00
Total Plant Assets . . . . . . . . . .         ─────────
                                                          10,800.00
                                                          ─────────
Total Assets . . . . . . . . . . . .                      $89,140.75
                                                          ═════════

LIABILITIES AND OWNERS' EQUITY

Accounts Payable . . . . . . . . . . .         13,775.60

OWNER'S EQUITY . . . . . . . . . . . .         75,354.15
                                                ─────────

TOTAL OWNERS' EQUITY AND LIABILTIES                       $89,140.75
                                                          ═════════
```

Typist—add leaders

RIVERSIDE PAINT COMPANY *DS*
Balance Sheet
March 31, 19--

ASSETS

Use commas throughout

Cash		$10,200.20
Petty Cash		520.00
Accounts Receivable	895.55	
Less Allowance for Bad Debts	100.00	795.00
Merchandise Inventory		50,225.00
Supplies - Office		3,250.00
Supplies - Store		2,500.00
Total Current Assetts		67,540.75
Plant Assets:		
Office Equipment	5,000.00	
Less Accumulated Depreciation	1,200.00	3,800.00
Store Equipment	9,000.00	
Less Accumulated Depreciation	2,000.00	7,000.00	10,800.00
Total Plant Assets		
		$89,140.75
Total Assets		

LIABILITIES *and Owners' Equity*

Accounts Payable	13,795.60
	75,345.15

OWNER'S EQUITY

TOTAL OWNERS' EQUITY AND LIABILITIES $89,140.75

Chapter 3—Keyboarding Errors, Part 2

COMPUTERIZED PROOFREADING

Job 4 **Minutes of a Meeting**

1. Load the file C3JOB4 from the template.
2. Proofread the minutes, making all of the corrections. Use the spell checker if it is available.
3. Format the minutes with 1" side margins and a 1½" top margin.
4. Save the revised minutes as C3JOB4R and print them.
5. Proofread the printed document. If you find additional mistakes, revise, save, and reprint it.

CHAPTER 4

ABBREVIATION ERRORS

Objectives: *After completing this chapter, you should be able to*
- Apply rules of abbreviation correctly.
- Use the appropriate proofreading symbols to indicate changes in text.
- Spell correctly a list of frequently misspelled words.

ABBREVIATIONS

Another form of keyboarding error occurs in the proper use and form of abbreviations. Abbreviations are shortened forms of words or phrases used to save time and space. Although abbreviations are not suitable for all business communication, they are generally used in business forms, catalogs, tabular material, footnotes, and bibliographies. Use abbreviations sparingly when a more formal style is desired, as in correspondence or reports.

Debate still exists as to whether periods should be used in various abbreviations. The trend is toward eliminating periods, especially when the elements are capitalized (NATO, TVA). Do not eliminate periods in abbreviations that could be mistaken for words in themselves, such as *in.* (*inch*). Although you will find variations in the use of periods, spacing, and capitalization of abbreviations, be consistent within a document. If the reader may not be familiar with an abbreviation, spell it out the first time it is used and place the abbreviation in parentheses—*computer-aided instruction (CAI)*. From that point on use only the abbreviation.

Space once after the final period of an abbreviation; do not space after a period within an abbreviation (*a.m.*).

When you note errors in the form or use of abbreviations, use the following proofreading symbols to mark your corrections:

sp	Spell out.	(Adm) Walker will join us for dinner at 7 p.m.
⊙	Insert a period.	Ms Jarvis will be present for the briefing.
⌒	Delete the period and close up the space.	Is there an F/D/R/ Memorial?

33

4-1   Spell out first names.

> William (*not* Wm.) Taft
> George (*not* Geo.) Fitzgerald

4-2   Spell out titles appearing with last names only. Titles such as Governor, President, and Professor may be abbreviated when used with a first and last name.

> Senator Proxmire
> General Washington *but* Gen. George Washington

▶ Abbreviate personal titles whether used with full names or last names only.

Mr.	Messrs.	(plural of Mr.)
Mrs.	Mmes.	(plural of Mrs.)
Ms.	Dr.	

▶ Do not abbreviate the title of a position following a name.

Avery Clements, treasurer, prepared the report.

▶ Do not abbreviate a position title when it is a part of the letter address. In this case, the position title should be capitalized.

Mr. Avery Clements, Treasurer
CNP Trucking Lines
681 Van Ness Street
San Francisco, CA   94109-7681

▶ Abbreviate titles, academic degrees, and professional designations after names.

Betsy H. Sparrow, Ed.D.
Antonio Pappas, CPS

▶ Do not set off *Jr.*, *Sr.*, or *II* with a comma unless you know that the person addressed prefers that a comma be used.

George Calhoun Sr.
Michael D. Hause II

▶ Follow initials in a name by a period and one space. When persons are known only by their initials, no periods are used.

Franklin D. Roosevelt
JFK (John Fitzgerald Kennedy)

✓ Proofread the following paragraph for abbreviation errors:

Pres. Richard R. Eakin Jr. announced a $1.3 million gift to the university from the estate of the late Prof. Thom. Waters. Prof. Waters' daughter, Dr. Margaret R Anders, presented the check to Pres. Eakin at the news conference.

4-3 The names of agencies, network broadcasting companies, associations, unions, and other groups are often abbreviated. These abbreviations are usually written without periods.

AAA	CBS	NAACP
AFL-CIO	FBI	NFL
AMA	IRS	UN

Company names often contain abbreviations such as *Bros., Corp., Inc., Ltd.,* or *&.* Check the letterhead for the proper style. (In some situations, such as in straight text, these words are written in full.)

4-4 Common time designations, such as *A.D., B.C., a.m.,* and *p.m.*, are usually abbreviated. Standard time zones and daylight saving time zones are also abbreviated.

EST (Eastern Standard Time)
EDT (Eastern Daylight Time)

▶ Days of the week and months of the year should not be abbreviated, except in tables, when space is limited, or in business forms.

Wednesday, December 12
On a time card, you could write: Wed., Dec. 12

✓ Use the appropriate proofreading symbols to mark errors in abbreviations in the paragraph below:

Messrs Pena, Adams, and Tonelli have reservations on TWA Flight 22 on Fri., October 22, arriving Kennedy International Airport at 1:45 p.m. E.S.T. They will be demonstrating the newest STAR word processing software at the American Vocational Association (AVA) Convention. The camera crews from the educational station W.C.I.M.-TV will be at the A.V.A. Convention to tape the presentations for later broadcasting.

4-1, 4-2
Thom. — sp
Prof. Waters' — sp
Margaret R⌃Anders
Pres. Eakin — sp

Chapter 4—Abbreviation Errors 35

4-5 Street addresses are spelled out. Exceptions are the abbreviations *NW*, *NE*, *SW*, and *SE*, which are used in some cities after the street name.

Avenue	Boulevard
Drive	Place
Road	Street
North	

1817 Hamilton Avenue, NW

▶ Two-letter state abbreviations are used only with ZIP Codes. They are keyed in all capitals without periods or internal spaces. In all other cases, the traditional state abbreviations are used. A list of the state, district, and territory abbreviations appears in the Appendix. Always check these abbreviations carefully in letter addresses and on envelopes.

Name	Standard	Two-letter
Alabama	Ala.	AL
Arizona	Ariz.	AZ
District of Columbia	D.C.	DC

▶ Country names are spelled out in text. The exception is *USSR*. When used as an adjective, *U.S.* is acceptable: *U.S. affairs*.

✓ Proofread the following copy for errors in abbreviations:

August 28, 19--

Dr. R.D. Kalmus
3851 S. Oak St.
Rapid City, S.D. 57702

Dear Doctor Kalmus

Your new credit card is enclosed. Please note that it can now be used in many foreign countries, including W. Germany and the U.S.S.R.

Sincerely yours

4-3, 4-4

Messrs.
Friday
EST
WCIM-TV
AVA Convention

---

36   Chapter 4—Abbreviation Errors

4-6 Weights and measurements are spelled out in text but may be abbreviated in technical writing and on business forms.

8 1/2- by 11-inch sheet
9′ × 12′
20 pounds of nails

4-7 Abbreviate expressions commonly used in business forms, tables, and statistical documents.

acct.	accounting
agt.	agent
a.k.a.	also known as
amt.	amount
ASAP	as soon as possible
att.	attachment
CEO	chief executive officer
EOM	end of the month
FYI	for your information
hdlg.	handling
mdse.	merchandise
mfg.	manufacturing
No.	number (used when a number follows)
pd.	paid
pkg.	package
PO	purchase order
P.O.	post office
pstg.	postage
rm.	ream(s) or room(s)
SASE	self-addressed stamped envelope
std.	standard
wt.	weight

If in doubt about whether an abbreviation is acceptable, check a dictionary.

Some business expressions are expressed in all CAPS on invoices and other forms. If they appear in text, use lowercase letters and periods.

COD or c.o.d.
EOM or e.o.m.

4-5

R. D.
South Oak **Street**
Rapid City, **SD**
Dear **Dr.** Kalmus
West Germany
USSR

Chapter 4—Abbreviation Errors

✓ Proofread the following copy for errors in abbreviations:

July 2, 19--

Ms. Ashley Barrett
Ozarks Wholesale Corp.
2842 Washington Boulevard, SE
Little Rock, AR   72201-9581

Dear Ms. Barrett:

Your order for 100 reams of 20-pound 8 1/2- by 14-in. copy paper was shipped by Fed. Express today. The total amt. of the invoice, including shipping and hndlg. charges, is $368.47. Payment is due by the EOM.

Very truly yours,

SPELLING REVIEW

To improve your ability to detect spelling errors, master the words below. Watch for them in the exercises that follow and in succeeding chapters.

accidentally	representative
annual	sponsored
compatible	surprise
competitive	therefore

PROOFREADING TIPS

Study these tips and apply them as you proofread:

1. Spell out an unfamiliar abbreviation the first time it is used and follow it with the abbreviation: American Management Society (AMS).
2. Although two forms of an abbreviation may be correct, use only one form throughout the same letter or report.
3. Check the spellings of cities and the state abbreviations in all addresses.

4-7
14-**inch**
Federal
amount
handling
end of the month.

38   Chapter 4—Abbreviation Errors

Proofreading Applications

Proofread the correspondence using the appropriate proofreading symbols to mark errors you find in spelling or abbreviations. To aid you in proofreading, the number of errors to be found is indicated in parentheses for Exercises P-1 and P-2; however, you must find the errors on your own in P-3.

P-1

January 28, 19--

Ms Gretchen K. Sorensen
Customer Service Mgr.
ICM, Inc.
1020 E. First Street
Butte, MT 59405-4125

Dear Ms. Sorensen:

Would you like to have one of your representatives present your acctg. software to the eight members of our software purchasing committee? Either Feb. 28 or March 14 will fit our schedule.

Please let me know if either of these dates is compatable with your schedule.

Sincerely yours,   (6 errors)

P-2

INTEROFFICE MEMORANDUM

TO: Software Purchasing Committee
FROM: Van Zoeller
DATE: February 12, 19--
SUBJECT: ICM Software Demonstration

An I.C.M. software demonstration is scheduled for Tuesday, March 14, at 9 a.m. in Conference Rm. B-101 by our representative Geo. Armstrong Sr. He will demonstrate four accounting software packages.

The date of the next committee meeting was accidently omitted from the schedule; it will be April 4.

(4 errors)

P-1
Ms. Gretchen
Service **Manager**
1020 **East**
accounting
February 28
compatible

Chapter 4—Abbreviation Errors

P-3

ITINERARY
for
Van K. McLaurin II

Helena - Chicago   April 27, 19--

6:00 a.m. (MST)	Leave Helena Municipal Airport, Western Airlines Flight 428
10:15 a.m. (C.S.T.)	Arrive O'Hare Airport, Chicago
12:00 noon	Lunch with Tony Dattilo, sales manager, in Alfredo's Restaurant at the airport
2:00 p.m.	Appt. with Hunter McKenzie, pres. of Pacific Foods, in Executive Suite 10, Western Airlines Terminal
3:00 pm.	Tour of Pacific Foods facilities, located at 7204 South Kennedy Avenue
6:15 p.m.	Leave O'Hare on Western Airlines Flight 187
8:30 p.m.	Arr. Helena Municipal Airport

P-2

ICM
Conference **Room**
George Armstrong
accident**ally**

P-3

10:15 a.m. (**CST**)
Appointment
president of
3:00 **p.m.**
Arrive Helena

PROGRESSIVE PROOFREADING

You are an office assistant in a computer sales and service company. One of your responsibilities is to proofread the materials that are produced to ensure that they are accurate. Four jobs have been given to you for proofreading. Using the proofreading symbols that you have learned, mark all errors.

Job 1 Proofread this seminar announcement. Correct errors in spelling, keying, or abbreviations.

WALLACE COMPUTER SOLUTIONS

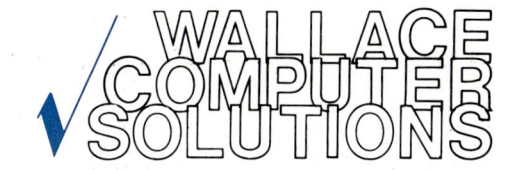

MANAGING INFORMATION WITH COMPUTERS

Seminar co-sponsored by Wallace Computer Solutions and
the College of Businesss, Montana State University
Friday, January 27, 19--
Bus. Admin. Bldg., Room 1311

Consultants

Prof. Paul Uhr Senior, MBA, School of Business, Mont. St. U.
Ms. Lillie Taylor, CPS, Office Manager, Quadrangle Products, Inc.
Dr. William R. Joyner, Chairperson, Information Sciences Dept., Montana State Univ.

Program

Registration	8:30 a.m. – 8:55 am
Morning Session	9:00 a.m. – 12:15 p.m.
Lunch	12:30 p.m. – 1:45 p.m.
Afternoon Session	2:00 p.m. – 4:30 p.m.

Registrants limited to 25
Seminar fee: $99 per person
Enrollment deadline: January 20
Send check to Business Education Services, P.O. Box 2136, Bozeman, Montana   59717-4368

Chapter 4—Abbreviation Errors

Job 2 Printed on the next page is a list of customers who wish to form a computer users' group. Check for keying errors in the printed list by comparing it carefully with the handwritten list. Check the printed addresses carefully for proper use of abbreviations. Do not assume the abbreviations are listed correctly on the handwritten list.

Customer Names and Addresses

1. Ms. Carmen Alvarez
   4012 Exeter Drive, NE
   Rocky Mount, NC 27801-4439

2. Mr. Davidson Tyler
   1518 Bennett St.
   Washington, NC 27889-6902

3. Mrs. Charles Varlashkin
   P.O. Box 30561
   New Bern, NC 28560-5713

4. Mr. D.L. Pate Sr.
   217-B North Meade Street
   Greenville, NC 27834-4209

5. Dr. Jacqueline Harris
   470 Shoreline Ave.
   Elizabeth City, NC 27909-8261

6. Mr. Christopher Churchill
   1036 Dogwood Trail
   Greenville, NC 27835-3479

7. Mr. Kevin Curran
   8941 Graystone Lane
   Pinetops, NC 27864-2297

8. Ms. Susan Haines
   235 Windsor Blvd.
   Greenville, NC 27834-6140

9. Mr. Jim Gothard
   602 Fairview Drive
   Wilson, NC 27893-4230

10. Ms. Geo. Herndon
    2018 Garrett Avenue
    Farmville, NC 27828-9817

11. Mrs. Valerie Beckman
    301-C Westbrook Apartments
    105 S. 11th Street
    Goldsboro, NC 27530-6346

12. Sen. Jackson
    1442 18th Street, S.E.
    Jacksonville, N.C. 28540-7294

```
File      Edit       Print       Select       Format      Options      Query      Report       Window
```

	Name	Address	City	St	ZIP
1	Ms. Carmen Alvarez	4012 Exeter Drive, N.E.	Rocky Mount	NC	27801-4439
2	Mr. David Tyler	1518 Bennett Street	Washington	NC	27889-6902
3	Mrs. Charles Varlashkin	P.O. Box 30651	New Bern	NC	28560-5713
4	Mr. D.L. Pate Sr.	217-B North Meade Street	Greenville	NC	27834-4209
5	Dr. Jacqueline Harris	470 Shoreline Drive	Elizabeth City	NC	27909-8261
6	Mr. Christopher Churchill	1036 Dogwood Trial	Greenville	NC	27835-3479
7	Mr. Kevin Curran	8941 Graystone Lane	Pinetops	NC	27864-2297
8	Ms. Susan Haines	253 Windsor Blvd.	Greenville	NC	27834-6140
9	Mr. Jim Gothard	602 Fairview Drive	Wilson	NC	27893-4230
10	Ms. Geo. Herndon	2018 Garrettt Avenue	Farmville	NC	27828-9817
11	Ms. Valerie Beckman	301-C Westbook Apartments			
12		105 South 11th Street	Goldsboro	NC	27530-6346
13	Sen. Jackson	1442 18th Street, SE	Jacksonville	NC	28540-7294
14					
15					
16					
17					
18					
19					
20					

```
1 Name                             LIST                      <F1=HELP>
Press ALT to choose commands, or F2 to edit.
```

Chapter 4—Abbreviation Errors

Job 3 Proofread the announcement on the next page by comparing it with the rough draft below. Remember, errors may occur on the original document. Mark your corrections on the typed copy.

STAR USERS' GROUP
Organizational Meeting

You are invited to attend the ~~initial~~ *stet* meeting of the STAR Computer User's Group to be held in the Prince Rm. of the Tryon Hotel on Feb. 20 at 7:30 p.m.

Anyone using or interested in STAR Computers, software, and STAR-compatible products is ~~encouraged~~ *eligible* to join, so pass this announcement along to your friends.

The STAR Users' Group will meet monthly to discuss PC-related topics. Guest speakers from industry will share how they are using their STARS. New products, software, and PC-compatible peripherals will be demonstrated and discussed. All product demonstrations will be video-taped and made available to chapter members ~~to hear and see.~~ *(by the manufacturers. These)*

The goals of the STAR Users' Group are to provide a network so that all members will be able to use their computers most effectively and to keep mfrs. aware of the consumer's needs.

Members attending the first organizational meeting will determine the best time and location of the monthly meetings and will appoint a nominating comittee for board members.

Remember: February 20, 7:30 p.m., Tryon Hotel

Typist: Please set up in an attractive format

SPECIAL NOTICE

```
                    STAR USERS' GROUP

                   Organizational Meeting


        You are invited to attend the initial meeting of the
   STAR Computer Users' Group to be held in the Prince Room
   of the Tryon Hotel on Feb. 20 at 7:30 p.m.

        The STAR Users' Group will meet monthly to discuss
   PC-related topics.  Guest speakers from industry will
   share how the are using their STARS.  New products,
   software, and PC-compatible peripherals will be demon-
   strated and discussed by the manufacturers.  These
   product demonstrations will be videotaped and made
   available to chapter members.

        Anyone using or interested in STAR Computers, soft-
   ware, and STAR-compatible products is eligible to join,
   so pass this announcement along to you friends.  The
   goals of the STAR Users' Group are to provide a network
   so that all members will be able to use their computers
   most effectively and to keep mfrs. aware of consumer's
   needs.

        Members attending the first organizational meeting
   will determine the best time and location of the monthly
   meetings and will appoint a nominating comittee for board
   members.

        Remember:   February 20, 7:30 p.m. Tryon Hotel
```

Chapter 4—Abbreviation Errors 45

COMPUTERIZED PROOFREADING

Job 4 Interoffice Memorandum

1. Proofread the rough draft of the memorandum and correct any errors that you find.
2. Load the file C4JOB4 from the template.
3. Revise the memorandum on the template according to the rough draft. Make all needed corrections. Use the spell checker if it is available.
4. Format the memorandum using 1" margins.
5. Save the memorandum as C4JOB4R.
6. Print the memo.
7. Proofread the printed memo. If you find any mistakes, revise, save, and reprint it.

---

memo

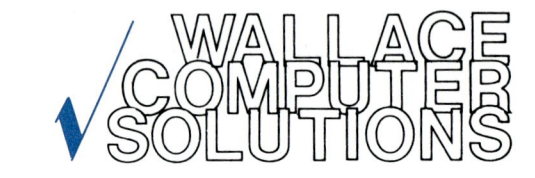

WALLACE COMPUTER SOLUTIONS

TO: Department Managers and Supervisors

FROM: Garry Morrison, Gen. Manager

DATE: ~~September 26~~ January 20, 19--

SUBJECT: Expense Reduction

Please analize your *tentative* budget carefully; then let me have your strategies for reducing our costs. *review the budget*

As you will see *that* our utilities expense is almost double what it was four years ago. Advt. expense has increased about 30 percent. Taxes are up more than 20 percent. The cost of ins. rises every year. If we are to remain competitive in the busi. enviroment, we must reduce our expenses.

~~Please let me have your suggestions~~ ASAP but no later than ~~October 10.~~ February 1

My goal is to incorporate your ideas into the management plan for the ~~November 7~~ February 15 anual meeting.

dw

Chapter 4—Abbreviation Errors

CHAPTER 5

WORD DIVISION ERRORS

Objectives: *After completing this chapter, you should be able to*
- ▸ Identify words that are divided incorrectly.
- ▸ Recognize items that should not be divided.
- ▸ Use the appropriate proofreading symbols to indicate changes in text.
- ▸ Spell correctly a list of commonly misspelled words.

GUIDELINES FOR CORRECT WORD DIVISION

Words are divided at the ends of lines to give the document an attractive, well-balanced appearance. The right margin should be as even as possible, yet the reader should not be interrupted with *excessive* word divisions.

Word division has become easier as a result of the automatic hyphenation feature found on most of today's word processing programs. With this feature turned on, words are hyphenated automatically; however, undesirable breaks are common. With automatic hyphenation turned off, words that do not fit completely on one line wrap to the next line, which results in an extremely ragged right margin. A good proofreader must be alert for excessive word division, words incorrectly divided, or an extremely ragged right margin.

Words may be divided only between syllables. A word division manual or dictionary can be used to determine correct syllabication; however, a knowledge of the rules presented in this chapter will prevent extensive searching in reference materials, reduce word division errors, and save valuable keyboarding time.

Read each of the rules that follow and study the examples given. Then complete the word division exercises. Use the insert hyphen symbol, illustrated below, to indicate the preferred division of each word according to the rule being reviewed (even if a word can be divided correctly at other points). If a word cannot be divided, place a check mark (✓) after the last letter in the word.

⸗   Insert hyphen.   proof⸗reading
                        type⸗writer

47

If a word is divided incorrectly, correct it as shown below.

formal plan of merg- er
~~er~~ was approved.

5-1 Divide words between syllables only; a one-syllable word cannot be divided.

    height   ac- com- mo- date   for- eign

✓
- a. volunteer
- b. disposable
- c. convenience
- d. accusation
- e. straight

5-2 Do not divide after a one-letter syllable at the beginning of a word or before a two-letter syllable at the end of a word. An easy way to remember this rule is: Key 2, Carry 3. This means that at least two (and preferably more) letters must be keyed before a word is divided, and at least three letters must be carried to the next line.

    re- cently   print- ers   *but* about or eighty

✓
- a. painter
- b. elusive
- c. wealthy
- d. uniform
- e. already

5-3 Divide a compound word between the elements of the compound. If the compound word contains a hyphen, divide only after the hyphen.

    sales- person (*not* salesper- son)   self- esteem

✓
- a. timesharing
- b. go-between
- c. eyewitness
- d. masterpiece
- e. troubleshoot

5-1
a. vol‖un‖teer
b. dis‖pos‖able
c. con‖ven‖ience
d. ac‖cus‖ation
e. straight ✓

5-2
a. painter ✓
b. elu- sive
c. wealthy ✓
d. uni- form
e. al- ready

5-4 When a single-letter syllable occurs within a word, divide *after* it. However, divide *before* a single-letter syllable that immediately precedes a terminating two-letter syllable (such as *clar-ify*) or one of these syllables: -ble, -bly, -cle, -cal, and -ly.

    stipu-late   *but* bus-ily

✓
- a. positive
- b. beneficial
- c. teleprinter
- d. clarification
- e. miracle

5-5 When two single-vowel syllables occur together in a word, divide between them.

    gradu-ation   physi-ological

✓
- a. anxiety
- b. humiliation
- c. evaluation
- d. insinuation
- e. valuable

5-6 Divide after prefixes or before suffixes when possible. (A prefix is a syllable placed at the beginning of a word to form a new word; a suffix is a syllable placed at the end of a word to form a new word.)

    trans-form   consign-ment

✓
- a. preparedness
- b. anticlimax
- c. repelled
- d. substandard
- e. misfortune

5-3
a. time- sharing
b. go- between
c. eye- witness
d. master- piece
e. trouble- shoot

5-4
a. posi- tive
b. bene- ficial
c. tele- printer
d. clari- fication
e. mir- acle

5-5
a. anxi- ety
b. humili- ation
c. evalu- ation
d. insinu- ation
e. valu- able

Chapter 5—WORD DIVISION ERRORS

5-7 You may usually divide a word between double consonants. However, if a word ends in double consonants and has a suffix ending, divide after the double consonants, provided the suffix creates an extra syllable.

> hur-ried   *but* pressed

✓
- a. bulletin
- b. bluffing
- c. fulfillment
- d. installed
- e. embarrass

▶ When addition of a suffix to a word *results* in double consonants, divide between the two consonants, provided the suffix creates an extra syllable.

> compel-ling   recur-ring   *but* preferred

✓
- a. referral
- b. planning
- c. omitted
- d. shipped
- e. cancellation

WORDS THAT SHOULD NOT BE DIVIDED

Although most words can be divided, some words should not be divided. The rules for words that should not be divided are stated in the following paragraphs.

5-8 Do not divide a word containing five or fewer letters regardless of the number of syllables. If possible, avoid dividing a word containing six letters.

> exit   being

✓
- a. forget
- b. admit
- c. number
- d. insert
- e. renew

5-6
a. pre- pared- ness
b. anti- climax
c. re- pelled
d. sub- standard
e. mis- fortune

5-7
a. bul- letin
b. bluff- ing
c. fulfill- ment
d. installed ✓
e. embar- rass

a. refer- ral
b. plan- ning
c. omit- ted
d. shipped ✓
e. cancel- lation

---

50   Chapter 5—Word Division Errors

5-9 Do not divide abbreviations, acronyms, contractions, and numbers.

    assoc.   M.A.   NABTE   haven't   852,741,639

✓
- a. $2 million
- b. e.o.m.
- c. N. Dak.
- d. mustn't
- e. NAACP

5-10 Avoid separating parts of a date, parts of a proper name, or parts of an address. If it is necessary to separate one of the above, do so at a logical point. Include as much of the proper noun as possible.

Date	December 15, 19--
Name	Mr. Carmen Garcia
Street address	1490 Third Street
City and state	Greenville, NC 27834-2930
Proper noun	Margaret

✓ Proofread the following paragraph using the insert hyphen symbol to indicate preferred item division.

NOTICE

East Federal 24, East Federal Savings Bank's automatic teller machine service will begin operation at 329 Arlington Boulevard on September 18. The bank's vice president, Mrs. Sue D. Briley, invites you to stop by the office to apply for your East Federal 24 access card and personal identification number today.

5-8
a. forget
b. admit
c. number
d. insert
e. renew

5-9
a. $2 million
b. e.o.m.
c. N. Dak.
d. mustn't
e. NAACP

Chapter 5—Word Division Errors

5-11 Keep word groups together that need to be read together, such as *6:30 p.m.* and *page 103*. Do not divide the last word of more than two consecutive lines, the last word of a paragraph, or the last word on a page.

✓ Proofread the following paragraph, using the insert hyphen symbol to correct word division errors and to indicate preferred item division.

> You can use your ATM card any hour of the day to get cash, make deposits, and transfer funds between your accounts. You can use it to receive instant information about checking and savings accounts, loans, and overdraft privileges. If you are interested, come by our office at 329 Arlington Boulevard on the afternoon of November 8 for a free demonstration by Wendy C. Wright.

SPELLING REVIEW

To improve your ability to detect spelling errors, master the words below. Watch for them in the exercises that follow and in succeeding chapters.

announcement	foreign
approximately	height
beginning	nickel
calendar	schedule
category	similar

PROOFREADING TIPS

Study these tips and apply them as you proofread:
1. Pronounce words carefully to determine syllabication.

chil- dren	*not* child- ren
knowl- edge	*not* know- ledge
prob- lem	*not* pro- blem
sched- ule	*not* sche- dule

5-10
329 Arlington
September 18
Mrs. Sue D.

5-11
de- posits
re- ceive
overdraft
329 Arlington

2. Be alert for words that change syllabication as pronunciation changes.

min- ute	(*n.*) 60 seconds
mi- nute	(*adj.*) tiny
pre- sent	(*v.*) hand over
pres- ent	(*n.*) gift; not absent
proj- ect	(*n.*) undertaking
pro- ject	(*v.*) throw forward
re- cord	(*v.*) write down
rec- ord	(*n.*) written account

3. Check a word division manual or a dictionary whenever you are in doubt about the division of a word.

Proofreading Applications

Each of the following exercises contains ten words that have been divided. Some of the words are divided incorrectly or do not follow the preferred style of word division. If an item is divided incorrectly, indicate the correct division by using the symbol for inserting a hyphen.

P-1	blind- ly	e- nough
	paper- weight	allowa- ble
	continu- ation	order- ing
	height	understate- ment
	tel- eprompter	presi- dent-elect

P-2	go- ing	spel- ling
	plan- ned	would- n't
	o' -clock	$3.4- billion
	neces- sary	aud-it
	dou- ble	Ph.D.

P-3	si- milar	cr- eate
	clie- nts	cat- egories
	progres- sive	Phoenix,- AZ 89534-0987
	March 21,- 1812	Dr. Beverly- Huber
	Philadel- phia	1034- North Avenue

P-1
blindly
tele- prompter
enough
allow- able
president- elect

P-2
going
planned
o'clock
double
spell- ing
wouldn't
$3.4 billion
audit

P-3
simi- lar
cli- ents
create
cate- gories
1034 North

Progressive Proofreading

You are working five hours a week as an office volunteer for Partners, Inc., a local charitable organization. Proofread the documents carefully for keyboarding, spelling, abbreviation, and word division errors. Remember that the original drafts may also contain errors.

Job 1 Proofread these form paragraphs, which will be used in correspondence with supporters of Partners, Inc.

FORM PARAGRAPHS:

    A.   You have been an enthusiastic and dependable supporter of Partners, Inc., for five years.

    B.   You have been one of Partners' most enthusiastic back-rs, and we appreciate the support you have given us.

    C.   Because you have so generously contributed your time or other resources to Partners, the Advisory Board members invite you tobe our guest at our annaul gala dinner on March 30 at the City Center at 6:30 p.m. You may bring a guest.

    D.   We are already at the heigth of planning the annual Partners' Auction. This year the auction will be held on February 15. As in the past, all proceeds will go to help the youth of of our community. May we count on your continuted support? If your answer is YES, and we hope it will be, please notify us by January 20.

    E.   As we prepare for this year's auction scheduled for Febuary 15, may we once again count on your support? If your answer is YES, and we hope it will be, please let us know the items or service that you will provide for the action by January 20.

    F.   If you will be aplbe to attend, please return the enclsoed reservation form by March 16 so that we can reserve a place for you.

    G.   Enclosure

Chapter 5—Word Division Errors

Job 2 Mark all errors in this letter using the appropriate proofreading symbols.

Partners, Inc.
1110 Logan Street
Denver, CO 80203-9176 (303) 555-6478

January 10, 19--

Ms. Jane Daniels, Mgr.
WEXZ Newstalk 1530
517 North Nineth Street
Denver, CO 80204-7825

Dear Ms. Daniels

PUBLIC ANNOUNCMENT

For the past four years, your station has very generously advertised the Partners' Auction as a public service announcement. The
Partners' Auction is held annually to raise money to support projects for the youth in our community. Can we count on your continued support this year?

If your response is YES, and we hope it will be, would you read
the enclosed news release onyour Community Calender program begin-
ing January 20 and running through February 5.

Sincerely yours

Joseph A. Ramirez
Executive Secretary

gg

Enclosure

---

56   Chapter 5—Word Division Errors

Job 3 Mark any errors you find in this news release, using the appropriate proofreading symbols.

Partners, Inc.

1110 Logan Street
Denver, CO 80203-9176
(303) 555-6478

NEWS RELEASE

January 10, 19--
To release January 29, 19--

FIFTH ANNUAL PARTNERS' AUCTION

The Fifth Annual Partners' Auction will be telecast on W.R.A.L.-T.V. from noon to midnight on Saturday, February 5. Local merchants have generously donated aproximately fifteen hundred gifts. Viewers can bid on any of then by calling one of the numbers that will be listed on the television screen. The retail value of each item will be given, and each item will be sold to the highest bidder.

All persons working with the acution donate their time; thus, every nickel goes directly to Partners to aid the youth of the community. Show your support for youth projects by supporting Partners' Auction.

# # #

Chapter 5—Word Division Errors

Job 4 Proofread the letter on the following page by comparing it to the rough draft below. Check for keyboarding, spelling, and word division errors. Errors may occur in the draft copy as well.

Typist: Please prepare in proper form

January 15, 19--

Mr. E. C. Troiano
AMS Electronics
5245 Trade Street
Denver, CO 80213-8275

Dear Mr. Troiano

Mark your calender for the Fifth Annual Partner's Auction to be held on Saturday, February 5, in Scott Pavilion. The auction is sponsored by area businesses for the benefit of Partners, Inc., an organization devoted to helping the youth of the community. ~~Since you are aware of the importance of~~ *As a loyal supporter of Partners, you know how vital* the auction is as a means of raising funds for the organization, ~~you will want to attend.~~

WRAL-TV will telecast the auction from noon to midnight. As each item is put up for bid, it will be shown on television, and its retail value will be given. You can place your bid for any item by calling the numbers listed on ~~the~~ *stet* television ~~screen~~ *stet*. Remember, too, that *should be for* if your bid ~~is~~ more than the retail value ~~of the item~~, the difference between the two ~~amounts~~ is ~~tax~~ deductible on your taxes.

We hope ~~that~~ you will ~~make a definite decsion to~~ participate in Partners' biggest fund-raiser of the year. When Partners benefits, the entire community benefits.

Sincerely yours

Persons working at the auction are volunteering their services; therefore, all proceeds go directly to Partners.

A. Joseph Ramirez
Executive Secretary

Partners, Inc.

1110 Logan Street
Denver, CO 80203-9176 (303) 555-6478

January 15, 19--

Mr. E. C. Troiano
AMS Electronics
5245 Trade Street
Denver, CO 80213-8275

Dear Mr. Troiano

Mark your calender for the Fifth Annaul Partner's Auction to be held on Saturday, February 5, in Scott Pavilion. The auction is sponsored by area businesses for the benefit of Partners, Inc., an organization devoted to helping the youth of the community. As a loyal supporter of Partners, you know how vital the auction is as a means of raising funds for the organization.

WRAL-TV will telecast the action from noon to midnight. As each item is put up for bid, it will be shown on television, and its retail value will be given. You can place your bid for any item by calling the numbers listed on television. Should your bit be for more than the retail value, the difference between the two is deductible on your taxes.

Persons working at the auction are volunteering their services; therefore, all proceeds go directly to Partners. We hope you will participate in Partners' biggest fund-raiser of the year. When Partners benefits, the entire community benefits.

Sincerely yours

Joseph A. Ramirez
Executive Secretary

re

COMPUTERIZED PROOFREADING

Job 5 Business Letter

1. Load the file C5JOB5 from the template.

2. Proofread the letter on the template and compare it with form paragraphs A, C, F, and G from Job 1.

3. Make all corrections. Use the spell checker if it is available.

4. Format the letter using 1½" side margins and begin the date on line 16. Save the letter using the file name C5JOB5R.

5. Print the letter.

6. Proofread the printed document. If you find additional mistakes, revise, save, and reprint the document.

CHAPTER 6

NUMBER EXPRESSION ERRORS

Objectives: *After completing this chapter, you should be able to*
- Identify errors in the expression of numbers.
- Identify keyboarding errors in numerical calculations.
- Use the appropriate proofreading symbols to indicate changes in text.
- Spell correctly a list of commonly misspelled words.

GENERAL GUIDELINES

An important aspect of developing proofreading skills is learning to detect errors in the expression of numbers. Because of the availability of vast amounts of information from computers, numbers occur frequently in business documents. Telephone numbers, credit card numbers, social security numbers, ZIP Codes, and product codes are just a few examples.

Because figures are quickly and easily perceived, numbers used in technical writing and business communication are usually expressed in figures. On the other hand, numbers used in formal documents, such as social invitations, are often spelled out. The rules presented here apply to the expression of numbers as they appear in business documents unless otherwise noted.

Use the following proofreading symbols to mark errors in the expression of numbers and in the calculation of numerical items:

sp	Spell out.	We enrolled 10 students in the class.
/	Change copy as indicated.	The nurse prepared 10 bandages, 5 five rolls of gauze, and 20 tongue depressors.

The first part of Chapter 6 deals with basic rules for expressing numbers in business communication. Because these are basic rules for expressing numbers, the proofreader must be thoroughly familiar with each one.

61

6-1 Write the numbers *one* through *ten* in words. Write numbers larger than ten in figures.

> It takes five years to qualify for membership.
>
> It takes 12 years to qualify for membership.

6-2 If a sentence contains a series of numbers, any of which is greater than ten, use figures for consistency.

> For the picnic, they bought 24 pounds of chopped beef, 8 dozen rolls, 36 quarts of lemonade, and 96 turnovers.

▶ If the numbers in a sentence can be grouped into different categories, examine each category separately. If figures are required for some numbers in a given category, use figures for all numbers within that category. (Categories may include numbers in a series, round numbers, ordinal numbers, dates, time, money, percentages, etc.)

The Per-Flo Company registered 37 women, 28 men, and 5 children for the *three* tours offered.

6-3 Spell out a number that begins a sentence. However, if the number requires more than two words when spelled out, rearrange the sentence so that it does not begin with a number.

Note: All compound numbers from twenty-one through ninety-nine should always be hyphenated when spelled out.

> Twenty-five persons have enrolled.
>
> *not* Seven hundred eighty-nine was the number of the lucky ticket.
>
> *but* The number of the lucky ticket was 789.

6-4 Spell out indefinite and round numbers that can be expressed in one or two words.

> About three thousand people attended the rally.
>
> Approximately fifty men entered the contest.

▶ Express round numbers such as 1,500 in hundreds rather than thousands.

> fifteen hundred balloons
>
> *not* one thousand five hundred balloons

▶ Express very large round numbers in figures followed by the word *million* or *billion*.

The population of Chicago is more than 3 million.

6-5 Spell out ordinal numbers that can be written in one or two words. (Consider a hyphenated number, such as thirty-five, as one word.)

Is this the sixth inning?

Harold and Sue celebrated their forty-fifth anniversary.

▶ If an ordinal number cannot be expressed in one or two words, use figures.

This is the 110th day of the strike.

✓ Proofread the following sentences for errors in the expression of numbers. If the sentence is correct, write a C to the right of the sentence.

a. Thirty-five people telephoned their regrets.

b. The requisition for 12 boxes of paper, two dozen printer ribbons, and three boxes of diskettes has been approved.

c. A plan for the city's needs in the 21st century has been drawn up.

d. Luis ranked twelfth in a class of six hundred thirty-seven.

e. Two hundred twenty-seven questions were on the test.

f. We received almost 200 inquiries about the ad.

GUIDELINES FOR SPECIFIC SITUATIONS

Specific situations require additional guidelines to clarify the message. These rules are covered in this section.

6-6 When two numbers are used together and one is part of a compound modifier, spell out one of the two—preferably the smaller number—and write the larger number in figures.

Calvin loaded two 40-pound cartons on the truck.

Martha bought 20 three-cent stamps.

6-1—6-5

a. C
b. **2 dozen, 3 boxes**
c. **twenty-first** century
d. **637**
e. **There were 227** questions
f. **two hundred** inquiries

Chapter 6—Number Expression Errors

6-7 Spell out street names from one through ten and the house number one. Street names of ten and under are always expressed as ordinals (Third Street, Fifth Avenue). Street names above ten may be expressed in figures as cardinal numbers (15 Street) or as ordinal numbers (15th Street).

> 1609 Fifth Avenue
>
> One Park Avenue
>
> 2109 Sandcastle Drive
>
> 2 East 11th Street (or 2 East 11 Street)

6-8 In nontechnical, informal material, spell out ages ten and under; use figures for ages 11 and up. Use figures for ages expressed in years and months.

> When will Chris be 21?
>
> Jim is 3 years and 9 months old.

6-9 Use figures to express numbers preceded by nouns.

> Please refer to page 16 in Chapter 2 when you do your research.
>
> The meeting will be held in Suite 101.

✓ Proofread the following sentences for errors in the expression of numbers:

a. The school is located at Eight West 23 Street, not West 24 Street.

b. See page 88 in the book and page 257 in the appendix for the references.

c. We will need 60 10-ounce cups and 60 9-inch plates for the picnic.

d. Jonathan has moved from One Meade Street to 1270 Seventh Avenue.

e. Ms. Alfonso, who was sixty-seven on May 5, has been with the company for 40 years.

f. Proper use of abbreviations is discussed in Lesson 3.

6-10 Spell out a fraction when it occurs without a whole number. Hyphenate a fraction immediately preceding a noun.

> Only about one half of the members were present.
> Order one-half dozen ribbons.

▶ Use figures to express a mixed number (a whole number and a fraction).

> Manuel bought 4 1/2 boxes of potatoes.
> I need 1 1/4 rolls of red ribbon and 3 1/2 rolls of blue.

6-11 Spell out time when stated in numbers alone or before *o'clock*.

> I will meet you for coffee at eleven.
> The wedding will begin at six o'clock.

▶ Use figures for time when *a.m.*, *noon*, and *p.m.* are used. Zeros are not necessary for on-the-hour times of day.

> Henrietta has a meeting at 10 a.m. and another at 2 p.m.
> The announcement will be made at 12 noon and 5 p.m.

6-12 Use figures after a month to express the day and year. Set the year off by commas if the day directly precedes the year. Otherwise, do not use commas.

> The events of November 21, 1975, will be long remembered.
> The events of November 1975 will be long remembered.

▶ Express the day in ordinal figures when it precedes the month or the month is omitted. (In formal messages, ordinal words may be used.)

> It was due on the 4th, but it's still not here.
> He will arrive on the 2d of July and depart on the 3d.

Note: The preferred abbreviation of the ordinals second and third is *d* alone, not *nd* or *rd*.

> This is the 103d day of the year.

6-6—6-9

a. **8** West
b. C
c. 60 **ten**-ounce
   60 **nine**-inch
d. C
e. **67**
f. C

✓ Proofread the following sentences for errors in the expression of numbers:

a. Was the envelope postmarked on August 18th?

b. The staff worked from 8 a.m. to 5:45 p.m. to finish the project.

c. All merchandise has been marked 1/3 off the regular price.

d. To convert miles to kilometers, multiply the number of miles by one and three fifths.

e. Ronson's sale will begin on September 29 at 10 a.m.

f. Lunch will be served at noon on the fourth of November.

6-13 Use figures in expressing dimensions, measures, and weights.

The room was 9 feet by 12 feet.

The bucket of sand weighed 21 pounds.

The athlete was 6 feet 9 inches tall.

6-14 Use figures to express amounts of money. Decimals and zeros are not used after even amounts except when they occur in a column with amounts that contain cents. Then add a decimal and two zeros to all whole dollar amounts to maintain a uniform appearance.

Paul earned $60 in tips.

Please pay $120 now and $61.50 for the next two months.

$ 82.75
  9.00
 17.42
$109.17

▶ If the amount is less than a dollar, spell out the word *cents*.

There was an error of 25 cents on her statement. (*not* $.25)

▶ In legal documents, express amounts of money or important figures in capitalized words followed by figures.

William Casady agrees to pay to the order of Sara Chambers Fifteen Hundred Dollars ($1,500) without interest.

6-10—6-12
a. August **18**
b. C
c. **one third**
d. **1 3/5**
e. C
f. **4th**

6-15 Use figures to express percentages and decimals.

The loan was obtained at a rate of 9 percent.

Note: Spell out the word *percent* except in statistical material where the symbol (%) is used.

▶ Use a zero before the decimal point for amounts less than one.

The accuracy percentage for all documents produced in the word processing center was 0.95, and 2,113 documents were produced.

Placing the zero before the decimal point in 0.95 prevents misreading the amount as 95 percent.

6-16 Always use figures with abbreviations or symbols.

9' × 12'   No. 345
65 deg   I-95

✓ Proofread the following sentences for errors in the expression of numbers:

a. The lease read: "Rent will be due on the fifth day of each month in the amount of Four Hundred Twenty-Five Dollars ($425)."

b. All contributions are welcome, whether they are for $50 or for $.50.

c. A 25% discount is given on rooms reserved thirty days in advance.

d. The 200-acre farm yields 130 bushels of corn per acre.

e. With a temperature of 32 degrees on June 17th, Banff had a 6-inch snow.

f. I bought 200 sheets of bond paper on sale for $4.50, which is 88 cents less than the regular price.

SPECIAL RULES

This section provides special reminders concerning number usage. The proofreader must pay close attention to these reminders.

Chapter 6—Number Expression Errors

6-17 When a number consists of four or more figures, use commas to separate thousands, hundreds of thousands, etc.

    5,000   320,267   43,824,321

Note: Do not, however, use commas when expressing years; page numbers; house, building, or room numbers; ZIP Codes; telephone numbers; and decimal parts of numbers.

    page 1324

    1584 Bayberry Drive, Cincinnati, OH   45230-8976

    (513) 555-1789

    0.0125

6-18 Serial numbers are usually written without commas, but other marks of punctuation and/or spaces are sometimes used.

    Invoice 38162

    Model G-4356

    Social Security No. 238-58-6600

    License No. 5014 587 035

6-19 Verify the accuracy of all numbers. Check all calculations.

    The book was $3.50 and the card was 75 cents, making the total $4.35. (Cost is $4.25.)

✓ Proofread the following sentences for statistical errors or errors in the expression of numbers:

a. The paperback book cost $4.95, which is $5.25 less than the $10.25 hardback copy of the same book.

b. Your insurance policy number is 293,404,478-R.

c. If interested, you may call me at (703) 5557629.

d. The revised projected cost of the building is $4859600, a 4.5 percent increase over the anticipated amount.

e. With the $7500 gift, we are only $1500 short of our goal.

f. Purchase Order 7,362 is for a Model BC-1928 walnut desk.

6-13—6-16

a. C
b. **50 cents**
c. 25 **percent**, 30 days
d. C
e. June 17
f. C

SPELLING REVIEW

To improve your ability to detect spelling errors, master the words below. Watch for them in the exercises that follow and in succeeding chapters.

absence
accumulate
conscious
extension
fourth

license
mortgage
ninth
waive

PROOFREADING TIPS

Study these tips and apply them as you proofread:

1. When possible, proofread numbers with another person, one reading the copy aloud, the other checking the copy as it is read.
2. If numbers have been transferred from another document, verify that they have been copied correctly.
3. When figures are in columns, check that decimals are aligned.
4. Proofread columns of numbers across rather than down the columns. You will more easily detect omitted numbers.
5. Use a ruler or a straightedge to keep your place when proofreading numbers.

6-17—6-19

a. $5.**30**
b. **293404478**-R
c. (703) **555-7629**
d. **$4,859,600**
e. **$7,500, $1,500**
f. Order **7362**

PROOFREADING APPLICATIONS

Proofread the following memorandums, using the appropriate proofreading symbols to mark errors you find in expression of numbers and spelling. To aid you in proofreading, the number of errors to be found is indicated in parentheses at the end of the first two exercises.

P-1   **INTEROFFICE MEMORANDUM**

TO: Adam
FROM: Mary Catherine
DATE: May 14, 19--
SUBJECT: Prospective Clients

Today I talked with Mr. and Mrs. Joseph Morales who are interested in selling their ranch-style house located at 3284 Fourth Street. The house has 3 bedrooms and 2 baths and 1,680 sq. ft. of floor space. The Moraleses have spent more than $3500 in the past three yrs. for repainting and for installing new carpet. The lot, which is just under 3/4 acre, is about average for the neighborhood.

Would you like to talk with them to try to secure their business?

xx   (7 errors)

P-2   **INTEROFFICE MEMORANDUM**

TO: Mary Catherine
FROM: Adam
DATE: May 14, 19--
SUBJECT: Morales Appointment

I have set up an appointment with Mr. and Mrs. Morales for 3 o'clock tomorrow afternoon. I plan to use these points as reasons why they should choose our agency and me to sell their house:

1. Our company is affiliated with a national relocation service.

2. It has consistently commanded 24% of the local market.

3. All of our agents are experienced and liscensed.

4. I, personally, have accummulated 82 sales and listings over the past 2 years.

xx   (5 errors)

P-1

1. **three** bedrooms
2. **two** baths
3.-4. **square feet**
5. **$3,500**
6. three **years**
7. **three-fourths** acre

---

70   Chapter 6—Number Expression Errors

P-3   **INTEROFFICE MEMORANDUM**

TO: Mary Catherine
FROM: Adam
DATE: May 15, 19--
SUBJECT: Morales Contract

Today the Moraleses and I signed a listing contract for the sale of their home. During the meeting we discussed several options.

1. Finance options are available, including morgage with a fixed interest rate over the life of the loan.

2. Professional home inspections should not be waived.

3. Using the concept of pricing items at $.99 rather than $1.00, we discussed pricing their home at $89,900 rather than at $90,000.

xx

P-2

1. **three** o'clock
2. 24 **percent**
3. licensed
4. accumulated
5. **two** years

P-3

1. mortgage
2. at **99 cents**
3. **$1**

PROGRESSIVE PROOFREADING

You are employed as office manager for the Phelps Real Estate Agency. In your basket today are four items to be proofread. Check for spelling, abbreviation, word division, and number expression errors.

Chapter 6—Number Expression Errors   71

Job 1 Proofread this letter carefully and mark all errors.

Phelps Real Estate Agency
1125 Umstead Drive Indianapolis, IN 46204-6154 (317) 555-3222

January 20, 19--

Ms. Patricia Strum
1 Kildaire Farm Road
Indianapolis, IN 46205-9241

Dear Ms. Strum

Good news! The house you are interested in on Thirty-third Street has been reduced $5,000. The price is now within the range you mentioned to me on the 4th. May I urge you to act quickly.

Because of the favorable mortgage rates that are now available, you can own this 2200-square-foot house and still have mortgage payments of less than $900.00 per month. For a limited time, the Indianapoles Federal Savings and Loan Association will approve your application for an adjustable rate loan within thirty days. If it is not approved, you will not be charged the 1% discount rate.

Please call me at 555-3222 to set up an appointment. My office hours are from 9:00 to 5 p.m. Mon-Sat.

Sincerely

Terry B. Andrus
Agent

df

Job 2 Proofread the ad at the bottom of this page using the fact sheet below. In addition to looking for the usual proofreading errors found in keystroking, abbreviations, word division, numbers, and spelling, verify the accuracy of the information in the ad.

RESIDENTIAL FACT AND FEATURE SHEET

Property: 430 Charles Street

Price: $84,900

Location: Greenwood

Home Features:
- Style: ranch
- Total Square Feet: 1,923
- Exterior Finish: vinyl siding
- Age (years): building (21)   roof (2)
- Heat/AC: heat pump
- Garage: 19 feet by 14 feet
- Appliances: stove, dishwasher, refrigerator, and gas logs
- Bathroom (s): two (2)
- Bedrooms: three (3)
- Special Features: formal living room with fireplace
  - den could be used as fourth bedroom
  - large eat-in kitchen
  - beautiful deck 12 feet by 27 feet
  - hot tub deck 12 feet by 12 feet

Lot Features:
- Lot Size: 125 feet by 275 feet
- Landscaping: yes
- Site Features: nice family neighborhood, park located nearby

For further information call Chris at 555-4200.

GREENWOOD SUBDIVISION. Spaciouus and convenient ranch for economy-consious owner. While its main features are three bedrooms, a living room with fireplace, and and a den that could be a forth bedroom, it also has a semi-wooded backyard, a 12- by 27-foot deck, and a twelve- by twelve-foot area with a hot tub. A detached garage provides space for a car and cabinet storage. For more details, call Chris at 555-42000.

Chapter 6—Number Expression Errors

Job 3 Proofread these minutes very carefully. Assume the numbers are accurate; however, they may not be expressed accurately.

Delhi Association of Realtors
325 Alabama Street
Indianapolis, IN 46204-6154
(317) 555-7355

MINUTES OF MEETING
DELHI ASSOCIATION OF REALTORS

Place of Meeting
The Delhi Assoc. of Realtors held its monthly meeting on Tuesday, January 18, 19--, at The Heritage Restaurant. The social hour began at 6:00 o'clock, and dinner was served at 7. Seventy-eight of the 85 members were present in addition to four guests.

Call to Order
Immediately following dinner, J.R. Hawkins, president, called the meeting to order and welcomed the members and guests. She noted that the January attendance was 10% above the December attendance.

Approval of Minutes
The minutes were presented by Secretary Tom Phelps. Jim Miller noted that the state convention would be held on the nineth of March instead of on April 10 as stated in the minutes. The correction was made, and the minutes were approved.

Treasurer's Report
In the absense of Susan Peoples, Tom Phelps gave the treasurer's report. The Association has a balance of $1,210 in the treasury, and bills amounting to $76.10 ($35.10 to Rouse Printing Company and $41 to The Heritage Restaurant) are outstanding. An extension of 10 days has been granted to members who haven't paid their dues.

2

Market   Robert Blankenship was called on to give a summary
Review   of the developments that have taken place in the local
                real estate market. Phelps Real Estate Company has
                been selected as exclusive marketing agent for Brecken-
                ridge subdivision on Leesville Rd. The 79-lot single-
                family subdivision is a Drexter development. Northwoods
                Village, a 228-unit luxury apartment community developed
                by Dallas C. Pickford & Associates, will open on the 1st
                of August. The community is located at Ten Northwoods
                Village Drive, one-half mile south of Interstate 40.

Speaker   Following the business session, the president introduced
                Mrs. Sarah Dunbarton, president of Dunbarton Associates,
                as speaker for the meeting. Mrs. Dunbarton discussed
                the potential effects of recent tax legislation on the
                real estate market. She predicted that the prime rate
                will drop another half point before it hits bottom. In
                In the local area, there will probably be an increase
                of 12-15 apartment buildings on the market within the
                next 6 months.

Adjournment   Following the presentation, the treasurer drew the
                lucky number to determine who would win the center-
                piece. 320 was the lucky number, and winner was Joann
                Durham.

                The meeting was adjourned at 9:15 p.m. Members were
                reminded that the next meeting would be on the third
                Tuesday of February.

                                           Respectfully submitted,

                                           Tom Phelps, Secretary

Chapter 6—Number Expression Errors

COMPUTERIZED PROOFREADING

Job 4 Journal Article

1. Load the file C6JOB4 from the template.

2. Proofread the article on the template, making all needed corrections. Use the spell checker if it is available.

3. Format the article as follows:
   a. Use a top margin of 1½" for the first page and 1" for page 2 and 1" side margins.
   b. Double-space the article and indent paragraphs.

4. Save the article as C6JOB4R.

5. Print one copy of the article.

6. Proofread the printed document. If you find any mistakes, revise, save, and reprint the document.

CHAPTER 7

FORMAT ERRORS

Objectives: *After completing this chapter, you should be able to*
- ▶ Recognize format errors in letters, envelopes, interoffice memorandums, and reports.
- ▶ Use the appropriate proofreading symbols to indicate changes in text.
- ▶ Apply helpful tips when proofreading for format errors.
- ▶ Spell correctly a list of commonly misspelled words.

IMPORTANCE OF FORMAT

A favorable first impression of any business document is important. Why? Because the reader forms an opinion—favorable or unfavorable—of the writer and the message based on the appearance of the document. The overall appearance is affected by the neatness of the document, the quality of the print and stationery, and the format of the document.

Format is perhaps the most complex factor in the appearance of a business document. The format of a document includes margin settings, vertical spacing, and the placement of various parts. If the document is produced on a printer, the format may also include the use of various print sizes (or pitches) and print styles (such as boldface or italic).

The proper use of format is essential to the production of quality copy. Incorrect use of format can instantly destroy the credibility of a document. Chapter 7 will provide a review and apply the basic rules that govern the standard formats of letters, interoffice memorandums, and reports. To be a good proofreader, you must be very knowledgeable of these rules and apply them consistently.

Note: Solutions for the exercises in Chapter 7 begin on page 264.

7-1 The proofreading symbols that apply to formatting are shown below.

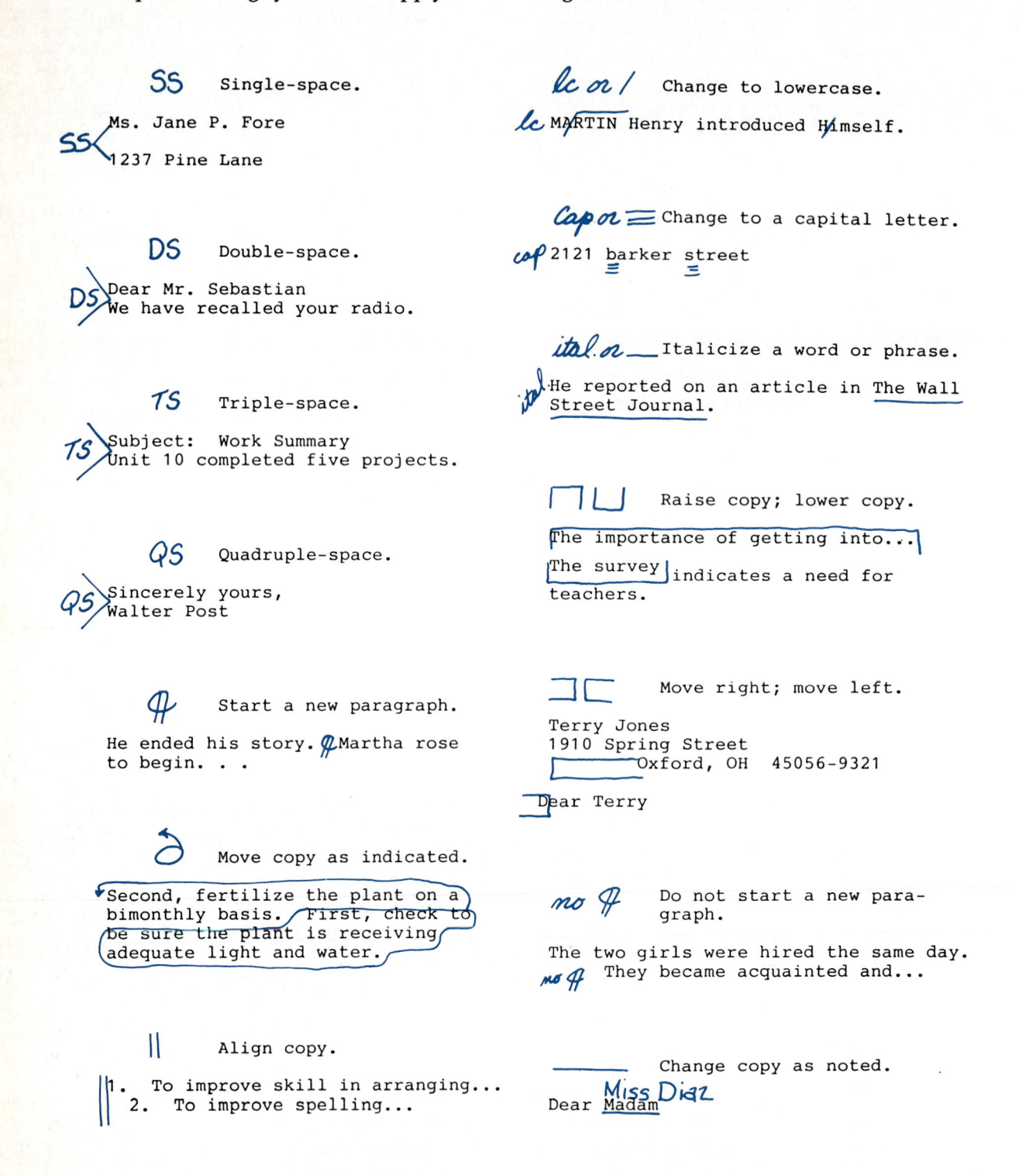

SS   Single-space.

SS Ms. Jane P. Fore
1237 Pine Lane

DS   Double-space.

DS Dear Mr. Sebastian
We have recalled your radio.

TS   Triple-space.

TS Subject: Work Summary
Unit 10 completed five projects.

QS   Quadruple-space.

QS Sincerely yours,
Walter Post

¶   Start a new paragraph.

He ended his story. *¶*Martha rose to begin. . .

↶   Move copy as indicated.

Second, fertilize the plant on a bimonthly basis. First, check to be sure the plant is receiving adequate light and water.

‖   Align copy.

‖1. To improve skill in arranging...
‖2. To improve spelling...

lc or /   Change to lowercase.

lc M/ARTIN Henry introduced H/imself.

Cap or ≡   Change to a capital letter.

cap 2121 ≡barker ≡street

ital. or ___   Italicize a word or phrase.

ital He reported on an article in The Wall Street Journal.

⊓ ⊔   Raise copy; lower copy.

⌐The importance of getting into...⌐
⌐The survey⌐ indicates a need for teachers.

⊐ ⊏   Move right; move left.

Terry Jones
1910 Spring Street
⊐Oxford, OH 45056-9321
⊏Dear Terry

no ¶   Do not start a new paragraph.

The two girls were hired the same day.
no ¶ They became acquainted and...

_____   Change copy as noted.

Dear <u>Madam</u> *Miss Diaz*

Review these marks carefully, and note how they are used in the rough draft shown on page 79. Then note the changes that have been made in the finished letter.

78   Chapter 7—Format Errors

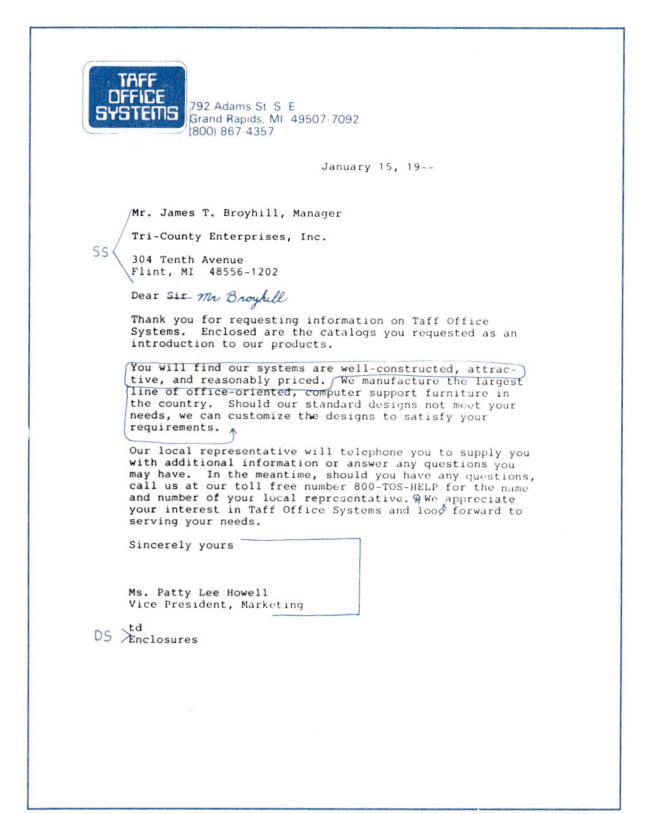

Rough Draft   **Finished Letter**

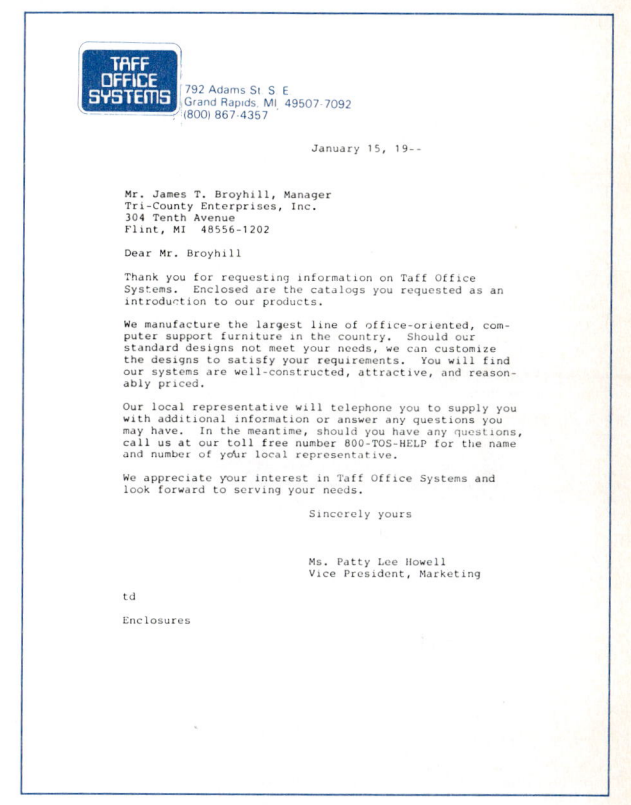

✓ Did the typist make all of the necessary changes? _____

LETTER FORMAT

Locating format errors in business letters requires that the proofreader be familiar with the correct sequence and placement of letter parts. Refer to Illustration 7-1 on page 80 as you review each of the letter parts. Placement of the letter parts and punctuation may vary with the style of letter used. These specific points will be discussed in the subsequent section on letter styles.

Date

To allow space for the company letterhead, the date should be placed between two and three inches from the top of the page depending on the length of the letter. Many businesses, however, use a standard or set placement for the date regardless of the letter length. When using either convention, allow at least a double space below the last line of the letterhead and the date.

ILLUSTRATION 7-1 Model Letter with Special Features

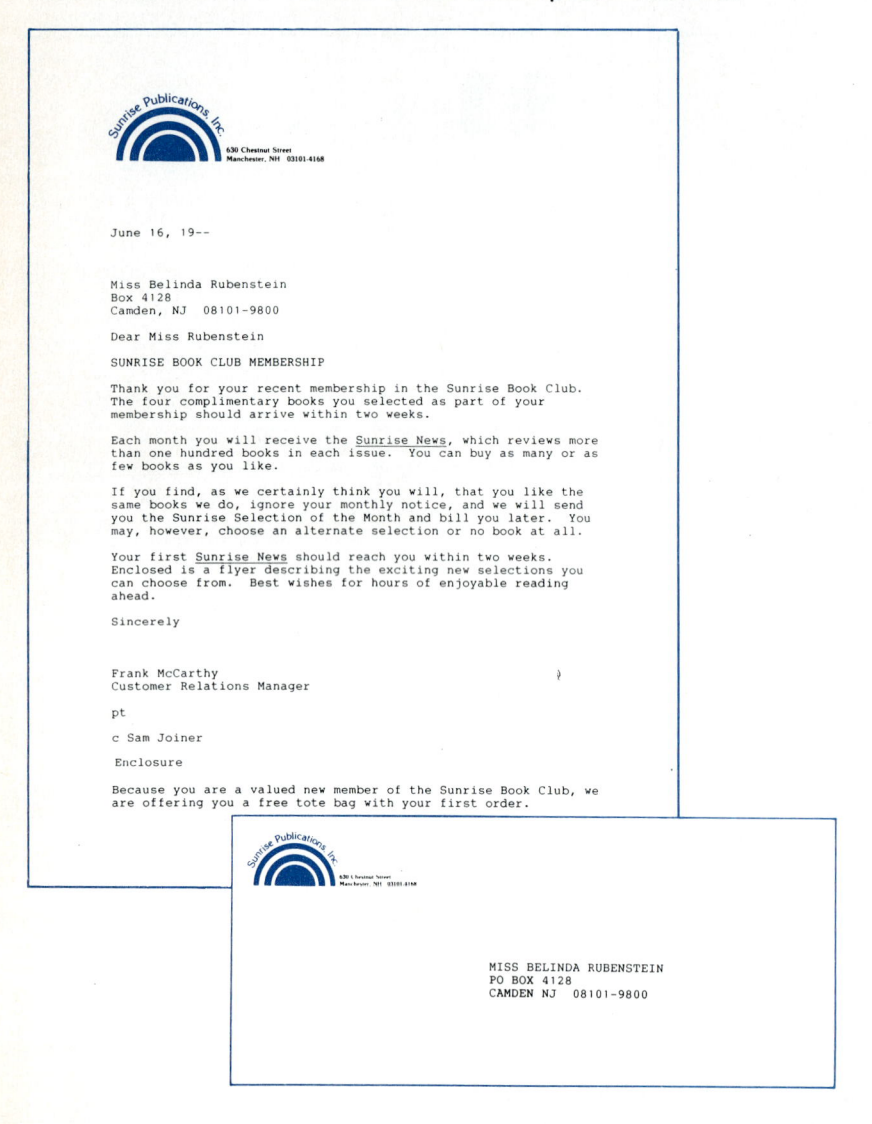

Note: Because of automated scanning equipment, the U.S. Postal Service requests that envelopes be prepared in ALL CAPS with no punctuation.

If the letter is prepared on plain stationery rather than on letterhead, the writer's return address is placed immediately above the date.

Letter Address

The letter address gives complete information about the person to whom the letter is directed. It should contain the recipient's name, job title (when appropriate), and complete address. If the letter is addressed to a company, an attention line may be included as the second line of the letter address. The letter address should begin on the fourth line, also known as a quadruple space (QS), below the date. The proofreader should always check the spelling of the name, street, and city to be sure they are correct.

80   Chapter 7—Format Errors

If the addressee is an individual, a personal title (Mr., Miss, Ms., Dr., etc.) should precede the name. If the letter is addressed to a woman whose personal title is not known, use *Ms*. If the gender of the addressee is unknown and cannot be determined by the first name (Examples: Lee, Kelly, Alex, Terry), then omit the personal title. Official titles (Chairman, Vice President of Operations) in the letter address should be capitalized.

Note: The address on the envelope should agree with the letter address. Refer to Illustration 7-1 for proper envelope format.

Salutation

The salutation (greeting) used must agree with the first line of the letter address. The salutation is placed a double space below the letter address. The examples below show the proper salutations to be used in different situations. Note that only the first word, nouns, and titles are capitalized in a formal salutation.

Addressed to a company:	Fisher-Price Securities
	31 St. James Avenue
	Boston, MA 02116-4255
	DS
	Ladies and Gentlemen
Addressed to a job title:	Advertising Manager
	Fisher-Price Securities
	31 St. James Avenue
	Boston, MA 02116-4255
	DS
	Dear Sir or Madam
Addressed to an individual:	Mrs. Ruby B. Speight
	1500 Sauls Street
	Covington, KY 41011-9750
	DS
	Dear Mrs. Speight

Subject Line

The subject line, which indicates the topic of the letter, is placed a double space below the salutation. The subject line is usually keyed in ALL CAPS at the left margin, but it may be centered or aligned with the first word of paragraph 1 depending on the letter format. A letter may or may not have a subject line.

Body

The body, or message, begins a double space below the salutation or subject line. The body is single spaced with a double space between paragraphs.

Complimentary Close

The complimentary close provides a cordial farewell. It should be placed a double space below the body of the letter. Only the first word of a complimentary close is capitalized.

Company Name and Writer's Name and Title

When letterhead stationery is used, the company name is rarely included in the closing lines. If the company name is used, it should be placed a double space below the complimentary close in ALL CAPS.

The sender's name should be entered on the fourth line (three blank lines) below the complimentary close (or the company name if it is included). If needed, the personal title is included as part of the sender's name so that others may address correspondence correctly (Examples: Mrs. Florence Sofiatti, Dr. Leo Thomas, Mr. Lee Burke). The sender's official title may be placed on the same line as the typed signature and separated from the signature by a comma or may be placed on the next line. The individual's title should be capitalized.

Reference Initials

Reference initials identify those involved in the creation of a business letter. These initials should be located at the left margin, a double space below the signer's keyed name and title.

Enclosure Notation

The enclosure notation is used when one or more documents accompany the letter. For the notation, the word *Enclosure* or *Enclosures* is spelled out in full. The notation should be placed at the left margin, a double space below the reference initials.

Copy Notation

The copy notation indicates other persons who will receive a copy of the letter. The copy notation appears in lowercase at the left margin as *c* followed by the name(s) of the person(s) receiving a copy. The copy notation should be placed a double space below the enclosure notation, if one is used, or a double space below the reference initials.

Postscript

Occasionally, writers use a postscript to emphasize information in a letter. The postscript is keyed a double space below the last notation on the letter.

7-2 When proofreading a business letter, make sure all appropriate letter parts are included and properly keyed and positioned.

✓ Proofread the following letter parts for format errors, using appropriate proofreading symbols to mark errors. Refer to page 264 for the solutions.

a. Ms. Katrina Ann Dewar
8577 Estate Drive South
West Palm Beach, FL   33411-9753

Sales Promotion

Dear Madam

b. Please let me know when we can get together to discuss the property.

Very Sincerely Yours,

Ms. Donna Raynor

Enclosure

ah

c. Carson Real Estate Enterprises
1860 Memorial Drive
Greenville, SC   29605-8642

Dear Mr. Carson

d. Mr. M. C. Alexander
1620 Quantico Court
San Jose, CA   95230-1009

Dear Mr. M. C. Alexander

e. Ms. Ilo Carlson
8090 Pinetree Street
Little Rock, AR   72201-0057

Dear Mrs. Carlson

f. Sincerely,

Brian Davis, Manager

dt

c Carolyn Walston

Chapter 7—Format Errors

LETTER AND PUNCTUATION STYLES

As mentioned in the previous section, punctuation and placement of some letter parts vary with the style selected. The following paragraphs describe the various letter and punctuation styles that may be used in letter preparation.

Although various letter styles are acceptable, the most popular are block style and modified block style. Usually organizations prepare all correspondence using the same style. Refer to Illustration 7-2 for a review of block and modified block letter styles. Paragraphs may be either blocked (begun at the left margin) or indented in modified block style.

Letters may be prepared using either open or mixed punctuation. Open punctuation includes no punctuation after the salutation or the complimentary close. Mixed punctuation includes a colon after the salutation and a comma after the complimentary close.

ILLUSTRATION 7-2 Block Style   Modified Block Style

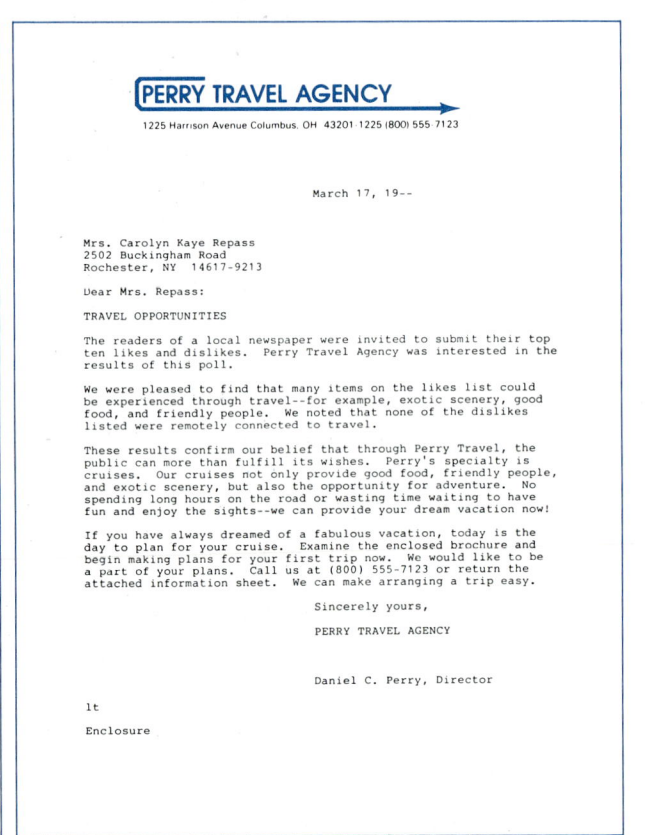

7-3 Remember to use the correct format consistently, regardless of the letter style chosen.

Proofread the letter shown below and mark the errors using appropriate proofreading symbols. Pay attention to the letter style, placement of letter parts, and punctuation style. The letter should be prepared in block style with open punctuation. Then compare your work with the solution given on page 265.

```
                        WALSH PAPERS
                         2250 Harris Road
                        Huntsville, AL 35810-2250
                          (509) 555-5892




                                              June 16, 19--

Ms. Jennifer Elaine Carson
Route 2, Box 507B
Huntsville, AL  35807-8615

PURCHASE ORDER 471

Dear Ms. Carson

Thank you for your order for six boxes of stationery,
Stock No. 331.  The quality of the stationery you have
selected will let your customers know that they are
important to you.

Because of the recent shipping strike, there has been a
delay in our receiving the merchandise from the factory.
We have been informed that the shipment has been sent,
however, and we should receive it within a week.  Your
order will be on its way to you as soon as we receive the
shipment.  We hope this delay will not inconvenience you
too much.

We appreciate the business you have given us in the past,
and we look forward to serving you in the future.

Sincerely,


Audrey D. Leapley, Manager
Shipping Department

ec
c R. P. Michaels
```

LETTER PLACEMENT

The spacing and placement of the various letter parts contribute to the readability of a document as well as to its overall attractiveness. Placing a letter too high or too low on the paper or too far to the left or the right upsets the balance and detracts from the letter's appearance. In order for a letter to have an attractive overall appearance, the operator must use appropriate side, top, and bottom margins. These margins depend on the size of stationery used (standard size, executive size, or half-size) and the length of the letter to be keyed.

Chapter 7—Format Errors

As a proofreader, you should be more concerned with the overall balance of a letter than with its exact margins. Regardless of the size of the stationery and the length of the document, the letter should appear "balanced" on the page. Your goal in proofreading will be to train your eye to identify an improperly placed letter. To help you place letters attractively on the page, use the following letter placement table as a guide.

LETTER PLACEMENT TABLE

Letter Classification	Side Margins	Dateline Position*
Short	2"	line 18
Average	1½"	line 16
Long	1"	line 14
Two-page	1"	line 14
Standard 6" line**	1¼"	line 16
Standard 6½" line**	1"	line 16

*When a deep letterhead prevents use of this dateline position, place the date a double space below last line of letterhead.

In letters containing special features or tables, adjust dateline position upward on letterhead.

When a window envelope is to be used, the dateline position is line 12.

**In some offices, the same line length and specific dateline position are used for all letters, regardless of classification.

7-4 Begin now to develop good judgment concerning letter placement by making a conscious appraisal of the placement of every letter you see.

✓ Study the three letters given and indicate which letter is properly placed.

Letter A   Letter B   Letter C

The correct placement is shown in Letter _____.

Chapter 7—Format Errors

MEMORANDUM FORMAT

Interoffice memorandums (memos, for short) are used to send informal messages within an organization. Memorandums cover one subject or topic that can be discussed in a few paragraphs. Even though the interoffice memorandum is for internal use, accuracy of the message and the proper format are still important. Co-workers and managers often judge the writer's overall job abilities by the quality of the message sent. Additionally, improper format tends to distract the reader. Two formats are generally used: *standard* and *simplified*. (See Illustrations 7-3 and 7-4.)

Standard Format

Standard style memos are placed on a printed form, on plain paper, or on company letterhead. Printed interoffice memorandum forms are used by many businesses. The forms usually have four main headings: **TO**, **FROM**, **DATE**, and **SUBJECT**.

If the organization does not use a form with printed headings, headings should be positioned so that the same margin setting can be used to fill in the headings and to enter the body. Set side margins of 1 inch and a tab setting 10 spaces from the left margin to key in heading information.

    TO: John Carlton
  FROM: Francis James
  DATE: February 14, 19--
SUBJECT: Purchase Requisition No. 039103

Many word processing packages have the ability to store memo formats that can be recalled and filled in the same way as a memo form.

The message begins a double space below the last line of the heading and is single spaced with a double space between paragraphs. Memos are usually signed or initialed by the originator. Reference initials are placed a double space below the body.

Simplified Format

The simplified memo, easily produced on automated equipment, omits the headings TO, FROM, DATE, and SUBJECT.

Using plain paper or company letterhead, set side margins of about 1 inch (or default margins on your equipment) and begin all lines at the left margin. Key the dateline 1½ inches (line 10) from the top of a plain sheet or a double space below the letterhead.

Quadruple-space after the date and key the recipient's name, followed by a double space with the subject line either in all capital letters or in capitals and lowercase. The message begins a double space below the subject line, with double spacing between paragraphs. Key the sender's name a quadruple space below the last line of the body, followed by a double space and the reference initials.

Chapter 7—Format Errors

ILLUSTRATION 7-3 Standard Memo Format, Interoffice Memorandum

KRIEGER PHARMACEUTICALS

Internal Memorandum

TO: All Employees

FROM: Pat Brooks, Personnel Manager

DATE: May 20, 19--

SUBJECT: Vacation Policies

The new vacation policy issued last week will be implemented beginning June 1. Please submit your request for vacation time as soon as you can so that we can try to accommodate your preferences.

Plan to take the full vacation to which you are entitled. Studies show that taking only a day or two of vacation at a time does not maximize the benefits to you of time taken off from work.

lj

ILLUSTRATION 7-4 Simplified Memo Format

March 17, 19--

Carla Sanders

OFFICE AUTOMATION TOUR BY CLINTON COLLEGE STUDENTS

Carla, please schedule an office automation tour on April 3 at 10 a.m. for 18 Clinton College students. These students are enrolled in a desktop publishing class and are interested in a demonstration of our desktop publishing equipment and software. Their instructor, Lillian Thomas, will accompany them.

Could you ask your staff to include a brief explanation of each of the three systems we use and appropriate printouts. About 20 minutes should provide a good overview. Thanks for making these arrangements.

Joyce Bickson

mp

7-5 Apply the guidelines above when proofreading memorandums.

✓ Proofread the following interoffice memorandum and mark the errors in format using the appropriate proofreading symbols. Check your solution on page 265.

Martindale Publishing   **Internal Memorandum**

TO: Associate Editors

FROM: Danny Bright, Executive Editor *DB*

DATE: Production Meetings

SUBJECT: April 10, 19--

    On Monday, April 25, all associate editors should plan to meet in Conference Room C, third floor, at 10 a.m. The purpose of this meeting is to identify topics that are of concern to you as a supervisor.
    You are a vital member of our editorial team, and your input is essential to keeping production running smoothly during this very heavy copyright year. Based on your input, we will establish an agenda for future meetings.

re

REPORT FORMAT

Reports are used extensively by business and educational institutions to provide information on specific topics. Standard parts of a report include the title page, main heading, body, side headings, paragraph headings, and reference page. Reports may be long, formal documents consisting of a number of parts; or they may be short, informal documents consisting of only a heading and the body of the report.

Reports may be prepared in unbound, leftbound, or topbound format. Most reports, however, are prepared in unbound format and are simply held together by a staple at the top.

Just as with business letters and memorandums, reports should be positioned in an attractive, easy-to-read format. Refer to Illustration 7-5 as you review the format for the main parts of a report.

Title Page

The title page contains the title of the report (line 16), the author's name (line 32) and title (line 34), and the date (line 50).

Margins

In unbound report format, 1-inch margins are used for the side and bottom margins. A top margin of about 1½ inches is used for the first page. On the second and succeeding pages, a top margin of 1 inch is used, the page number is on line 6, and the text continues a double space below.

In leftbound report format, the left margin should be 1½ inches to allow space for the binding. All other margins are the same as for an unbound report.

Headings

The *main heading* is centered about 1½ inches from the top of the page and is entered in ALL CAPS. If two lines are required, the lines may be either single spaced or double spaced. If a *secondary heading* is used, it is centered a double space below the main heading, and important words are capitalized.

Side headings indicate subdivisions of the main topic. Side headings are entered in capital and lowercase letters (important words capitalized) and underlined. A double space precedes and follows a side heading.

Paragraph headings indicate subdivisions of the side headings. Paragraph headings are placed at the beginning point of paragraphs. The first word is capitalized, and the heading is underlined and followed with a period. The text of the paragraph begins on the same line as the heading.

Body

The body, or the text, of a report begins a quadruple space below the main heading. The body is either double spaced with five-space paragraph indentions or single spaced with block paragraphs. Leave at least two lines of a paragraph at the top and bottom of a page. Single-space quotes of four lines or more and indent five spaces from the left margin.

Page Numbers

The first page of a report usually is not numbered. On the second page and subsequent pages, the page number should be placed on line 6 at the right margin. The body of the report continues on line 8.

ILLUSTRATION 7-5 Unbound Report Format

TIPS FOR GETTING ORGANIZED **(line 10)**
QS

    Do you have trouble getting everything done in the time available? Do you often lose important papers? Do you lose papers on top of your desk? If you're like most people, the answer to some of these questions is a resounding yes! Perhaps a few tips for getting organized would be helpful.

<u>Identify Your Time Wasters</u> **DS**

    The first step to becoming better organized is to identify your time wasters. Some may be external factors that you cannot easily control such as telephone interruptions, meetings, and socializing. However, you can control internal factors such as procrastination and failure to delegate, to plan, or to set priorities.

    Once you identify your time wasters, find out how you spend your time by taking a time inventory.

<u>Time Inventory</u>

    Record the amount of time you spend each day in various activities on a time log. Then analyze your time log to try to discover ways in which you can improve the management of your time. Ask yourself these questions:

    1. What was the most productive period of the day and why?

    2. What was the least productive period of the day and why?

    3. On what activities could I spend less time and still get the desired results?

    4. Do I have all my supplies and materials ready before beginning an activity?

(line 6) 2

    After you have analyzed your time log, develop an action **DS** plan to increase your time management efficiency.

<u>Develop a "Things to Do" List</u>

    Develop a list of tasks to be completed, placing the most urgent items first. Depending on the type of work you do, your list can be compiled on a daily, weekly, or project basis.

<u>Maintain a Recording and Filing System</u>

    Keep pertinent information in an accessible place. Two such places are a pocket organizer and your personal files.

    <u>Pocket organizer</u>. Carry a pocket organizer to record appointments, expenses, addresses and telephone numbers, reminders, and jobs to be done.

    <u>Filing system</u>. Store important papers in one place--your files. Label folders appropriately; for example, automobile, credit card statements, medical, taxes, travel, and warranties.

    Time is a valuable resource that few people have enough of. The aim of time management (Kallus and Keeling, 1991) is to provide for efficient use of resources, including time, so that individuals are productive in achieving their goals.

REFERENCES

Bell, Carol Lynn, and Brian H. Kleiner. "Orchestrating Your Time," <u>The Secretary</u>, January 1990.

Fulton, Patsy J., and Joanna D. Hanks. <u>Procedures for the Office Professional</u>. Cincinnati: South-Western Publishing Co., 1990.

Kallus, Norman F., and B. Lewis Keeling. <u>Administrative Office Management</u>. Cincinnati: South-Western Publishing Co., 1991.

References

When quoting another writer or when using another's ideas, writers must document (identify) their source(s). A common method of documentation is to cite the source of the information within the body of the report. This reference includes the author's last name, the year of publication, and the page number.

    According to Macey (1990, 74)

Complete information about the sources is found on the reference page, which contains a list of references at the end of the report. Each entry on the page consists of the name(s) of the author(s), the title and date of the referenced publication, and the page number(s) of the material cited. Refer to Illustration 7-5 for an example of a reference page.

Note: The references should begin on a new page if all references will not fit on the last page of the body of the report.

Memo Reports

Memo reports are frequently used in business to communicate routine information. A memo report uses standard memo headings; internal headings may be used for ease of reading. Should the report be longer than one page, a second-page heading is used consisting of the reviewer's name, the page number, and the date. Refer to Illustration 7-6 for an example.

ILLUSTRATION 7-6 Memo Report Format

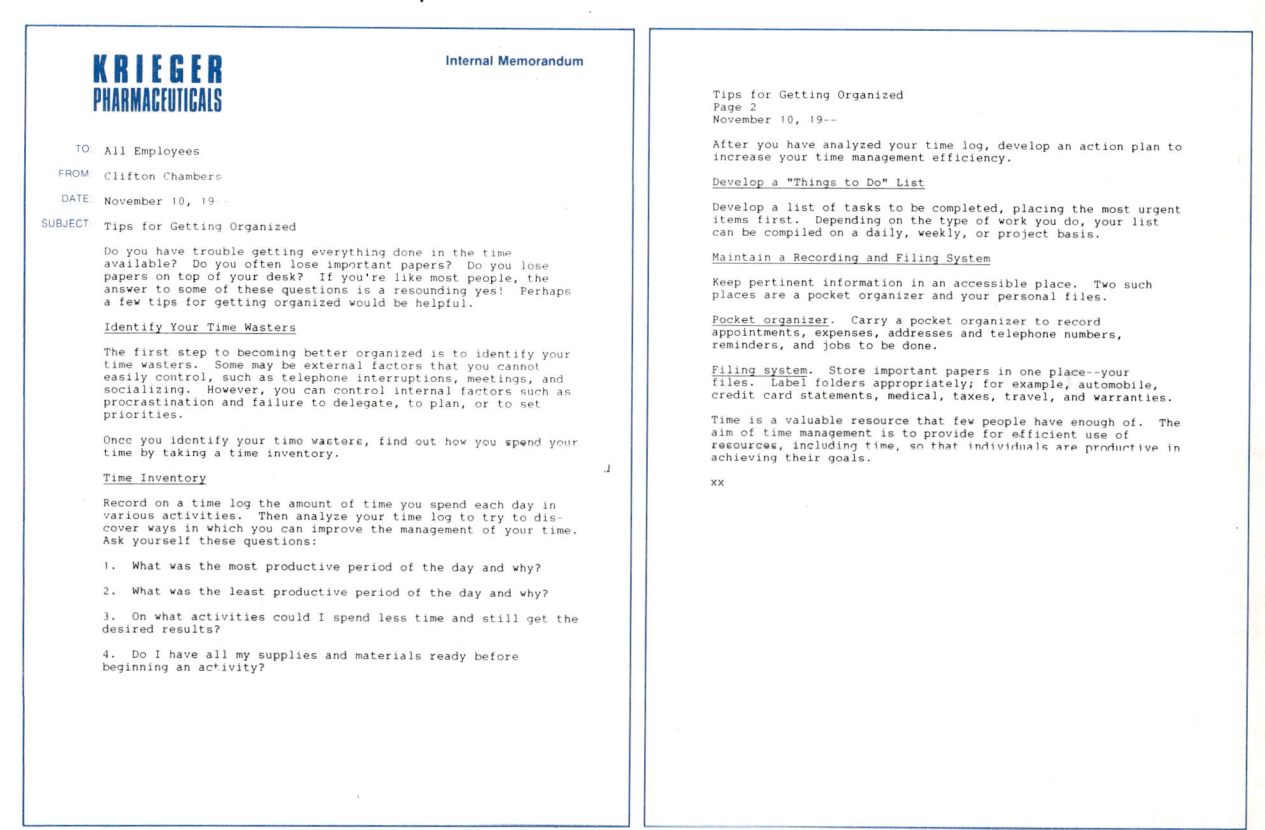

7-6 Follow these tips whenever you are proofreading a report, especially a long report.

▶ Develop a style sheet or a list showing how unusual terminology, features, punctuation, capitalization, names, or titles will be handled. Using a style sheet will help you to treat items consistently.
▶ If the report has been prepared from a draft copy, check to be sure that copy has not been omitted in typing.
▶ If the text refers to a particular illustration, figure, or page within the report, check to be sure the reference is correct.
▶ If you are responsible for checking the references given in the report, look each one up to verify it.

Chapter 7—Format Errors

▶ As a final check, proofread separately similar parts of a lengthy report. For example, check all the side headings to see if they are handled consistently; then check all the paragraph headings. Also, check that all pages have been numbered in sequence.

Refer to the Progressive Proofreading section for an opportunity to exercise your skills in proofreading reports.

SPELLING REVIEW

To improve your ability to detect spelling errors, master the words below. Watch for them in the exercises that follow and in succeeding chapters.

column	particularly
description	precede
eliminate	separate
judgment	sufficient
opportunity	usable

PROOFREADING TIPS

Study these tips and apply them as you proofread:

1. Watch for the places where errors tend to occur: in words located near the margins; in lines close to the bottom of the page; in long words; in titles, headings, and subheadings.

2. Use an up-to-date reference guide. (Because of increased use of the personal computer, some format rules may change.)

3. Be sure to proofread the date, letter address, salutation, and closing lines within a letter.

4. Be sure that the format of the letter is not a mixture of block and modified block and that the punctuation styles are not mixed.

5. When completing a large mailing, make sure letters are put in the proper envelopes and all enclosures are included.

PROGRESSIVE PROOFREADING

You are employed as executive secretary to Ms. Emily Simpson, regional manager of Perin Office Systems, Inc. You have just finished keying three documents that she dictated. In addition to proofreading them, you need to proofread the documents prepared by a typist who works with you. Check for errors in keying, spelling, word division, number expression, and format.

Job 1 Proofread the following letter. Ms. Simpson prefers block letter style and open punctuation.

PERIN OFFICE SYSTEMS
3903 Spaulding Drive, Atlanta, GA 30338-3903
(404)555-1719

March 17, 19--

Ms. Cleo Mendoza
Phillips and Solomon
431 N. Main Street
Champlain, NY 12919-4300

Dear Ms. Mendoza

    Thank you for the oportunity to demonstrate our new DataPhone telephone system for you at the TeleCom Exhibition last week. As you make your decision on a new system, keep in mind the following features that DataPhone offers:

1. **Speed dialing.** This feature can bring as many as 20 often-called numbers together in one place on the desktop console. By pressing a preprogrammed button, you can place a call in less than 3 seconds. Speed dialing eliminates searching for phone numbers.

2. **Call pickup.** This feature helps to elimintae unanswered calls by allowing anyone to answer a ringing phone.

3. **Conferencing.** This feature provides an easy, convenient way to bring people together without having to travel or even to leave their desks.

4. **Call forwarding.** This feature is particularly useful since it allows a person away from his or her desk to automatically forward calls to another extension.

5. **Speaker.** An optional feature, this is an extremely convenient way to talk with your hands free to take notes or operate the computer keyboard.

Perin Office Systems provides installation and employee training free of charge to companies that purchase the DataPhone system. Call us today to discuss your phone needs.

                Sincerely,

                Ms. Emily E. Simpson
                Regional Manager

ri

Chapter 7—Format Errors

Job 2 Proofread this letter to Eastman Brothers.

PCS PERIN OFFICE SYSTEMS
3903 Spaulding Drive, Atlanta, GA 30338-3903
(404)555-1719

March 17, 19--

Mr. Roger Moe
Eastman Brothers, Inc.
7861 Monroe Street
Tallahassee, FL 32301-7654

Ladies and Gentlemen

Enclosed is a short report reviewing the preliminary
design factors that your project committee must consider
when planning the 15,000-square-foot addition to your
existing facilities.

We will provide complete documentation for these reccomen-
dations atour initial planning session on Apirl 7. In
the mean time, good luck with your planning.

Sincerely yours,

Ms. Emily E. Simpson
Regional Manager

jp

Enclosure

Job 3 Proofread this report to Eastman Brothers. Check correct figures of the floor area with the note supplied by one of the realtors (page 99).

OFFICE DESIGN FACTORS

Eastman Brothers, Inc.

Because office design does affect job performance and job satisfaction, several factors should be considered in the preliminary stages of planning the construction or renovation of any facility. This report discusses these factors and gives recommendations that may increase employees' productivity by as much as 30% and decrease absenteeism.

Work Space

The area where workers spend most of their time is their work space. The factors to be considered when work space is designed are discussed below.

Enclosures. The open office plan with enclosures gives workers the privacy they need, supports communication, and improves productivity more than either the fully open or fully closed office plan. To be effective, the partitions surrounding each work area should be higher than standing height on 3 sides.

Floor area. The amount of usable flour space a worker can call his or her own is based on job need and status. According to Quible (1989), the minimum requirements for various employees are as follows:

         Top-level executives   400 square feet
         Middle-level executives   300 square feet
         Supervisors   200 square feet
         Office employees   100 square feet

Chapter 7—Format Errors

2

Layout. The physical arrangement (layout) of furniture and walls greatly affects job performance, comfort, status, and ease of communication. Workers should have two good work surfaces and a single front entrance. The layout should be designed so that others are not seated directly in front of the employee.
Lighting.

Proper lighting is determined by the quality and quantity of light. Approxmately 150 footcandles are recommended for computer usage. Most lightning problems are caused by too much light, resulting in in glare on documents or reflections on monitors. Although most workers prefer to be near a window, windows do cause glare.

Ambient light fixtures (which illuminate the entire office area) combined with task lighting (which lights specific work surfaces) create the most effective lighting system.

<u>Noise</u>

Office conversations, ringing telephones, and outside nose account for most office noise. Sound-absorbent materials used throughout the building, acoustical enclosures on printers, and layout are effective means of reducing office noise. Office noise should be less than 65 decibels (Casady 1989).

<u>Energy</u>

Energy needs include lines for power, phones, and data. To determine these needs, these questions need to be answered: Do you expect high growth in computer usage? Do you expect to rearrange workstations frequently? If so, how often?

Access floors raised of the structural slab provide an excellent solution for distributing heat, air conditioning, and wiring for data and telephone services. These floors have unlimited capacity and may be accessed at any point by service units without calling an electrician. Additionally, quality and speed of transmission will not be affected as your transmission needs grwo.

From the desk of ROGER MOE Date 3/17

To *Emily Simpson*

Here are the correct figures on minimum floor space requirements.

Top level executives	425 sq ft
Middle level "	350 sq ft
Supervisors	200 sq ft
Office employees	75-100 sq ft

rm.

Chapter 7—Format Errors

Job 4 Proofread the document for the typist, following the instructions left for you.

PCS PERIN OFFICE SYSTEMS
3903 Spaulding Drive, Atlanta, GA 30:
(404)555-1719

Please check to be sure that I haven't missed any errors! Mr. Holms prefers the modified block letter style with mixed punctuation. Thanks tr

March 17, 19--

Ms. Jessica Shimer
2905 Sandcastle Dr.
Tallahassee, FL 32308-9625

Dear Ms. Shimer:

Thank you for your interest in the Perin Laser Copier, Model 212. Enclosed is a brochure detailing its unique features, its specifications, and its cost.

The Perin Laser Copier is the most technologically sophisticated copier on the marked today. This laser-driven copier uses a scanner to digitize originals. Text (including columns can be manipulated before printing begins. Because it is digital, the laser copier can transmit images to other printers and produce high-resolution copiers in seconds.

After you have had a chance to review this brochure, I will give you a call to provide you with additional product or price information or to set up a demonstration. In the meantime, please call me at the number listed above if you have any questions.

Sincerely yours,

Robert C. Holms
Saels Representative

tr

100   Chapter 7—Format Errors

COMPUTERIZED PROOFREADING

Job 5 Memorandum

1. Load C7JOB5 from the template.
2. Format the memo in simplified style, addressing it to **All Product Managers** from you. Use the current date and **Computer Maintenance** as the subject.
3. Proofread the memo for all types of errors, including keying, formatting, spelling, and word division. Correct any errors that you find.
4. Spell check the document if possible.
5. Save the memo using the file name C7JOB5R.
6. Print the memo.
7. Proofread the printed document. If you find any additional errors, revise it, save, and reprint.

NOTE these procedures for the following chapters:

▶ Beginning in Chapter 8, specific formatting instructions will not be provided for letters, memos, or reports. If necessary, check the placement table or the models in this chapter.
▶ The procedures of saving, printing, proofreading the printed document, and, if necessary, reprinting the document are standard procedures that you should implement each time you process a job on the template. These instructions will not be repeated.

CHAPTER 8

GRAMMAR ERRORS: SUBJECT AND VERB AGREEMENT

Objectives: *After completing this chapter, you should be able to*
- Recognize sentence fragments.
- Identify errors in subject-verb agreement.
- Use the appropriate proofreading symbols to indicate changes in text.
- Spell correctly a list of commonly misspelled words.

IMPORTANCE OF CORRECT GRAMMAR

The proofreader must be alert for grammatical errors. In addition to clarifying the message, correct grammar conveys a message to the reader about the writer. It reflects the writer's abilities and attention to detail. The reader will have greater confidence in the writer if the message is grammatically correct. If it is not correct, the reader will react negatively and lose confidence in the writer or the person or company the writer represents. This chapter will review the rules concerning basic sentence structure and subject-verb agreement. Because correct grammar is essential to effective communication, study carefully the rules reviewed here and in Chapter 9.

PARTS OF A SENTENCE

A sentence is a group of words that expresses a complete thought. It requires both a subject and a verb. The **subject** is the person, place, or thing spoken of in the sentence, and the **verb** indicates what the subject is or does. The verb expresses action (*eat, sleep, think*) or a state of being (*is, am, are, seem*).

8-1 An incomplete sentence, termed a *sentence fragment*, does not contain both a subject and a verb and does not express a complete thought. Rewrite sentence fragments to change them into complete sentences.

    Sentence Fragment: Promoted the clerk and hired a replacement.

    Complete Sentence: Martha promoted the clerk and hired a replacement.

✓ Identify each of the following groups of words as either a sentence or a fragment by writing *S* or *F* after each group. Correct sentence fragments by adding words to make complete sentences.

  a. The project consultant is an expert in urban planning.

  b. Two new computer programs developed by Phil.

  c. Hannah became the editor of her hometown newspaper.

  d. Miles and Sam will work as census takers.

  e. Because the word processing center is undergoing renovation.

8-2 The subject of a sentence is usually a noun (Barbara, New York, hat) or a personal pronoun (*I, you, he, she, it, we, they*). A **pronoun** is a word used in place of a noun.

      S   V
Dr. Morgan signed the contract.
    (noun used as a subject)

                S   V
Before Phil left, he signed the contract.
    (pronoun used as a subject)

✓ Indicate whether the subject of each sentence is a noun or a pronoun by writing either *N* or *P* above the subject.

  a. Mr. Ormond wants the report on his desk by noon.

  b. Three new laser printers have been installed in the office.

  c. She will conduct a leadership workshop at the district conference.

  d. Many people are working as volunteers in their communities.

  e. You may take your vacation the second week in November.

8-1
a. S
b. programs **were** developed
c. S
d. S
e. renovation, . . .

SUBJECT-VERB AGREEMENT

The verb must agree with its subject in number. Rules on subject-verb agreement are given in the frames that follow.

8-3 A singular subject must have a singular verb, and a plural subject must have a plural verb.

       S   V
  The author writes clearly.

           S   V
  The two books appear to be lost.

▶ The personal pronouns *I, he, she,* and *it* require a singular verb; *you, we,* and *they* require a plural verb. *You* always requires a plural verb even when it is used in the singular sense.

S   V
I am going to exercise daily.

S   V
We are going to jog weekly.

S   V
You know the limitations of the program.

S   S   V
You and Pat know the limitations of the program.

S   V
She writes very concisely.

S   V
They make an excellent team.

✓ Correct errors in subject-verb agreement by crossing through the incorrect verbs and writing in the correct verbs. If the subject and verb are in agreement, write a C to the right of the sentence.

  a. She doesn't want to study any foreign languages or science.

  b. Mr. Huggins employ 1,300 workers in his Augusta plant.

  c. You and Art enters all the sweepstakes contests.

  d. Jolie writes effective communications.

  e. You was gone when the call came to close the store early.

8-2
a. Mr. Ormand — N
b. printers — N
c. She — P
d. people — N
e. You — P

Chapter 8—Grammar Errors: Subject and Verb Agreement

8-4 When a sentence contains an irregular verb (such as *to be* or *to have*), subject-verb agreement can be difficult to determine. Because irregular verb forms are used frequently, be alert for their proper usage.

FORMS OF TO BE

	Singular	Plural
Present Tense:	I *am* you *are* he, she, it *is*	we *are* you *are* they *are*
Past Tense:	I *was* you *were* he, she, it *was*	we *were* you *were* they *were*
Future Tense:	I *will be* you *will be* he, she, it *will be*	we *will be* you *will be* they *will be*

TO HAVE

	Singular	Plural
Present Tense:	I *have* you *have* he, she, it *has*	we *have* you *have* they *have*
Past Tense:	I *had* you *had* he, she, it *had*	we *had* you *had* they *had*
Future Tense:	I *will have* you *will have* he, she, it *will have*	we *will have* you *will have* they *will have*

✓ Proofread for errors in subject-verb agreement; cross out any incorrect verbs and write in the correct verb form. If a sentence is correct, write a C to the right of it.

a. A price list and an order blank is enclosed for your order.

b. Terry have written several books about migratory birds.

c. You are ready to proceed to the next level, if you wish.

d. The concert programs was printed on heavy bond paper.

e. Have the representative decided to collect the money today?

8-3
a. C
b. **employs**
c. **enter**
d. C
e. **were**

8-5   The subject and the verb must agree in number even though they may be separated by a group of words containing nouns of a different number.

        S   V

The employees working on that job have to finish it by September 4.

        S   V

The bus driver, in addition to the students, was injured.

✓ Proofread for errors in subject-verb agreement. If a sentence is correct, write a *C* to the right of it.

  a. The need for service employees is greater today than ever before.

  b. Employees trained for data entry has been hired by the company.

  c. Skills as well as knowledge is necessary for success in business.

  d. His sister who works as a cashier in a bank has been promoted.

  e. The criteria for selecting my successor has been defined.

8-6   A compound subject (more than one subject) joined by *and* usually requires a plural verb.

        S   S   V

Larry Mann and Blair Jordan are seniors.

     S   S   V

Chris and I were classmates in school.

Note: When using the pronoun *I* as part of a compound subject, always put the other subject first.

There are only two exceptions to the above rule:

▶ When the compound subject is considered to be one unit, use a singular verb.

     S   S   V

My teacher and advisor, Dr. Underwood, is a Pirate fan.

▶ When the compound subject is preceded by *each, every, many a,* or *many an,* use a singular verb.

      S   S   V

Each teacher and student is expected to attend the assembly.

       S   S   V

Many an honor and award is presented at graduation.

8-4
a. **are**
b. **has**
c. **C**
d. **were**
e. **Has**

8-5
a. **C**
b. **have**
c. **are**
d. **C**
e. **have**

✓ Proofread for errors in subject-verb agreement. If a sentence is correct, write a C to the right of it.

  a. Records and letters are to be placed in the lateral filing cabinet.
  b. The quarterback and captain of the team, Tony Webber, have been drafted by a pro team.
  c. Every man and woman in the room are eligible to vote in the election.
  d. Each employee and supervisor has a private parking space.
  e. Many a publisher and author have sent complimentary books to prospective customers.

8-7 A compound subject joined by *or* or *nor* may require either a singular verb or a plural verb. The verb should agree with the subject nearest the verb.

$$\text{S} \quad \text{S} \quad \text{V}$$
Either you or I am responsible for paying the bills.
$$\text{S} \quad \text{S} \quad \text{V}$$
Neither Jon nor they are qualified for that position.

✓ Proofread for errors in subject-verb agreement. If a sentence is correct, write a C to the right of it.

  a. Either Eric or Heather has to attend the board meeting.
  b. Neither the employer nor the employees is willing to admit an error.
  c. Are James, Marion, or Al responsible for planning the program?
  d. Ms. Winters or her secretary have called the meeting for tomorrow.
  e. Neither the children nor Evelyn is going to Europe this summer.

8-8 *There* and *here* are adverbs; therefore, they are never the subject of a sentence. In sentences that begin with *there* or *here*, the subject follows the verb.

$$\text{V} \quad \text{S}$$
There is an incentive for increased productivity.
$$\text{V} \quad \text{S} \quad \text{S}$$
Here are an example and an illustration for you to follow.

8-6
a. C
b. **has**
c. **is**
d. C
e. **has**

8-7
a. C
b. **are**
c. **Is**
d. **has**
e. C

108   Chapter 8—Grammar Errors: Subject and Verb Agreement

✓ Proofread for errors in subject-verb agreement. If a sentence is correct, write a *C* to the right of it.

a. There is only 350 shopping days left until Christmas!

b. Here are several reasons why Jon did not receive a promotion.

c. There is a large bag of glass containers to be recycled.

d. Here are the secretary and treasurer of the company, Ms. Eady.

e. Here is the information you requested for your tax report.

8-9 Collective nouns identify groups. When the group acts as one unit, use a singular verb.

      S   V
The family is moving to its new home.

     S   V
The staff is meeting on Thursday.

▶ If the members of the group act individually, use a plural verb.

The staff are rescheduling their vacations in response to the crisis.

Note: The article preceding the collective noun may indicate whether the group is acting as a unit or individually. *A* usually indicates the need for a plural verb; *the*, a singular verb.

     S   V
A number of people are enrolling in the computer classes.

     S
The number of people enrolling in computer classes
  V
is increasing.

✓ Proofread for errors in subject-verb agreement. If a sentence is correct, write a *C* to the right of it.

a. The number of reports sent to stockholders has increased to 325,000.

b. A number of new cars has been recalled by several major companies.

c. The editorial staff are having a meeting in Mr. McLean's office.

d. A majority were in agreement on the decision to amend the motion.

e. Our company have given its employees large bonuses for increased productivity.

8-8
a. **are**
b. C
c. C
d. **is**
e. C

Chapter 8—Grammar Errors: Subject and Verb Agreement

8-10 Some pronouns do not refer to definite persons or things. They are called *indefinite pronouns*. The following indefinite pronouns are always singular:

another	everyone	nothing
anyone	everybody	one
anybody	everything	someone
anything	many *a/an*	somebody
each	(see Frame 8-6)	something
either	neither	
every	nobody	
(see Frame 8-6)	no one	

     S   V
Somebody is bringing a stereo to the party.
    S   V
Another one of the companies has put its employees on 12-hour shifts.

▶ The following indefinite pronouns are always plural: *both, few, many, others, several*.
 S   V
Both of the computers are used each hour the lab is open.
 S   V
Several were boxed for storage until needed.

▶ The words *all, none, any, more, most,* and *some* may be singular or plural depending on how they are used.
 S   V
More than 20 programs were assigned to the class.
 S   V
Some of the paper is being sold at reduced prices.

✓ Proofread for errors in subject-verb agreement. If a sentence is correct, write a C to the right of it.

   a. Someone has volunteered to chair the fund-raising event.

   b. Several of the managers have participated in the AMS seminars.

   c. None of the seven packages was delivered to the warehouse.

   d. All of the money she earned working at the fair were used to pay her tuition.

   e. Few of the workers are able to complete their quota in an hour.

8-9
a. C
b. **have**
c. **is**
d. C
e. **has**

SPELLING REVIEW

To improve your ability to detect spelling errors, master the words below. Watch for them in the exercises that follow and in succeeding chapters.

bulletin	profited
concession	quantity
emergency	recommend
necessary	restaurant
pamphlet	unanimous

PROOFREADING TIPS

Study these tips and apply them as you proofread:

1. When determining agreement of subject and verb, be alert for the following troublemakers that are frequently used in business.

   a. Foreign words containing both singular and plural forms:

Singular	Plural
addendum	addenda
analysis	analyses
basis	bases
crisis	crises
criterion	criteria
medium	media
memorandum	memorandums or memoranda
parenthesis	parentheses

   b. Nouns that are spelled the same in both their singular and plural forms:

   means   series

   c. Nouns that are usually considered plural:

belongings	grounds
credentials	premises
earnings	proceeds
goods	

2. As you proofread, adjust your level of effort to the job. A one-time reading of an interoffice memo may be sufficient, but a letter or a report may need to be read more than once.

8-10
a. C
b. C
c. **were**
d. **was**
e. C

Chapter 8—Grammar Errors: Subject and Verb Agreement

Proofreading Applications

Proofread the paragraphs, using the appropriate proofreading symbols to mark errors you find in grammar and spelling. To aid you in proofreading, the number of errors is indicated in parentheses for Exercises P-1 through P-3; you must find the errors on your own in P-4.

P-1 The snows of December has turned the higher elevations into magnificent ski trails. So our friends, Lillie and Richard tell us. Many of the resorts in Alpine Valley is offering special vacation packages to lure skiers. If you would like to have information about these packages, such as dates, pamphets, and maps, call the National Ski Area Association. To obtain the latest weather bullentin before heading for the slopes, dial 1-555-SNOW. (5 errors)

P-2 The majority of ski resorts is promoting themselves as four-season vacation spots. Fine accommodations, year-round recreation, and amenities (including indoor pools, fitness centers, and saunas), as well as a variety of resturants and shops, appeals to persons of all ages. Resorts find it necessary to make these concesions to meet the needs of nonskiers and families and as well as skiers. (4 errors)

P-3 Most of the ski resorts have profitted from installing snow-making equipment. It guarantee sufficient quanties of snow from November through April, the quality of the snow is always good, and thus more people are skiing more often. Consequently, many a resort have expanded its services to include ski schools, service centers, and emergensy health care facilities. (5 errors)

P-1
1. **have** turned
2. trails**, so** our friends . . .
3. **are** offering
4. pamphlets
5. bulletin

P-2
1. **are** promoting
2. restaurants
3. shops **appeal**
4. concessions

Chapter 8—Grammar Errors: Subject and Verb Agreement

P-4 Accommodations at a typical resort varies from rustic lodges to bed and breakfast places (B&Bs) to charming inns. The lodges and inns are generally located near the slopes. B&Bs, a European concept, provides food and lodging in a private residence. Unanimusly, skiers recomend B&Bs to persons who enjoys a homey atmosphere and a touch of pampering from the host or hostess.

P-3
1. profited
2. guarantee**s**
3. quantit**ies**
4. resort **has** expanded
5. emergency

P-4
1. vary
2. provid**e** food
3. Unanim**ou**sly
4. recom**m**end
5. **enjoy**

PROGRESSIVE PROOFREADING

You are the office supervisor for the Louisville Chamber of Commerce. One of your responsibilities is to verify the correctness of all communications produced. Letters in your office are prepared in modified block style with mixed punctuation. Proofread the following items indicating any corrections that need to be made.

Chapter 8—Grammar Errors: Subject and Verb Agreement

Job 1 Proofread this welcome statement, marking any errors you find using the appropriate proofreading symbols. (The copy has been keyed using 1½ spacing to provide additional space for proofreaders' marks.)

Louisville Chamber of Commerce

Civic Plaza Building
701 West Jefferson Street
Louisville, KY 40202-4161

WELCOME, ROSE SOCIETY MEMBERS

A gracious welcome awaits you and the other 2,500 Rose Society members and guests who will be attending the Society's convention in Louisville. This meeting is the second Society meeting to be held here, the first one having been held 23 years ago. Both the organization and the city was a bit younger and smaller then.

Louisville, a fun-filled vacation city, is located right on the northern edge of southern hospitality. You'll find it has lots of new things going for it--things like River City Mall in the heart of downtown, turn-of-the-century neighborhoods offerring boutiques and restaruants, and Churchill Downs, home of the Kentucky Derby. Louisville is also located near many other Ky. attractions.

Maps and broshures highlighting points of interest is included in your registration packet. We hope that your stay in Luisville will be enjoyable and that you will visit our city again.

BULLETIN

114   Chapter 8—Grammar Errors: Subject and Verb Agreement

Job 2 Using the proofreading symbols you have learned, mark all the errors in this business letter.

*Louisville
Chamber of Commerce*

Civic Plaza Building
701 West Jefferson Street
Louisville, KY 40202-4161

May 29, 19--

Ms. June Davidson
3162 North Tenth Street
Wichita, KS 67203-9149

Dear Ms. Davidson:

We are delighted to send you the information you requested about Queen's Park.

From the map on the enclosed brochure, you can see that the park is divided into 5 areas. Each of the areas include games and rides, exhibits, live entertainment, concession stands, a restarant, and a zoo. Something is available for every member of the family to enjoy.

On the enclosed list of rates, you will note that persons under 6 and those over 70 is admitted free. Note, too, there is always group rates available.

The park operates on a daily schedule in the summer but is open only on weekends during the spring and fall. The staff post announcment on the bulletin board at the entrance to the park.

The enclosed pamphlet contains a coupon good for a $5 discount on one adult admission ticket. We hope you will be able to use it soon.

Yours very truly,

Alexis J. McQuillan
Department of Tourism

rl

Enclosure

Chapter 8—Grammar Errors: Subject and Verb Agreement   115

Job 3 Proofread the letter below, using the appropriate proofreading symbols to make corrections.

Louisville
Chamber of Commerce

Civic Plaza Building
701 West Jefferson Street
Louisville, KY 40202-4161

February 10, 19--

Ms. Alita Guitterez, President
National Sales Company, Inc.
3910 Trade Street
Louisville, KE 66044-5133

Dear Ms. Guitterez:

Welcome to Louisville! We are delighted that your company chose to locate in our city.

As a member of the business community, you are elegible for membership is the Louisville Chamber of Commerce. On the first Tuesday of each month, we have a breakfast meeting to which each new businessman and businesswoman are invited. This meeting provides an opportunity for us to get to no each other. Each third Tuesday, we have have a dinner and a business meeting at the Arbor Inn.

We hope your schedule will permit you to attend the next meeting, which will be at Tom's Restaurant on the 6th at 7:30 a.m. The Hospitality Committee are in charge of this function. If you can attend, please call 555-2361.

To welcome you as a new member of the business community, we plan to feature a story about your company in the next issue of our newsletter. Will you submit an article of about 500 words about your company? To meet our deadline, we will need the material by the 25th.

        Again, welcome to our city!

                        Very truly yours,

                        Ms. Cynthia Shepherd,Director
                        Public Relations

tr

116   Chapter 8—Grammar Errors: Subject and Verb Agreement

COMPUTERIZED PROOFREADING

Job 4 Business Letter

1. Load the file C8JOB4 from the template. This file was keyed from the following handwritten copy.

2. Compare the letter on the disk with the handwritten copy. Make sure that any errors in the handwritten copy have been corrected.

3. Using the current date, address the letter to **Ms. Ruth Niemer, Director, Convention Housing Bureau, United States Chamber of Commerce, P.O. Box 54321, Des Moines, IA 50318-4126.** Provide an appropriate salutation and complimentary closing. The letter is being sent by **Alex F. Stevens, Director of Tourism**.

4. Format the letter in modified block style with mixed punctuation. Save it as C8JOB4R.

5. Produce the document by following the standard procedures.

> Don Jenkins, our pres. and I am planning to attend the (U.S.) Chamber of Commerce Convention in your city, Aug. 20-25.
>
> Since the number of rms. reserved for this convention are limited, we want to make our reservations now. Both of us wants single rooms. Although it is not necessary, we would like to have adjoining rooms. ¶ We would prefer to stay at the convention hotel; however, if it is not available, either the Plaza or the Palmer Hotel are all right.
>
> There are a no. of Chamber members planning to attend. They or their sec. has the housing info; so you should be hearing from them soon.

Chapter 8—Grammar Errors: Subject and Verb Agreement

CHAPTER 9

GRAMMAR ERRORS: PRONOUN AGREEMENT AND SELECTION

Objectives: *After completing this chapter, you should be able to*
- Identify errors in pronoun-antecedent agreement.
- Recognize errors in the use of pronoun and case.
- Recognize errors resulting from language stereotyping.
- Use the appropriate proofreading symbols to indicate changes in text.
- Spell correctly a list of commonly misspelled words.

GRAMMATICAL ACCURACY

The study of effective communication and proofreading skills continues in Chapter 9. Your grammatical accuracy should improve as pronoun-antecedent agreement, pronoun cases, and language stereotyping are reviewed.

PRONOUN-ANTECEDENT AGREEMENT

Personal pronouns have various forms to indicate *person* (first person, the person speaking; second person, the person spoken to; and third person, the person spoken about), *number* (singular or plural), and *gender* (masculine, feminine, or neuter). You applied the concept of pronoun number in Chapter 8 when you proofread for errors in subject-verb agreement. In Chapter 9, you will learn to identify errors in agreement of pronouns and the words they refer to and in pronoun selection.

9-1 The word the pronoun refers to is called an *antecedent*. A pronoun must agree with its antecedent in person, number, and gender.

> When *Karen* visited, *she* surprised us with a gift.
> (third person, singular, feminine)
>
> When *David* visited, *he* surprised us with a gift.
> (third person, singular, masculine)
>
> When *Karen and David* visited, *they* surprised us with a gift.
> (third person, plural)

9-2 When the antecedent is a collective noun, the proofreader must determine whether the noun represents a group acting as a unit or a group acting as individuals. When the group acts as a unit, use a singular pronoun. When the group acts as individuals, use a plural pronoun.

> The *jury* made *its* decision.
> (group acting as a unit)
>
> The *staff* submitted *their* vacation schedules.
> (group acting as individuals)

✓ Proofread the sentences below inserting the correct pronoun wherever necessary. If a sentence is correct, write a C to the right of it.

   a. Everybody made their own costume for the Fine Arts Ball.

   b. The committee will select their chairperson at the March meeting.

   c. Most of the employees spend their time working diligently.

   d. Either Katelyn or Katherine will make their presentation on Friday.

   e. The group voted at their last meeting to support the blood drive.

PRONOUN CASES

Pronouns are divided into three different categories according to their use in sentences. These categories are termed *cases* and include the following: subjective, objective, and possessive. A personal pronoun changes its case according to how it is being used. Using the incorrect pronoun case is one of the most common errors made by writers and proofreaders.

9-3 The subjective case pronouns include *I, you, he, she, it, we,* and *they*. Use the subjective case for a pronoun that is the subject of the sentence.

    S   V
We are making plans for the business seminar.

    S   V
You are well informed.

   S   S   V
He and I finished the report.

Note: To determine the correct case when a compound subject is used, consider each subject alone with the verb. You would say "I finished the report," not "Me finished the report."

▶ Use the subjective case when the pronoun refers to the subject and follows a form of the verb *to be* (*be, am, is, are, was, were*) or a verb phrase ending in *be, being,* or *been.*

It is *I.*

It was *she* who found the solution to the problem.

It could have been *they* who won.

Note: This sentence, while grammatically correct, is awkward. Normally it is best to reword to avoid such constructions: They could have won.

✓ Proofread the sentences below inserting the correct pronoun wherever necessary. If a sentence is correct, write a C to the right of it.

    a. Would you change jobs now if you were him?

    b. It was she who designed the program cover.

    c. Was it them who were responsible for getting volunteers?

    d. The officer promoted to captain was him.

    e. It was she who won first prize in the speaking contest.

9-4 The objective case pronouns include *me, us, you, him, her, it,* and *them*. Use the objective case when the pronoun is the object of the verb. A pronoun is an object if it (1) follows the verb and answers the question "what" or "whom" about the verb or (2) follows the verb and answers the question "to whom," "for whom," or "for what" something is done.

Chapter 9—Grammar Errors: Pronoun Agreement and Selection

9-1, 9-2
a. **his or her**
b. **its**
c. **C**
d. **her**
e. **its**

9-3
a. **he**
b. **C**
c. **they**
d. **he**
e. **C**

John asked *us* for a contribution.
    (Asked whom?)

Please put *them* in the file.
    (Put what?)

Sarah gave *him* and *me* a pen.
    (Gave to whom?)

Michael bought *them* tickets.
    (Bought for whom?)

▶ Use the objective case when the pronoun is the object of a preposition. A pronoun is the object of a preposition if the pronoun follows the preposition. (Prepositions include *among, at, between, by, for, from, on, to,* and *with*.)

This telegram came for *us* today.

Just between *you* and *me*, I think it is a great idea.

▶ Use the objective case when the pronoun is the subject or object of an infinitive. An infinitive is a phrase containing the word *to* plus the present form of a verb. When a pronoun immediately precedes or follows an infinitive phrase, use the objective form of the pronoun.

Carlos expected *them* to help.
(*Them* is the subject of the infinitive.)

Carlos expected to help *them*.
(To help whom? *Them* is the object of the infinitive.)

✓ Proofread the sentences below inserting the correct pronoun where necessary. If a sentence is correct, write a C to the right of it.

    a. Our supervisor is considerate of we employees.

    b. Between you and I, his idea was not practical.

    c. Vivian showed us her newly decorated office.

    d. We expect Marion to help Juan and he with registration.

    e. The president asked her to be the secretarial assistant.

9-5 While it may appear difficult, mastering usage of the pronouns *who* and *whom* and *whoever* and *whomever* is really quite simple. Whenever *who* or *whom* appears in a dependent clause, determine the pronoun's use within the clause. Do not consider the rest of the sentence. (A dependent clause contains a subject and a verb but does not express a complete thought.)

▶ *Who* and *whoever* are the subjective forms. Use *who* or *whoever* when *he, she, they, I,* or *we* could be used as the subject of the *who* clause.

An executive wants a secretary **who** *is dependable*.
(*He* is dependable.)

Who *shall I say is calling*?
(I shall say *she* is calling.)

Whoever *ate the fruit* should replace it.
(*They* ate the fruit.)

Note: If the sentence is a question, mentally change the question to a statement. Then substitute *he/she/they* or *him/her/them* for *who* or *whom*.

▶ *Whom* and *whomever* are the objective forms. Use *whom* or *whomever* when *him, her, them, me,* or *us* could be used as the object of the verb or the object of the preposition in the *whom* clause.

The person **whom** *you recommended* for the position starts work tomorrow.
(You recommended *her*.)

Whom did you wish to speak *with*?
(You wished to speak with *him*.)

We will promote **whomever** *you suggest*.
(You suggest *him*.)

✓ Proofread the sentences below inserting the correct pronoun where necessary. If a sentence is correct, write a C to the right of it.

  a. Give the extra copy of the book to whoever can use it.

  b. This order for copier supplies was taken by who?

  c. We must respect the wishes of whomever is in charge.

  d. Who is going to prepare the agenda for the meeting?

  e. We do not know who to call about the needed repairs.

9-4
a. **us**
b. **me**
c. C
d. **him**
e. C

Chapter 9—Grammar Errors: Pronoun Agreement and Selection

9-6 Use the possessive case to show ownership. Possessive case pronouns usually have two forms.

▶ Use *my, your, his, her, its, our,* or *their* when the possessive pronoun precedes the noun it modifies.

That is *my* piano.

It was *their* fault.

▶ Use *mine, yours, his, hers, its, ours,* or *theirs* when the possessive pronoun is separated from the noun to which it refers.

That piano is *mine*.

The fault was not *theirs*.

Each idea has *its* own merit.

Note: Do not confuse the possessive pronouns *its, your,* and *their* with their soundalike contractions *it's, you're,* and *they're*.

▶ Use the possessive case of a pronoun immediately before a gerund (a verb form ending in *ing* that is used as a noun).

His leaving the company was a surprise.

The teacher approved of *our* going on the field trip.

✓ Proofread the following sentences for errors in pronoun selection. If a sentence is correct, write a *C* to the right of it.

   a. You returning by plane really surprised us.

   b. The best reorganization plan submitted was theirs.

   c. Is this biology notebook yours or mine?

   d. Because the policy is reasonable, the staff voted it's adoption.

   e. With him leaving the company on such short notice, Jamie will have to take over his work.

LANGUAGE STEREOTYPING

Today's society frowns on the stereotyping of particular jobs or roles as either "men's work" or "women's work" because men and women are now employed in a greater variety of occupations than they once were. Using the pronouns *she* or *he* alone to refer to a person may be incorrect and reflect stereotyping.

9-5
a. C
b. **whom**
c. **whoever**
d. C
e. **whom**

9-7 Eliminate *he* or *she* from copy when it is impossible to determine which pronoun is accurate.

    not   Who is the lawyer and what is his address?

    but   What is the name and address of the lawyer?

▸ Use a plural noun and *their* to avoid using gender-specific pronouns.

    not A good teacher praises his students.
    but Good teachers praise their students.

▸ Address the reader in the second person to avoid using gender-specific pronouns.

Praise your students.

▸ Reword the sentence to avoid the use of gender-specific pronouns.

    not Each contestant signed *her* entry form.
    but Each contestant signed *an* entry form.

▸ Use neutral terms when referring to both men and women.

businessperson, business people	*not* businessman
salesperson, sales representative	*not* salesman
mail carrier	*not* mailman
members of Congress, representatives	*not* congressmen
people, humanity	*not* mankind
flight attendant	*not* stewardess

✓ Proofread the following sentences for language stereotyping and make any necessary corrections.

    a. The company is proud of their growth rate.

    b. Each salesman distributed copies of his sales report.

    c. The sales manager expressed her appreciation for the employees' work.

    d. The manager asked each salesperson to write his plan for increasing sales.

    e. If anyone inquires about the company's newest product, tell him it will be available in six months.

9-6

a. **Your**
b. C
c. C
d. **its**
e. **his** leaving

Chapter 9—Grammar Errors: Pronoun Agreement and Selection

SPELLING REVIEW

To improve your ability to detect spelling errors, master the words below. Watch for them in the exercises that follow and in succeeding chapters.

criticism	possession
enthusiasm	recognize
incidentally	regard
miscellaneous	relevant
permanent	responsible

PROOFREADING TIPS

Study these tips and apply them as you proofread:

1. If you spot a grammatical error, write a question mark in the margin next to the sentence and query the originator.
2. Reading aloud to yourself is a good way to detect grammatical errors.

9-7
a. **its** growth
b. **salesperson**
   his or her
   OR
   all salespersons
   their
c. omit *her*
d. **his or her**
   OR **a** plan
e. tell **him or her**

Proofreading Applications

Proofread the following paragraphs and use the appropriate proofreading symbols to mark errors you find in spelling and grammar. To aid you in proofreading, the number of errors to be found is indicated in parentheses for Exercises P-1, P-2, and P-3.

P-1 In the 90's, more women and minorities will enter the work force, many of who will need additional training. Because their skills may not be relavent to the jobs, employers will find theirselves responsable for educating the unskilled. To meet the employment challenge, employers are turning to people who can do his or her jobs at home with the aid of personal computers and facsimile machines. (5 errors)

P-2 A worker who once took fringe benefits for granted won't have that luxury in this decade. They will have to make critical choices about his or her benefits. Benefits are reguarded as an integral part of an employee's compensation, but it comes at a price. For example, our benefit plan enables us to exchange some health care benefits for child care benefits. Also, contributions to the benefit plan may be applied either to a savings plan or to miscallaneous medical or dependent expenses. (5 errors)

P-3 Today, employers are generally more flexible with the benefits they offer to its employees. For example, one employer may underwrite the cost of health insurance for both the employee and his dependents. Another company may cover health insurance premiums for it's employees but not medical care for their dependents. Incidentaly, one criticism of some health care plans is that subscribers must utilize the services of preferred provider organizations (specified hospitals or doctors). (4 errors)

Chapter 9—Grammar Errors: Pronoun Agreement and Selection

P-1
1. many of **whom**
2. relevant
3. find **themselves**
4. responsible
5. **their** jobs

P-2
1. **Workers** who once
2. **their** benefits
3. regarded
4. but **they come**
5. miscellaneous

P-4 Brian O'Malley, an economist whom spoke to our economics class, said that businesses have become more concerned about its employees' personal time. Today, for example, employees may often select the hours that fit their personal schedules. A secretary who has a long commute to her job might prefer a 10 a.m. starting time while a nurse who is at her best early in the day would prefer taking the 7 a.m. shift. Employers recognise that a satisfied employee is a more productive one and is more likely to remain a permenant one.

P-3
1. to **their** employees
2. both the **employees** and **their** dependents
OR
both the employee and **his or her** dependents
3. for **its** employees
4. Incidentally

P-4
1. economist **who**
2. about **their** employees'
3. **his or her** job
4. **her or his** best
5. recognize
6. perma**n**ent

PROGRESSIVE PROOFREADING

You have applied for a position as a secretary in the School of Technology at City College. Dr. Brian Layman, your prospective employer, is seeking a person who has exceptionally good language arts skills. To determine whether you can do the job, you are given some drafts of typical correspondence to proofread. Dr. Layman uses block letter style with open punctuation.

Job 1 Proofread the letter for errors in spelling, abbreviations, number expression, format, and grammar.

SCHOOL of TECHNOLOGY
CITY COLLEGE
989 Johnstown Road
Chesapeake, VA 23310-4961

January 10, 19--

Mr. Greg West
4572 East Ninth Street
Chesapeake, Va. 23310-4572

Dear Mr. West

Your request for readmission to City College has been reviewed by members of the Admissions Committee and I at our January 8 meeting.

After the 3d semester, a a student must have earned 36 hours, and he must have a grade-point average (g.p.a.) of 1.80 in order to stay in school.

You was enrolled for three semesters. During that time you earned 27 hours with a gpa of 1.67. Consequently, admission is not possible at this time.

We reccomend that you attend summer school. If you do so, you must take 2 3-hour courses that are relevant to your major area of study. With a grade of C or better in each of these courses, the committee and I will be happy to reconsider your petition for admission.

Sincerely yours

Joseph W. Wrenn
Associate Dean

rv

Chapter 9—Grammar Errors: Pronoun Agreement and Selection

Job 2 Proofread the memorandum carefully for errors.

SCHOOL of TECHNOLOGY CITY COLLEGE — MEMO

TO: All Staff

FROM: Brian Layman, Dean

DATE. January 10, 19--

SUBJECT: Establishment of Task Force

At the suggestion of numerous staff members, the College is pursuing the idea of purchasing a new computer system. Members of the staff with who I have talked have shown enthusaism for this idea.

A task force of interested staff members are being formed to conduct a more through study of the needs of the staff. Based on its findings, the task force will then make recommendations for the purchase of a computer system and software. I need to know who among the staff are interested in serving on the task force.

Responsibilities of the task force includes the following: (1) assessing the staff's needs, (2) gathering information about computer systems, (3) evaluating the available software, and (4) making recommendations to the purchasing agent and I.

If your interested in actively researching this topic and meeting this challenge, please send me a memo indicating your interest.

rv

Job 3 Mark any errors in keying, spelling, and grammar.

SCHOOL of TECHNOLOGY CITY COLLEGE — *MEMO*

TO: Department Charipersons

FROM: Brian Layman, Dean

DATE: January 10, 19--

SUBJECT: Parking Regulations

In an effort to improve staff parking conditions, the Campus Traffic Committee have developed the following parking regulations. Will you please see that all members of your department receives this information reguarding the new regulations.

1. All current campus parking permits expire on September 14. Beginning September 15, new permits are required.

2. Parking is prohibited in areas other then those designated for staff members.

2. Permanant premits must be displayed in the rear window of all vechicles.

3. Any staff member in possession of more than 5 unpaid parking tickets will forfeit their right to park on the campus.

Because Chief Security Officer Calder has been aware of the numerous problems in parking, he was very receptive to the recommendations made by the staff. In fact, it was him who suggested that such a committee be formed.

rv

Chapter 9—Grammar Errors: Pronoun Agreement and Selection

Computerized Proofreading

Job 4 Edit Letter

1. Load file C9JOB4 from the template.
2. Format the letter in block style with open punctuation.
3. Save the letter as C9JOB4R.
4. Produce the document by following the standard procedures.

CHAPTER 10

ERRORS IN CONFUSING WORDS

Objectives: *After completing this chapter, you should be able to*
- ▶ Recognize the correct usage of words that sound alike but have different meanings.
- ▶ Recognize the correct spelling of words that sound alike but have different spellings.
- ▶ Use the appropriate proofreading symbols to indicate changes in text.
- ▶ Spell correctly a list of commonly misspelled words.

One of the major difficulties of the English language is that so many words sound similar but are spelled differently and have different meanings. To be a good proofreader, you must be able to distinguish between the words so that you will be able to detect and correct errors in their usage. Study each group of words and their definitions. Then read each of the sentences and write the correct word in the space provided.

10-1
accept—*v.* to receive; to take
except—*prep.* with the exclusion of

a. You should _____ the responsibility for completing the payroll.

b. All of the officers _____ the secretary attended the meeting.

c. We will fight the courts about the ruling rather than _____ it.

d. No one _____ the treasurer can unlock the bank vault.

10-2 addition—*n.* increase; enlargement or gain
edition—*n.* form in which a text is published

a. In six months the new _____ to the office building will be completed.

b. She autographed a copy of the latest _____ of her book.

c. Do you think the _____ to the laboratory will be approved?

d. Since the _____ of Mario to the staff, we have caught up with our work.

10-3 advice—*n.* recommendation; suggestion
advise—*v.* to counsel; to inform

a. Mark received the _____ he needed from his attorney.

b. Please _____ your supervisor about your vacation plans.

c. I did _____ my son about handling his allowance, but he did not take my _____.

d. Most people like to offer _____ to their friends.

10-4 affect—*v.* to influence
effect—*n.* an outcome or a result; *v.* to cause to happen

a. What _____ will the change in the law have on us?

b. Your performance will _____ your rating.

c. The plans to _____ a change in policy have been approved.

d. How will her resignation _____ our previous plans?

10-1
a. accept
b. except
c. accept
d. except

10-2
a. addition
b. edition
c. addition
d. addition

10-3
a. advice
b. advise
c. advise, advice
d. advice

10-5 a lot—*n.* a number of; many
allot—*v.* to assign; to distribute

✓
a. The hotel will _____ ten meeting rooms for our conference.

b. Did you find _____ of errors in the transcription paper?

c. We will _____ 5 percent of the total amount for printing expenses.

d. There are _____ of people who are uncomfortable working with computers.

10-6 all ready—*adj. phrase* completely prepared
already—*adv.* by or before this time

✓
a. The boxes have _____ been packed by the movers.

b. We are _____ to begin the remodeling job.

c. Have you _____ prepared the financial report?

d. Since we are _____ to start to work, let's begin.

10-7 cite—*v.* to quote or mention
sight—*n.* a view; vision; *v.* to see
site—*n.* a location

✓
a. Can you _____ the source of that quotation?

b. As soon as the company finds the proper _____, it will begin construction of its building.

c. The Grand Canyon is an inspiring _____.

d. The coliseum is located on a _____ about three blocks away.

10-4
a. effect
b. affect
c. effect
d. affect

10-5
a. allot
b. a lot
c. allot
d. a lot

10-6
a. already
b. all ready
c. already
d. all ready

Chapter 10—Errors in Confusing Words

10-8 complement—*n.* something that fills up, completes, or makes perfect; *v.* to complete or make perfect
compliment—*n.* recognition; praise; *v.* to praise

✓ a. Did you _____ the actor on his performance?

b. The drapes and the carpet _____ the color of the walls.

c. I consider that remark to be a _____.

d. When the ship left the shore, it had a full _____ of personnel.

10-9 council—*n.* an assembly; a governing body
counsel—*v.* to give advice; advise; *n.* a lawyer; advice

✓ a. New employees need to receive _____ about the fringe benefit options.

b. The mayor is the presiding officer of the city _____.

c. Did you know the person who was appointed _____ for the defense?

d. Students gain many experiences by serving on the student _____.

10-10 envelop—*v.* to surround; to enclose
envelope—*n.* a flat (usually paper) container for a letter

✓ a. If the fog continues, it will quickly _____ the entire area.

b. Use the enclosed _____ for mailing your contribution.

c. While disciplining your children, _____ them with love.

d. Why not use a small _____ for returning the copy of the receipt?

10-7
a. cite
b. site
c. sight
d. site

10-8
a. compliment
b. complement
c. compliment
d. complement

10-9
a. counsel
b. council
c. counsel
d. council

Chapter 10—Errors in Confusing Words

10-11 every day—*adv. phrase* each day
everyday—*adj.* ordinary; customary

✓ a. The girls have been jogging _____ this week.

b. Proofreading is an _____ task for the word processing secretary.

c. Why not use the _____ dishes for the picnic?

d. When you retire from your job, _____ will be a holiday!

10-12 its—*adj.* possessive form of *it*
it's—contraction of *it is* and *it has*

✓ a. _____ too early to determine the winner of the election.

b. When the postal system increased _____ rates, business declined by 5 percent.

c. Do you realize _____ been four years since you joined our company?

d. Universal Bank is moving _____ headquarters to Dallas.

10-13 loose—*adj.* not fastened or tight; having freedom of movement
lose—*v.* to fail to win, gain, or keep; to mislay

✓ a. Too many traffic violations caused Kevin to _____ his license.

b. When the belt is too _____, it will not pull the motor.

c. The loss of the key will cause us to _____ access to the safe-deposit box.

d. We lost several pages of the book when its binding came _____.

10-10
a. envelop
b. envelope
c. envelop
d. envelope

10-11
a. every day
b. everyday
c. everyday
d. every day

10-12
a. It's
b. its
c. it's
d. its

Chapter 10—Errors in Confusing Words   137

10-14 moral—*adj.* ethical; pertaining to right and wrong
morale—*n.* a mental and emotional condition; mood

✓
a. Keeping up the _____ of its employees is important to a company.

b. Today's society has to face several _____ issues.

c. After its third loss, the tennis team's _____ was pretty low.

d. One admirable trait is that of high _____ standards.

10-15 passed—*v.* past tense of *pass*, meaning to go by or to circumvent or to receive favorable results on an examination
past—*n.* the time before the present; *adv.* go beyond

✓
a. Ying was happy to have _____ the statistics test with only a minimum score!

b. The bus went _____ my house without stopping.

c. Do you realize that we _____ the road to the park?

d. A knowledge of the _____ is necessary for an understanding of the present.

10-16 personal—*adj.* private; relating to an individual
personnel—*n.* a body of employees

✓
a. I wish to obtain a _____ loan from the bank.

b. Katie had an interview with the head of the _____ department.

c. All of the company _____ received end-of-the-year bonuses.

d. Employers are not permitted to ask their employees for certain _____ information.

10-13
a. lose
b. loose
c. lose
d. loose

10-14
a. morale
b. moral
c. morale
d. moral

10-15
a. passed
b. past
c. passed
d. past

10-17 precede—*v.* to go or come before or in front of
preceding—*adj.* previous
proceed—*v.* to move forward; advance

✓
a. Mario Parker _____ Mr. Brumfield as principal.

b. Can you apply the procedures you learned in the _____ lesson?

c. The council will _____ to the next item on the agenda.

d. The second edition has enjoyed over $375,000 in sales this year; that is more than the sales for the two _____ years.

10-18 principal—*n.* a leader; a sum of money; *adj.* highest in importance
principle—*n.* a general truth; an accepted truth

✓
a. How much interest will the company have to pay on the _____?

b. The superintendent has just appointed a new _____ for the elementary school.

c. May I borrow your _____ of accounting book?

d. Are you familiar with the economic _____ of supply and demand?

10-19 sales—*n.* distribution by selling; *adj.* relating to or used in selling
sells—*v.* singular present tense of *to sell*, to achieve a sale, to exact a price for

✓
a. The _____ tax adds 5 percent to the cost of the goods.

b. Bradley will win a cruise if he _____ nine cars this month.

c. The store's charge _____ have doubled in the past five years.

d. To earn extra income, Margo _____ stationery products.

10-16
a. personal
b. personnel
c. personnel
d. personal

10-17
a. preceded
b. preceding
c. proceed
d. preceding

10-18
a. principal
b. principal
c. principles
d. principle

Chapter 10—Errors in Confusing Words

10-20 stationary—*adj.* immobile; fixed in one position
stationery—*n.* materials (paper, pens, ink) for writing

a. That card shop also sells _____.

b. Every physical fitness enthusiast should have a _____ bicycle.

c. In the business world the use of colored _____ appears to be a trend.

d. Nailing the desk to the floor will certainly keep it _____.

10-21 their—*adj.* the possessive form of *they*
there—*adv.* at that place; *pron.* used as an introductory word in a sentence
they're—contraction of *they are*

a. The twins were standing _____ by the door when I left.

b. Next year _____ going to remodel the entire building.

c. Seven employees celebrated _____ retirement from the company.

d. During spring vacation _____ going to see _____ relatives.

10-22 to—*prep.* in the direction of; used before a verb to indicate an infinitive
too—*adv.* also; more than enough
two—*adj.* more than one but less than three

a. Brad and I are going, _____, if there's room.

b. Did you know that only _____ candidates showed up for the forum?

c. "_____ be rather than _____ seem" is the motto of what state?

d. He, _____, can go to the _____-day conference if he can get someone _____ drive him there.

10-19
a. sales
b. sells
c. sales
d. sells

10-20
a. stationery
b. stationary
c. stationery
d. stationary

10-21
a. there
b. they're
c. their
d. they're, their

---

140   Chapter 10—Errors in Confusing Words

SPELLING REVIEW

To improve your ability to detect spelling errors, master the words below. Watch for them in the exercises that follow and in succeeding chapters.

experience	psychology
grammar	receiving
occasionally	reference
omitted	valuable
prerequisite	writing

PROOFREADING TIPS

Study these tips and apply them as you proofread:

1. When in doubt about the meaning or spelling of a word, consult the dictionary. The correct word usage shows that you have proofread all communications carefully so that the reader can understand the intended message.

2. Be aware of the standard pronunciation of words because mispronunciation frequently leads to misspelling and misuse of words.

10-2
a. too
b. two
c. To, to
d. too, two, to

Proofreading Applications

Proofread the following ads and use the appropriate proofreading symbols to mark errors you find in word usage or spelling. To aid you in proofreading, the number of errors is indicated in parentheses for the first three ads.

P-1 THE PRICE IS RIGHT!

Well-built two-story house on 3-acre sight, complemented by professional landscaping. House overlooks a lush green valley—a beautiful sight to see every day. Valuable property all ready for occupancy. Sales for $112,000. Directions: Proceed 1 mile passed the water tower on Highway 28; first house on the right. For additional information, call Kendra at Four-Star Realty, telephone 555-4607. (3 errors)

P-2 OUR LOSS—YOUR GAIN

Must sell personal items, including valuable date-of-issue stamped envelops; boxes of bond stationery; exercise equipment, including stationary bicycle; books on principles of counciling, psychology, investment advise, reference, how-to-loose weight, cookbooks, morale-building, and valuable first editions; and more items to numerous to list. Saturday from 8 a.m. to 11:30 a.m. at 3153 Highland Avenue. (5 errors)

P-3 SECRETARY NEEDED

Secretary, City Council. Principal duties include allot of correspondence and writing of council minutes and memoranda. Ocasionally, some travel will be necessary. Prerequisits for the job include three years of experience, excellent keyboarding skills, and good grammar skills. Applicants should be able to accept every day secretarial responsibilities with minimum supervision. Send resume, including referances, to Personnel Department, City Hall, 401 Sixth Street, Sioux City, IA 51101. (5 errors)

P-1
1. 3-acre **site**
2. **Sells** for $112,000.
3. 1 mile **past**

P-2
1. stamped **envelopes**;
2. **counseling**
3. investment **advice**
4. how-to-**lose** weight
5. items **too** numerous

P-4 **NOTICE TO CITIZENS**

The City Council will be receiving comments about the redistricting proposal at it's April 3 meeting. The Counsel members voted on the proposal at the last meeting; however, the city attorney advised the members that there vote was not binding for two reasons:

1. The item was omitted from the announced agenda.
2. Their was no quorum because to many members were absent.

Citizens wishing to express their views on this proposal should be in Room 207 of the City Hall 30 minutes preceding the April 3 meeting.

P-3
1. **a lot** of correspondence
2. Occasionally
3. Prerequisit**e**s
4. **everyday**
5. references

P-4
1. **its**
2. **Council** members
3. **their** vote
4. **There** was
5. **too** many

PROGRESSIVE PROOFREADING

One of your duties as an administrative supervisor in the Ridge Hills Real Estate office is to proofread the correspondence. You proofread not only for the usual keyboarding, spelling, and number expression errors but also for errors in grammar and word usage. Ridge Hill uses modified block letter format and mixed punctuation.

Job 1   Proofread the letter carefully.

RIDGE HILLS REAL ESTATE
3168 NORTHWOOD DRIVE
RUSTON, LA 71270-6653
318-555-8700

July 12, 19--

Mrs. Elizabeth Harris
Claims Representative
United Insurance Company
32940 South 3d Street
Ruston, LA 71272-8977

Dear Mrs. Harris:

On June 23 Todd Roberts suffered personal injuries from an accident in a car driven by Carol Shultz. Both are agents for our company and were on company business at the time of the accident.

Mr. Roberts was a passenger in Mrs. Shultz's car when she past another vehicle and entered into the path of an oncoming car. The site of the accident was on Highway 37 about 5 miles from Bloomington. Mrs. Shultz has been cited for negligent operation of a motor vehicle.

Brett Arnold, council for our company, advised Mr. Roberts not to proceed with a suit. Mr. Roberts agreed.

Should there be further developments in this situation, I will notify you.

                              Yours very truly

                              Walter T. Hartsell
                              Gen. Mgr.

xx

Job 2 Proofread the letter below to Mr. Whitehurst, client.

RIDGE HILLS REAL ESTATE
3168 NORTHWOOD DRIVE
RUSTON, LA 71270-6653
318-555-8700

July 19, 19--

Mr. Bryant Whitehurst
Plant Manager
Toggs Manufacturing Co.
P. O. Box 7022
Indianapolis, IN 46208-9865

Dear Mr. Whitehurst:

The one hundred-acre sight on Five-Mile Rd. you wanted for your new plant is available. Even though the owners have all ready had a lot of inquiries about the property, I believe they're prepared to accept your proposed offer.

If you are serious about obtaining this property, I suggest that you submit an offer immediately. Real estate prices are not likely to decrease further this year. In fact, it is likely to increase.

Because the owners insist on a cash transaction, you may want to get your counsel's advise about the best way to finance the principal loan. Please call me to discuss your plans about this matter.

                          Sincerely yours,

                          Walter T. Hartsell
                          General Manager

yri

Chapter 10—Errors in Confusing Words   145

Job 3 Compare the typed note of congratulations with the handwritten draft. Use the appropriate proofreading symbols to mark all errors.

Please type this note. Make corrections if needed

Hannah:

Congratulations on being named salesperson of the year! You have exceeded your sales quota every month for the passed six months. I know that its taken a lot of personal effort for you to achieve this success.

Your performance shows that you believe in the principle of hard work. Your attitude shows that your objectives are to sale property and to gain valuable experience. The total affect of your efforts are that we will not lose our #1 position among the real estate firms in the city.

Thank you, Hannah, I complement you, Hannah, for your achievements. Your enthusiasm for your work is inspiring. I am proud to have you as a member of our sales team.

Walter

146   Chapter 10—Errors in Confusing Words

July 12, 19--

Hannah

Congratulations on being named salesperson of the year! You have exceeded your sales quota every month for the passed six months. I know that it's taken a lot of personal effort for you to achieve this success.

Your performance shows that you believe in the principle of hard work. Your attitude shows that your objectives are to sell property and to gain valuable experience. The total affect of your efforts are that we will not lose our No. 1 position among the real estate firms in the city.

I complement you, Hannah, for your achievements. I am proud to have you as a member of our sales team.

Walter

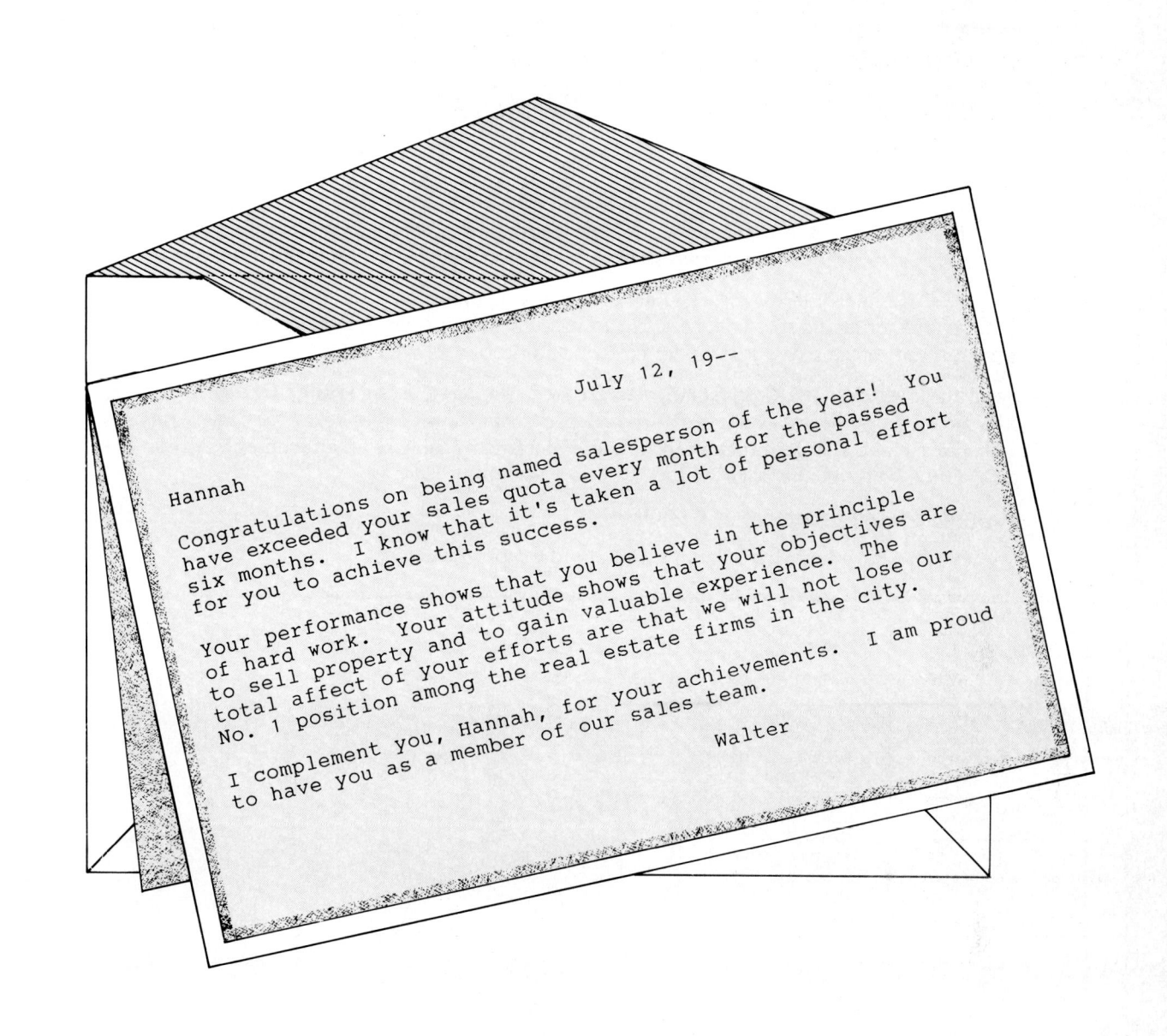

Chapter 10—Errors in Confusing Words

COMPUTERIZED PROOFREADING

Job 4 Proofread Memo with Table

1. Load the file C10JOB4 from the template. The document consists of a memorandum, including a table. The table was compiled from excerpts taken from the financial statements shown below.

2. Proofread the message for errors in abbreviations, spelling, grammar, number expression, format, and confusing words. Check the accuracy of the figures and text in the table by comparing them to the printed statements. Check all totals as well.

3. Send the memo to **Jill Carmichael, Advertising Manager**, from **Walter Hartsell, General Manager**. The subject is **Review of Advertising Costs from 1990 to 1992**; the date is **July 12, 19—**. Format as a standard memorandum and include the table as an attachment. Format the table attractively on the page with a 1½" top margin.

4. Save the revised document as C10JOB4R.

5. Produce the document by following the standard procedures.

```
                          1992

      OPERATING EXPENSES:
          ADVERTISING
              TELEVISION         $19,588.52
              CIRCULARS            5,047.90
              HOMEBUYER'S GUIDE    3,885.12
              NEWSPAPERS          14,589.70
              RADIO                1,409.61
              MISCELLANEOUS          961.80
                                                $45,482.65


                          1991

      OPERATING EXPENSES:
          ADVERTISING
              TELEVISION         $15,947.50
              NEWSPAPERS          12,785.63
              CIRCULARS            4,672.30
              HOMEBUYER'S GUIDE    2,933.88
              RADIO                1,180.12
              MISCELLANEOUS          769.44
                                                $38,288.87


                          1990

      OPERATING EXPENSES:
          ADVERTISING
              CIRCULARS          $ 3,597.28
              HOMEBUYER'S GUIDE    2,292.18
              NEWSPAPERS          11,096.79
              TELEVISION          14,795.72
              RADIO                  870.08
              MISCELLANEOUS          641.20
                                                $33,293.25
```

CHAPTER 11

PUNCTUATION ERRORS, PART 1

Objectives: *After completing this chapter, you should be able to*

▶ Identify errors in end-of-sentence punctuation.
▶ Identify errors in the use of the comma in compound sentences, in a series, with consecutive adjectives, with adjacent numbers, and in dates and addresses.
▶ Use the appropriate proofreading symbols to indicate changes in text.
▶ Spell correctly a list of commonly misspelled words.

IMPORTANCE OF CORRECT PUNCTUATION

Punctuation makes the meaning of messages clear and precise. When punctuation is omitted or used incorrectly, messages may become confusing, distorted, or inaccurate. Consider the change in meaning in the following sentences:

"The child," claimed the newscaster, "was abducted by an angry mob."

The child claimed the newscaster was abducted by an angry mob.

As you can see, the proofreader must know how to use the different marks of punctuation.

In this chapter you will review the correct use of terminal punctuation (punctuation used at the end of a sentence) and the most common internal punctuation mark, the comma. Additional uses of the comma and other internal punctuation are reviewed in Chapters 12 and 13.

TERMINAL PUNCTUATION

Terminal punctuation is used to indicate a distinct pause in the voice and, therefore, helps to clarify the meaning of sentences. Terminal punctuation marks consist of the period, the question mark, and the exclamation point. Internal punctuation marks, which will be discussed later in the chapter, signify shorter pauses and help to further clarify the meaning.

Use the following proofreading symbols to indicate changes in punctuation:

⊙	Insert a period.	Answer the telephone promptly⊙
?/	Insert a question mark.	Where are you going on vacation this year?/
!/	Insert an exclamation point.	I just won the lottery!/

11-1 Use a **period** at the end of a statement or a command, a polite request, or an indirect question. An indirect question is a statement that reports someone else's question.

> The sun is shining today.
> (statement of fact)

> Be sure to make the reservation this morning.
> (command)

> I asked if she had eaten.
> (indirect question)

▶ Remember to use a period rather than a question mark if the reader is requested to act rather than to answer.

> Would you please find the Anderson file for me.
> (polite request, action required)

> Did you go to the meeting?
> (direct question, answer required)

11-2 Use a **question mark** after a direct question. The first word of a direct question is capitalized.

> How much money have you saved this month?

> The question is, Which is the best software?

▶ Use a question mark after each item in a series of short questions related to one idea. The question mark is usually followed by two spaces. Use one space if the question mark is used as part of a series of similar questions begun with a capital letter. Begin each question in the series with a lowercase letter if the question is not a complete sentence. One space follows all but the final question mark.

> Who proofread this? Was it Mary? Was it Aaron?

> Is your objective to avoid failure? to protect your ego? to sell property?

11-3 Use an **exclamation point** to express strong emotion, surprise, or urgency or to give emphasis after an interjection. One space follows an exclamation point if it appears within a sentence.

Ramon won the scholarship!

Congratulations! You have completed your coursework.

One of the parachutes hasn't opened!

✓ Proofread the following groups of words for errors in terminal punctuation. If a sentence is correct, write a C to the right of it.

a. Will you please close the door?

b. Edward asked if we were joining him for lunch.

c. I can't believe English 201 is already closed!

d. Which class will you substitute? business communication? marketing?

e. The assistant exclaimed, "Finally. The last schedule has been processed!"

INTERNAL PUNCTUATION—THE COMMA

Internal punctuation is used when a brief rather than a distinct pause is needed. Internal punctuation marks consist of the comma (discussed below and in Chapter 12), the colon, the semicolon, the dash, parentheses, quotation marks, the underscore, and the apostrophe (all discussed in Chapter 13). Each internal punctuation mark has a specific function. The proofreader should know the function of each and keep in mind that punctuation is used to make the meaning clearer.

Use the following proofreading symbols to mark corrections in the use of the comma:

⁀	Insert a comma.	Our company has openings for computer operators⁀but we don't expect to begin hiring until next month.
(̷,)	Delete a comma.	The children are opening their gifts,̸ and sharing their toys.

Chapter 11—Punctuation Errors, Part 1   151

11-4 Use a comma to separate the main clauses of a compound sentence connected by the conjunctions *and, or, but,* or *nor*. (A compound sentence consists of two main clauses, each containing both a subject and a verb.) The comma comes before the conjunction. The subject and verb of each main clause are identified in the examples.

    S V   S V

I am not a member of that group, nor do I intend to become a member.

       S   V   S   V

Many resources were available, but we decided to use a computer search.

     S   V   S   V

Betty Robbins will attend the meeting, or she will send a substitute.

▶ If both clauses are short, do not use a comma.

   S   V   S   V

I caught the fish and my husband cooked them.
(short, compound sentence)

Note: Do not mistake a compound sentence for a simple sentence with two or more verbs. Such a sentence requires no comma before the conjunction.

                 S   V

The telephone transmits important business messages
     V
and allows friends to keep in touch.
(simple sentence containing one subject and two verbs)

✓ Proofread the following sentences for errors in the use of the comma. If a sentence is correct, write a C to the right of it.

   a. You can now purchase ultrasonic humidifiers, or you can still buy the warm-mist models.

   b. A humidifier will permit the thermostat to be set lower, but it will not work effectively if the temperature is too low.

   c. A humidifier can soothe dry throats, and help keep plants from withering.

   d. Low humidity allows static electricity to build up, and it accounts for minor electrical shocks received when touching a metal object.

   e. An acceptable humidity range is between 40 and 60 percent but higher ranges may cause paper to absorb moisture.

11-1—11-3

a. door?
b. C
c. C
d. C
e. Finally, processed!

11-5 Use the comma to separate three or more elements in a series. Use a comma before the conjunction preceding the last item in the series.

> We look for qualities such as integrity, sincerity, adaptability, and initiative in prospective employees. (word series)

> Tom, Dave, and Paul attended the game. (proper noun series)

> They picked up the tickets, attended the movie, and returned home that night. (phrase series)

> Jim cooked, Bob ate, and Susie cleaned up. (clause series)

✓ Proofread the following sentences for errors in the use of the comma. If a sentence is correct, write a *C* to the right of it.

a. Specialty temporary services in accounting, in computing and in medical technology will continue to grow in the 1990s.

b. This trend is increasing because hiring costs are less, fringe benefits do not have to be provided and workloads can be handled more easily in peak periods.

c. A nationwide survey indicates that temporaries can start expecting to receive health insurance, retirement plans tuition assistance, and child care.

d. More people are turning to temporary work because of the freedom, and flexibility it provides.

e. Temporaries will face more extensive pre-employment testing for personality, general aptitudes, and computer skills.

11-6 Use a comma to separate two consecutive adjectives that modify the same noun. A comma is needed between the two adjectives if they can be joined by *and*.

> This has been a long, hard trip. (long and hard)

> She bought a good used car.
> (*Good* modifies the idea expressed by the combination *used car*. It is not a good and used car.)

11-4
a. C
b. C
c. throats, and
d. C
e. percent, but

11-5
a. computing, and
b. provided, and
c. plans, tuition
d. freedom and
e. C

Chapter 11—Punctuation Errors, Part 1

✓ Proofread the following sentences for errors in the use of commas. If a sentence is correct, write a C to the right of it.

a. Many people choose real estate as a challenging, second career.

b. We often associate a residential real estate agent with signs posted on local front lawns.

c. Most real estate agents are concentrated in large, urban areas or in small but rapidly growing communities.

d. Many jobs exist in real estate if you consider the total career area.

e. An up-to-date annotated reference on jobs in real estate can be found in your local library.

11-7 Use a comma to separate unrelated adjacent numbers.

On page 15, 35 different kinds of birds are named.

▶ Use a comma to separate numbers with four or more digits, unless the number identifies (such as an invoice number) rather than enumerates.

A balance of $2,500 is due on Invoice 67412.

11-8 Use a comma to separate parts of addresses and dates.

We met on Tuesday, September 10, 1990, at 4 p.m.

Did you visit Seattle, Washington, last year?

Spring practice will be held in Toronto, Canada, this year.

Please send the shipment to Mark Dues, 528 Easy Street, Sunnyvale, CA 94088-9236.

Note: The comma may be omitted when only the month and year are given.

The next convention will be held in June 1992 in Las Vegas.

11-6
a. challenging second
b. C
c. large urban areas
d. C
e. up-to-date, annotated

✓ Proofread the following paragraph for errors in the use of the comma.

A secretarial want-ad survey was conducted from ads in the Sunday, March 26, editions of 14 U.S. newspapers and the Saturday, March 25 editions of three Canadian newspapers. Newspaper ads from Seattle, Washington, to Miami, Florida were surveyed. Results indicated that salaries ranged from $10,000 to $70000. In the report published on page 14 33 types of information were gathered in the survey.

SPELLING REVIEW

To improve your ability to detect spelling errors, master the words below. Watch for them in the exercises that follow and in succeeding chapters.

amateur	leisure
development	liaison
fulfill	privilege
immediately	transferred
itinerary	volume

11-7, 11-8
March 25, editions
Florida, were
$70,000
14, 33

PROOFREADING TIPS

Study these tips and apply them as you proofread:

1. Punctuation marks are used in order to make the meaning clear. Proofread to eliminate confusion caused by errors in punctuation.

2. If the material is interesting, read first for pleasure, then for errors.

3. Keep a reference guide ready in case you need to refer to it.

Proofreading Applications

Proofread the following paragraphs. Use the appropriate proofreading symbols to mark errors you find in terminal punctuation, comma usage, or spelling. To aid you in proofreading, the number of errors to be found is indicated in parentheses for Exercises P-1, P-2, and P-3.

P-1 Do you routinely use an automatic teller machine (ATM) to withdraw money from your checking account? to transfer funds between accounts? to pay regular monthly bills? Many of us are no longer amaters at this form of electronic funds transfer, and find it a convenient flexible method of banking. Did you know that these services may be available even if you are thousands of miles from your bank's ATM. Many of the thousands of ATMs in our country are linked into statewide, regional, or national networks. (4 errors)

P-2 The small plastic card you use at your ATM is actually a debit card. It allows you to withdraw from your account electronically without ever writing a check. Would you like to be able to use your debit card right at the cash register? You would merely put your debit card through a processing machine, enter your personal code and depress a computer-entry button. The amount of your purchase would be immediatly deducted from your checking account, and transfered to the store's account. (4 errors)

P-3 The developement of point-of-sale debiting has been slow but this debiting method has the enthusiasm of many persons. Retailers get their money almost immediately, and chances of a holdup are diminished because money is deposited in the store's account rather than into its cash register. Customers enjoy the priviledges of paying faster, carrying less cash, and not having to wait in line for check approval. Do you think banks will ever feel threatened that debit cards may cause them to lose their high-volume, profitable, credit card business. (5 errors)

P-1
1. amateurs
2. transfer and
3. convenient, flexible
4. bank's ATM?

P-2
1. code, and
2. immediately
3. account and
4. transferred

P-4 Would you like to receive current relevant information about our new All-in-One card. Just return the enclosed coupon to National Bank, 1987 Wilshire Boulevard, Los Angeles CA   90024-8765. Send in your coupon by February 15, 19-- and you will receive a rebate of 1 percent on all All-in-One credit purchases above the first $1000 in any 12-month period.

P-3
1. develo**pm**ent
2. slow**,** but
3. privil**eg**es
4. profitable credit
5. card business**?**

P-4
1. current**,** relevant
2. All-in-One card**?**
3. Los Angeles**,** CA
4. February 15, 19--**,**
5. $1**,**000

PROGRESSIVE PROOFREADING

You are the manager of McDowell Travel Agency. Because this is a relatively new business, only four people are employed in the office. You confer with customers and make travel reservations, but you are also responsible for seeing that all communication is correct. Today you have four documents to proofread. Follow the instructions given with each document. Your office uses block letter format and open punctuation.

Chapter 11—Punctuation Errors, Part 1

Job 1 Mark any errors you find.

McDowell Travel Agency
4500 West Kennedy Blvd.
Tampa, FL 33609-3421

November 5, 19--

Ms. Mary McCarthy
1166 Norwood St.
Cleveland, OH 44197-8032

Dear Ms. McCarthy

Thank you for your letter requesting brochures, price lists and information sheets about cruises leaving from Miami, FL. Your inquiry comes at a time when a number of interesting, exotic cruises are available at fabulously low prices.

You should receive up-to-date information within the next few days from three cruise lines about their winter cruises. Consider each line's total cost the cost of air travel to the point of departure, and the itinerary when you are making a choice. You will note that prices for a seven-day cruise range from $795 to $2150 per person.

The enclosed brochure will provide helpful information about choosing a cruise. After you make your desicion about the cruise, fill out and return the data sheet. You can then leave everything in our hands and rest assured that satisfactory arrangements will be made.

We look forward to serving as you laisison with the cruise line of your choice and assisting you in any way possible.

Sincerely

Mrs. Laura E. Spellman
Marketing Manager

dp

158   Chapter 11—Punctuation Errors, Part 1

Job 2 Proofread the printed copy by comparing it to the rough draft below.

PARADISE ISLAND
"Your Bahamas Getaway Vacation"

Add Art

Ask about our
- Golf and tennis clinics
- Island dance lessons
- Honeymoon packages

From $299
3 days / 2 nights including air
(3 nights from $329 including air)

1-800-555-2435

McDOWELL TRAVEL AGENCY
4500 West Kennedy Blvd.
Tampa, FL 33609-3421

Please rush FREE brochures and information to:
NAME _____
STREET _____
CITY _____ STATE __ ZIP ____

PARADISE ISLAND
"Your Bahamas Getaway Vacation"

Ask about our
- Golf and tennis clinics
- Honymoon packages

From $299
★ 3 days/3 nights including air
(3 nights from $339 including air)

1-800-555-2435

McDowell Travel Agency
4500 West Kennedy Blvd.
Tampa, FL 33609-3421

Please rush FREE brochures and information to:
NAME _____
STREET _____
CITY _____ STATE _____ ZIP _____

Chapter 11—Punctuation Errors, Part 1

Job 3 Check the following copy for errors. Be sure that all words are spelled correctly. The main headings and side headings should be in bold.

CHOOSING THE RIGHT CRUISE FOR YOU

As the winter cruise season approaches, discounts on ship fares are plentiful in the travel industry, and smart consumers are taking advantage of the special bargains. Now is the time to consider taking a liesurely cruise if it is one of those things that will fullfill a lifetime dream for you. If you have never pictured yourself as a passenger on a cruise ship, consider the following facts.

Passenger Profile

Once cruises were a pastime for the rich and the retired. Today cruises are taken by individuals from all walks of life and all income levels. Forty-eight percent of cruise passengers now earn less than $30,000 a year. Nearly half are under forty-five years of age, and ten percent are under twenty-five.

It is estimated that more than a million and a half people will take cruises on about one hundred cruise ships this year and cruise lines are competitively vying for this business. Two qualities of the cruise experience is being stressed: value and convenience. Now is a great time to participate in what some refer to as the ''cruise revolution.

Cost and Convenience

Consider the price of the average cruise. The price that you pay includes accomodations, baggage handling, meals, entertainment (including first-run movies and live performances), room service, daily activities ranging from computer lessons to disco dancing, travel to any number of ports, and reduced air fare from home.

Convenience is another factor that you must consider as you contemplate taking a cruise. In what other way can you travel from one country to another without having to unpack and repack your bags? Where else can you spend days or weeks without having to open your wallet or purse constantly. You don't even have to worry about arranging travel schedules, making plane reservations, or waiting long hours in airports.

Activities on Board

To be sure that your cruise proves to be all that you expect it to be, you should take the time to find out what the various cruise lines offer and to who they cater. For example, some cruise lines cater to children and make special provisions for them. Other lines cater only to adults. Some provide for academic pursuits while others primarily provide entertainment and recreation.

160   Chapter 11—Punctuation Errors, Part 1

You should give some thought to the types of activities that you might enjoy. Do you want entertainment. Do you want some physical fitness programs? Do you want to learn something? At least one cruise ship doubles on a regular basis as a floating university. There is no pressure to participate in any of the activities provided by the cruise line. If you wish, you can relax on the deck with a book or watch television in your own cabin. You can choose your own recreation.

Cruise Itinarary

Another important criterion that will effect your selection of a cruise is the planned itinarary of the ship. Consider the number of stops you would be making and the ports you would be visiting. Is there particular cities you have always wanted to tour. Your travel agent can provide you with a detailed list of port choices and itinerary options to help you decide on the best cruise.

How to Get Started

After you have made some of the major decisions reguarding your preferences in a cruise, see your travel agent. The agent can help determine which cruise suits your needs, and provide answers to any other questions that you might have. In other words, your travel agent is the liason between you and the cruise line. Contact your travel agent today and take the worry out of traveling.

COMPUTERIZED PROOFREADING

Job 4 Proofread Advertising Copy

1. Load the file C11JOB4 from the template.
2. Proofread the advertising copy and make all necessary corrections.
3. Format the document double spaced with 1" side margins. Divide the heading into two lines and format it in bold.
4. Save the document as C11JOB4R.
5. Produce the document by following the standard procedures.

CHAPTER 12

PUNCTUATION ERRORS, PART 2

Objectives: *After completing this chapter, you should be able to*

▶ Identify errors in commas used to set off introductory elements, nonessential elements, appositives, nouns of direct address, and contrasted elements.
▶ Use the appropriate proofreading symbols to indicate changes in text.
▶ Spell correctly a list of commonly misspelled words.

FUNCTIONS OF THE COMMA

Chapter 11 dealt with terminal punctuation and some simple uses of the comma. Chapter 12 discusses the more complex uses of the comma. This chapter covers rules for using commas to (1) separate introductory elements, (2) set off nonessential expressions, (3) set off appositives, and (4) set off nouns of direct address. Generally two commas set off nonessential elements that interrupt the flow of thought from the subject to the verb or complement. One comma is used to separate elements in a sentence to clarify their relationship.

INTRODUCTORY ELEMENTS

Introductory elements are words, phrases, or clauses that begin a sentence and come before the subject and verb of the main clause. Generally, a single comma is used to separate an introductory element from the rest of the sentence in order to clarify the meaning of the sentence. The subject and verb of each main clause are identified in the examples.

12-1 Use a comma after most introductory elements. The introductory words, phrases, or clauses are italicized in the examples.

       S   V
Yes, we can accommodate you on June 4.
    (introductory word)

              S   V
Remember, the books must be returned today.
      (introductory word)

                           S   V
Leaving the next morning, we drove through a scenic forest.
      (introductory phrase)

                    S   V
To assemble the kit, you must follow the directions.
      (introductory phrase)

                          V
If you come to Atlanta, be sure to visit Stone Mountain.
      (introductory clause, *you* is the subject)

▶ Do not mistake the main clause of the sentence for an introductory clause. A comma is usually not used when the main clause comes first.

When you join Phi Beta Lambda, you will have many professional opportunities.
      (introductory clause)

You will have many professional opportunities when you join Phi Beta Lambda.

▶ Do not use a comma after phrases or clauses that function as the subject of the sentence. The noun clauses are italicized.

            S   V
Finding the lost contact lens is their goal.
      (noun phrase used as subject)

            S   V
To accept sole credit for the idea would be unfair.
      (infinitive phrase used as subject)

         S   V
What he learned in school has helped him throughout his life.
      (noun clause used as subject)

12-2   Generally do not use a comma after introductory adverbs (*frequently, recently, now, tomorrow*) and introductory adverbial phrases.

In the morning things may look better.

Frequently the class visits the history museum.

Proofread the following sentences for errors in the use of the comma. Use the proofreading symbols you have learned thus far to mark any errors. If a sentence is correct, write a C to the right of it.

a. If you had a multimillion-dollar inheritance, how would you spend it?

b. In this workbook the author covers a spectrum of topics.

c. Although the two leaders disagreed on some points, the meeting was beneficial.

d. Yes I am a member of Professional Secretaries International.

e. We will not go to school, if it snows.

NONESSENTIAL AND ESSENTIAL ELEMENTS

A nonessential element is a word, phrase, or clause that provides additional information but is not necessary to the meaning of the sentence. An essential element is a word, phrase, or clause that is necessary to the meaning of the sentence. Nonessential elements include nonrestrictive elements, transitional expressions, and appositives. Essential elements are also referred to as *restrictive*.

To determine whether an expression is essential or nonessential, try omitting it from the sentence. If you can leave the expression out without changing the basic meaning of the sentence, the expression is a nonessential expression and should be set off with commas.

12-3 Use commas to set off nonrestrictive elements. Nonrestrictive elements provide additional descriptive information about the nouns or pronouns they modify. These elements often begin with *who*, *whom*, or *which*. Restrictive clauses often begin with *that*, *who*, *whom*, or *which*.

We knew that, late or not, we were expected to attend that meeting.

The new automated information delivery system, which was installed last Thursday, can function as a telephone receptionist and voice mail system.

Dr. Benita Moore, who is president of Georgia Business Education Association, has provided excellent leadership to business teachers.

12-1, 12-2

a. C
b. C
c. C
d. Yes**,** I
e. school if

Chapter 12—Punctuation Errors, Part 2

▶ Do not use commas to set off elements that are essential to the meaning of the sentence.

The student who studies hard and completes all assignments should make a good grade.

All orders that are postmarked by December 6 will be shipped before Christmas.

12-4 Use commas to set off such transitional expressions as *on the other hand, first, in fact, to tell the truth, however, that is, then, therefore,* and *for example* when they interrupt or change the flow of the sentence.

It is possible, theoretically, to make the experiment work.

The person who received the recognition, if you recall, was the supervisor.

She may, however, choose to spend the extra time watching a television special.

You could, on the other hand, refuse to accompany her.

✓ Proofread the following sentences for errors in the use of the comma. Use the proofreading symbols you have learned thus far to mark any errors. If a sentence is correct, write a C to the right of it.

a. The statements highlighted in yellow are important in this course.

b. The woman, who is standing by the punch table, is my wife.

c. Leisure activities, which include swimming and sailing are important to me.

d. She has not been to church since she returned home.

e. He was in fact the first member of the club.

12-5 Use commas to set off appositives. An *appositive* is a word or phrase that renames or can be substituted for the noun or pronoun that immediately precedes it.

Panama City Beach, one of my favorite vacation spots, is very crowded during Memorial Day weekend.

Theresa Fowlkes, a benefits consultant with Higgins Co., reported that only a small percentage of companies allow unused vacation time to accrue.

12-3, 12-4

a. C
b. woman who table is
c. sailing, are
d. C
e. was, in fact,

▶ Do not use commas to set off an appositive when it contains information that is essential to the meaning of the sentence or has a close relationship to the preceding word.

Her daughter Barbara is going on vacation.
    (She has more than one daughter; Barbara is the one who is going on vacation.)

The doctor himself did the testing.

✓ Proofread the following sentences for errors in the use of the comma. Use the proofreading symbols you have learned thus far to mark any errors. If a sentence is correct, write a *C* to the right of it.

   a. One of Salman Rushdie's books, *The Satanic Verses*, was offensive to many Moslems.
   b. Bill Burdette chair of the department is going to conduct the seminar.
   c. Have the materials delivered to Marjorie the chauffeur.
   d. According to Jim Clark of Clark Associates producers of on-line directory services, over half of the data bases provide business-related information.
   e. The author herself was there to autograph the books.

ADDITIONAL COMMA RULES

The following guidelines will help you use the comma correctly in special situations. Rules for direct address and contrasted elements are discussed along with guidelines for the use of the comma to prevent misreading.

12-6 Use a comma to set off a name or title addressed directly to the reader or listener.

   Frank, please assist me with conference registration.
   Ask the participants, Mr. Templeton, if they are planning to stay for lunch.

12-7 Use a comma to set off contrasted elements.

   The president, not the board, made the decision.
   Glennis, rather than Sandra, will make the presentation.

12-5
a. C
b. Burdette, chair department, is
c. Marjorie, the
d. Associates, producers
e. C

Chapter 12—Punctuation Errors, Part 2   167

▶ When a contrasted element is considered essential to the meaning of the sentence, the contrasted element is not set off by commas.

It was a busy but enjoyable trip.

12-8 Insert a comma to prevent misreading the sentence.

Confusing: Inside the house was a mess.
Better: Inside, the house was a mess.

Confusing: To Joe Alexander seemed the man for the job.
Better: To Joe, Alexander seemed the man for the job.

Note: Use this rule sparingly. Generally all commas are inserted to make reading easier.

12-9 Insert a comma to separate identical or similar words, except when the addition of a comma would increase the awkwardness of the sentence.

They walked in, in groups.

He felt that that statement was not in good taste.

▶ Insert a comma to separate unrelated numbers that fall next to each other.

In 1991, 800 people attended the city's annual fair.

Proofread the following sentences for errors in the use of the comma. Use the proofreading symbols you have learned thus far to mark any errors. If a sentence is correct, write a C to the right of it.

a. I believe Mrs. Clark that your order has been received.

b. Out of three, one choice was possible.

c. To a perfectionist like Anne Marie would not be acceptable for the assignment.

d. The personal computer not the typewriter is my choice.

e. I am happy that that goal was achieved.

168   Chapter 12—Punctuation Errors, Part 2

SPELLING REVIEW

To improve your ability to detect spelling errors, master the words below. Watch for them in the exercises that follow and in succeeding chapters.

appropriate	occurrence
conscientious	questionnaire
convenience	receipt
facilitate	strictly
integrate	utilization

PROOFREADING TIPS

Study these tips and apply them as you proofread:

1. When proofreading for comma errors, always look for the main thought in the sentence and determine if the main thought is changed by the use of commas. Do not use commas to set off material that is essential to the meaning.
2. Remember, only one comma is needed to set off an introductory word, phrase, or clause.
3. Two commas are required to set off words, phrases, or clauses within a sentence.

12-6—12-9

a. believe, Mrs. Clark, that
b. C
c. Anne, Marie
d. computer, not the typewriter, is
e. C

Proofreading Applications

Proofread the following paragraphs. Use the appropriate proofreading symbols to mark errors you find in spelling and the use of the comma. To aid you in proofreading, the number of errors is indicated in parentheses for Exercises P-1, P-2, and P-3.

P-1 Stress in the office environment is a major concern of all concientious managers. Actually this health hazard has been around for centuries. Health officials view stress as a factor that, properly controlled, can contribute to human growth by preparing the body for situations, that are frightening or unfamiliar. The trick, say these officials, is learning to cope with stress. A number of strategies have been designed to combat physical stress in the office environment. For example exercises have been designed to relieve such stress symptoms as backaches, headaches, and stiffness. (4 errors)

P-2 Backaches and other signs of tension are often caused by insufficient physical activity during the workday. This condition is particularly common in employees who "sit for long periods of time and move only their eyes and fingers," says Ruth Lindsey co-author of the book *Survival Kit for Those Who Sit*. "When you sit for long intervals several of your physical functions begin to slow down," says Ms. Lindsey. According to her muscles lose some of their flexibility and begin to weaken, if they are not worked and stretched. Without exercise oxygen levels in the blood decline, and the brain's supply of its most vital need is reduced. (5 errors)

P-1
1. conscientious
2. Actually,
3. situations that
4. For example,

P-3 An excellent way to help reduce work stress is to purchase appropirate seating for tasks, that need to be performed. A good work chair should provide support for the lower back. If the chair lacks lumbar support place a small cushion or rolled-up towel in the hollow of the back. Studies show that without this support, the shoulders become hunched, the head is thrust forward, and the lower back is flattened. Create a hollow area for the buttocks. A chair should be low enough so that the front edge of the seat does not cut off circulation to the legs. Use a footrest, if a chair is too high. (5 errors)

P-4 A recommended office chair according to Ms. Lindsey is one that rolls, swivels, and tilts like a rocker. The rocking motion aids circulation and helps to keep knee joints limber. Swiveling allows the user to change body position while keeping the eyes focused on the work. A rolling action allows for frequent changing of the distance from one's work surface. This changing reduces eye fatigue. Many of these features are built into chairs by the office seating industry a market whose value should reach $2.7 million by 1993. In short, find out about an office chair before purchasing it. After all the user will spend many hours in it and should be comfortable.

P-2
1. Lindsey, co-author
2. intervals, several
3. her, muscles
4. weaken if
5. exercise,

P-3
1. appropriate
2. tasks that
3. support, place
4. support the
5. footrest if

P-4
1. chair, according
2. Lindsey, is
3. industry, a
4. all, the

PROGRESSIVE PROOFREADING

You are employed as an editorial assistant for *The Jackson Herald*, a daily newspaper. You are responsible for proofreading the work of new reporters, and from time to time the chief editor asks you to proofread specific items.

Chapter 12—Punctuation Errors, Part 2

Job 1 Proofread the following ad.

(Cartoon: A man and a woman at a computer.)

Woman: "THAT'S GREAT, ANN! WHAT KIND OF SOFTWARE ARE YOU USING?"

Man: "CHRIS, DESKTOP PUBLISHING IS THE ANSWER TO OUR IN-HOUSE PUBLISHING NEEDS."

PERFECT-PAGE SOFTWARE: THE ANSWER TO YOUR IN-HOUSE PUBLISHING NEEDS.

For more information on our cost-effective plan for producing professional-quality reports, brochures, and forms right in your office, fill out and return the attached card today. Upon reciept of your inquiry we will sent you informatoin about PERFECT-PAGE desktop publishing software.

Name _____ Position _____

Company _____

Adress _____

City   State   Zip

Mail today to: The Upjohn Software Company
1010 Rives Street
Baltimore, MA   21226-2318

172   Chapter 12—Punctuation Errors, Part 2

Job 2 Proofread the news release below.

The Jackson Herald

News Release

April 22, 19--

RELEASE: IMMEDIATELY

CONTACT: Savella Marino

JACKSON COLLEGE HOSTS DESKTOP PUBLISHING SEMINAR

JACKSON, Ohio. More than fifty local companies expected to attend the second annual Desktop Publishing Seminar at Jackson College on May 5, 19--. This year the seminar will intergrate new graphics software packages with desktop publishing applications.

According to Dr. Sharon Hilltop seminar coordinator this seminar is paticularly designed for companies that want ot produce cost-effective, high-quality documents. The utalization of desktop publishing is especially appropiate in in producing company broshures, advertising flyers, reports and proposals, newsletters, and business forms.

The conference will begin at 9 a.m. and conclude at 4 p.m. Included in the $50 registration fee, will be a luncheon and seminar materials. To register, for the seminar, call 614/555-2208.

###

Chapter 12—Punctuation Errors, Part 2

Job 3 Proofread the following article on desktop publishing.

DESKTOP PUBLISHING

A New Concept in Document Production

What is deskop publishing? Why is it capturing the attention of so many people? Will it become the standard way to produce ads and brochures? to produce all corporate communications?

Although some of these questions may remain unanswered for some time the occurence of one thing is sure: Desktop publishing is definately changing the communication process for a number of organizations.

What is Desktop Publishing?

Desktop publishing describes the process by which a professional-quality document is produced using a microcomputer system and a special software.

"Desktop publishing may replace word processing software for final output."

Software

WYSIWYG which stands for "What you see is what you get" characterizes much of the composition software. WYSIWYG (pronounced "wisywig") means that what you see on the screen is exactly what you'll get when the copy is printed.

Printer

The utalization of laser printers facilatates the use of multiple type sizes and styles on the same page. Graphics (letterheads, logos, and freehand drawings done with a mouse) and scanned images (photographs or drawings) may be intergrated into the copy with ease.

Is There a Market?

Until recently, professional-quality printing was strickly limited to the domain of graphic arts professionals: typesetters, pasteup artists, and printers Desktop publishing enables typeset-quality pages to be produced in-house. With a little practice and some good design ideas, managers, office workers, or students can create their own layouts complete with borders, rules, columns of type and other graphic elements.

"Now companies can produce cost-effective near-typeset quality documents in-house."

How Is It Used?

A questionaire sent to more than ninty users, reveal that people are using desktop systems for an array of different purposes: ads, broshures, business forms, manuals, proposals, newsletters, resumes, and transparency masters.

Katherine Smith vice president of a publishing consulting firm predicts that desktop publishing will replace word processing software for final output. One consultant commented "Now companies can produce cost-effective near-typeset quality documents in-house."

This handout on destop publishing was prepared by Kim Stephens. For more information on desktop publshing systems call her at extension 212.

COMPUTERIZED PROOFREADING

Job 4 Proofread List of Registrants

1. Load the file C12JOB4 from the template.

2. Proofread the list of registrants on the screen by comparing it to the correct individual registration forms shown on pages 176 and 177. The ZIP Codes listed are for the company addresses. Correct any mistakes you find. The information on the forms is correct.

3. Format the list with 1/2" side margins and a 1" top margin.

4. Save the list as C12JOB4R.

5. Produce the list by following the standard procedures.

REGISTRATION FOR DESKTOP PUBLISHING SEMINAR, JACKSON COLLEGE, MAY 5, 19--

Name: _Burns_ (Last) _Jerry_ (First)   Date: _4/20/--_
Home Address: _4560 Lawndale St._
City: _Ridgeland_   State: _OH_   ZIP: _45692-0854_   Home Phone: _614_ / _562-9224_ (Area Code)
Company: _The Tripp Company_   Address: _P.O. Box 46213_
City: _Wellston_   State: _OH_   ZIP: _45692-6441_   Work Phone: _614_ / _562-8461_ (Area Code)

The $50 registration fee includes the luncheon and seminar materials. Please send your registration and check made out to Desktop Publishing Seminar—Jackson College to: Jackson College
Attention Joyce Chan
P.O. Box 667
Jackson, Ohio   45640

Deadline for Registration: April 25, 19--

REGISTRATION FOR DESKTOP PUBLISHING SEMINAR, JACKSON COLLEGE, MAY 5, 19--

Name: _Finlay_ (Last) _Jean_ (First)   Date: _4/21/--_
Home Address: _60 Fairlawn Circle_
City: _Jackson_   State: _OH_   ZIP: _45640-1241_   Home Phone: _614_ / _543-4126_ (Area Code)
Company: _Hammermill, Inc._   Address: _500 N. Orleans St., Suite 40_
City: _Jackson_   State: _OH_   ZIP: _45640-8462_   Work Phone: _614_ / _543-8942_ (Area Code)

The $50 registration fee includes the luncheon and seminar materials. Please send your registration and check made out to Desktop Publishing Seminar—Jackson College to: Jackson College
Attention Joyce Chan
P.O. Box 667
Jackson, Ohio   45640

Deadline for Registration: April 25, 19--

REGISTRATION FOR DESKTOP PUBLISHING SEMINAR, JACKSON COLLEGE, MAY 5, 19--

Name: _FREDERICKS_ (Last) _LAURIE_ (First)   Date: _4/24/--_
Home Address: _902 RIVER PARK DR._
City: _JACKSON_   State: _OH_   ZIP: _45640-2161_   Home Phone: _614_ / _543-2809_ (Area Code)
Company: _STEVENS INDUSTRIES, INC._   Address: _815 STONEHENGE DR._
City: _JACKSON_   State: _OH_   ZIP: _45640-8902_   Work Phone: _614_ / _543-1431_ (Area Code)

The $50 registration fee includes the luncheon and seminar materials. Please send your registration and check made out to Desktop Publishing Seminar—Jackson College to: Jackson College
Attention Joyce Chan
P.O. Box 667
Jackson, Ohio   45640

Deadline for Registration: April 25, 19--

REGISTRATION FOR DESKTOP PUBLISHING SEMINAR, JACKSON COLLEGE, MAY 5, 19--

Name _Pascarella_____Lou_____ Date _4/24/--_
        Last   First

Home Address _102 Williams Lane_____

City _Wellston_____ State _OH_ ZIP _45692-1664_ Home Phone _614/562-2250_
                                                                                      Area Code

Company _Cullen Business Systems_ Address _14 Meridian_____

City _Jackson_____ State _OH_ ZIP _45640-4416_ Work Phone _614/543-2949_
                                                                                      Area Code

The $50 registration fee includes the luncheon and seminar materials. Please send your registration and check made out to Desktop Publishing Seminar—Jackson College to: Jackson College
                                                                                                                                     Attention Joyce Chan
                                                                                                                                     P.O. Box 667
                                                                                                                                     Jackson, Ohio   45640

Deadline for Registration: April 25, 19--

REGISTRATION FOR DESKTOP PUBLISHING SEMINAR, JACKSON COLLEGE, MAY 5, 19--

Name _Konica_____Michelle_____ Date _4/23/--_
        Last   First

Home Address _6150 Touhy Ave. Dr._____

City _Jackson_____ State _OH_ ZIP _45640-1665_ Home Phone _614/543-0260_
                                                                                             Area Code

Company _Gaylord and Mortensen_ Address _45 Harvey Rd._____

City _Jackson_____ State _OH_ ZIP _45640-8148_ Work Phone _614/543-9112_
                                                                                              Area Code

The $50 registration fee includes the luncheon and seminar materials. Please send your registration and check made out to Desktop Publishing Seminar—Jackson College to: Jackson College
                                                                                                                                     Attention Joyce Chan
                                                                                                                                   P.O. Box 667
                                                                                                                                     Jackson, Ohio   45640

Deadline for Registration: April 25, 19--

REGISTRATION FOR DESKTOP PUBLISHING SEMINAR, JACKSON COLLEGE, MAY 5, 19--

Name _Radwan_____Lee_____ Date _4/23/--_
        Last   First

Home Address _402 Mayhill St._____

City _Danville_____ State _OH_ ZIP _43014_____ Home Phone _614/581-7742_
                                                                                             Area Code

Company _UMI Lighting_____ Address _4260 Darrow Rd._____

City _Jackson_____ State _OH_ ZIP _45640-2316_ Work Phone _614/543-9444_
                                                                                              Area Code

The $50 registration fee includes the luncheon and seminar materials. Please send your registration and check made out to Desktop Publishing Seminar—Jackson College to: Jackson College
                                                                                                                                     Attention Joyce Chan
                                                                                                                                  P.O. Box 667
                                                                                                                                     Jackson, Ohio   45640

Deadline for Registration: April 25, 19--

Chapter 12—Punctuation Errors, Part 2

CHAPTER 13

OTHER INTERNAL PUNCTUATION ERRORS

Objectives: *After completing this chapter, you should be able to*
- ▶ Detect errors in the use of these punctuation marks: semicolon, colon, apostrophe, quotation marks, underscore, dash, and parentheses.
- ▶ Use the appropriate proofreading symbols to indicate changes in text.
- ▶ Spell correctly a list of commonly misspelled words.

PUNCTUATION TO CLARIFY

As discussed in the last two chapters, punctuation marks have specific, prescribed functions. Punctuation helps the reader interpret the meaning of the communication. The proofreader must know the function of each mark of punctuation to be able to evaluate its use in clarifying the message.

Chapter 13 reviews the use of the semicolon, colon, apostrophe, quotation marks, underscore, dash, and parentheses. Use the following proofreading symbols to mark errors in the use of these punctuation marks:

⋏;	Insert semicolon.	Join us for dinner tonight we're having steak.
⋏:	Insert colon.	You will need to bring three things notepaper, pen, and pencil.
⋎	Insert apostrophe or single quotation mark.	Tennessees economic climate is continually improving.
⋎⋎	Insert quotation marks.	When interest rates are down, invest in stocks, advised the broker.
___ or *ital*	Underline or italicize.	The word articulate should be included in the list.

179

	Insert dash.	The thief took everything—my car, my wallet, and my luggage.
	Insert parentheses.	The committee (consisting of five students and three teachers) presented the report on time.

SEMICOLON

A semicolon is used when a sentence needs a stronger break than would be provided by a comma. The semicolon is not as abrupt as a period and does not signal the end of a thought as a period does. The semicolon is a strong separator and is used only between equal parts. A semicolon is followed by one space.

13-1 Use a semicolon to separate the main clauses of a compound sentence when the clauses are not joined by a coordinate conjunction (*and, but, or,* and *nor*).

> I must go to vote; the polls will close in an hour.

> Send the report by Federal Express Mail; we need an answer tomorrow.
> (*You* is the understood subject in the first clause.)

13-2 Use a semicolon to separate the main clauses of a compound sentence when either of the clauses contains a comma. Confusion could occur if a comma were used to separate the clauses.

> When you receive the document, sign it; but do not mail it until Friday, March 10.

> I requested files for Carlson, Carson, and Davison; but files for Carlsen, Carson, and Davidson were delivered.

13-3 Use the semicolon to separate the main clauses of a compound sentence joined by an adverb or transitional expression such as *accordingly, consequently, furthermore, hence, however, in fact, likewise, otherwise, therefore,* and *thus*.

> It was past midnight; consequently, they had to adjourn before the issue was settled.

> The cost was minimal; however, he chose not to attend the meeting.

13-4 Use the semicolon to separate items in a series when at least one of the items contains a comma.

> Copies of the report were sent to Elaine Carson, president; Janet Wukman, vice president; and Trilby Mays, secretary.

✓ Proofread the following sentences for errors in the use of commas and semicolons. If a sentence is correct, write a C to the right of it.

a. Budgeting is crucial to financial planning, however most people don't enjoy the recordkeeping.

b. I will carry only the essentials, the nonessentials require too much space.

c. I like to visit North Carolina, South Carolina and Georgia but Florida, Alabama, and Louisiana will be my destination this year.

d. I detest dieting; it takes too much willpower.

e. Imperial Airlines serves Miami, Florida, Atlanta, Georgia, Birmingham, Alabama, and Raleigh, North Carolina.

COLON

A colon represents a break in the sentence that is greater than the semicolon but less than the period. Usually the writer uses the colon after a statement to introduce and emphasize what follows the colon. The colon usually means *as follows*. Two spaces follow a colon except in expressions of time and reference initials.

13-5 Use a colon to introduce a question, a lengthy quotation, or a phrase or clause that explains what has gone before. The first word of a main clause following a colon may be capitalized for emphasis.

> The speaker raised an interesting question: Which comes first, enthusiasm or success?

> The researcher made these recommendations:
> (long quote)

> Watson's philosophy was simple: Give the best service, strive for superior performance, and respect the individual.

13-1—13-4

a. planning; however,
b. essentials; the
c. South Carolina, and Georgia, but
d. C
e. Florida;
   Georgia;
   Alabama;

Chapter 13—Other Internal Punctuation Errors   181

13-6 Use a colon to introduce a list or a series. (Omit periods after items in a vertical list unless one of the items is a complete sentence.)

The steps are as follows:
1. Insert the disk into drive 1.
2. Turn on the computer.

These criteria are considered important:
1. A quality education
2. Meaningful work experience
3. Academic grade-point average
4. Leadership experience

▶ Do not use a colon to introduce a list that immediately follows a preposition or a verb.

The supervisor has the responsibility to (1) assist the staff, (2) establish procedures, and (3) resolve conflicts.

13-7 Use a colon to separate hours and minutes expressed in figures.

Dinner will be served at 5:30 p.m.

13-8 Use a colon to punctuate reference initials or the salutation when mixed punctuation is used in a letter.

JP:df   Dear Ms. Fine:

✓ Proofread the following sentences for errors in the use of commas, semicolons, and colons. If a sentence is correct, write a C to the right of it.

a. It's as true with documents as it is with people: First impressions count.

b. Three criteria are used when booking a hotel; location, value, and reputation.

c. The "Employment Policies" section of the Policy Manual states: "Spouses will not be permitted to continue their employment when one of them occupies a confidential position."

d. The article was sent to the following newspapers: *The News and Observer*, Raleigh, *The Bethel Beacon*, Bethel, and *The Daily Southern*, Tarboro.

e. In one hour I plan to do the following; Spin the barrel of entries, draw ten slips from the barrel, and announce the winners.

APOSTROPHE

An apostrophe is used to form possessives and some plurals. It is also used to indicate the omission of letters and figures. The apostrophe is followed by a single space unless the next character is part of the same word.

13-9 Use an apostrophe and *s* to form the possessive case of a singular noun.

>   Janie's friend   (friend of Janie)
>   a year's work   (the work of a year)
>   Michael's hat   (the hat of Michael)

Note: The possessive case for some nouns is formed by adding only an apostrophe. Addition of an apostrophe and an *s* makes the word too difficult to pronounce.

>   for appearance' (conscience', goodness', old times') sake
>
>   species' habits

13-10 Use an apostrophe and *s* to form the possessive case of an indefinite pronoun.

>   anyone's guess
>   everybody's friend
>   somebody's glove

Note: A personal pronoun does not require an apostrophe.

>   my/mine   our/ours
>   your/yours   their/theirs
>   her/hers   its
>   his

This notebook is mine; yours is on the desk.

The building has exceeded its capacity.

13-11 Use an apostrophe alone to form the possessive case of a plural noun ending in *s* or *es*.

>   employees' rights   (rights of the employees)
>   three years' work   (the work of three years)
>   Davises' house   (house of the Davises)

13-5—13-8

a. C
b. hotel: location
c. C
d. Raleigh; Bethel;
e. following: Spin

Chapter 13—Other Internal Punctuation Errors

▸ Use an apostrophe and *s* to form the possessive case of a noun that does not form its plural by adding *s* or *es*.

    children's field trip   (field trip of the children)
    men's coats   (coats of the men)
    women's coats   (coats of the women)

13-12 To form the possessive of a compound noun, make the last element possessive.

    my daughter-in-law's schedule   (the schedule of my daughter-in-law)

    my daughters-in-laws' schedules   (the schedules of my daughters-in-law)

    somebody else's

13-13 To show joint ownership, make the last name possessive. To show separate ownership, make each name possessive.

    Marvin and Joyce's condominium   (one condominium owned by both)

    Brian's and Ben's rackets   (two rackets, one Brian's and one Ben's)

13-14 Use an apostrophe to form the plural of a letter, an abbreviation containing periods, and a word that would otherwise be confusing if only an *s* were added.

    B.A.'s
    A's and S's
    &'s (ampersands)
    too many that's

13-15 Use an apostrophe to indicate the omission of letters or figures.

    OK'd (okayed)
    it's (it is)
    o'clock (of the clock)
    class of '91 (class of 1991)

✓ Proofread the following sentences for errors in the use of the apostrophe. If a sentence is correct, write a C to the right of it.

   a. Managers will need to spend more time with clients as the nation's economy becomes more service oriented.

   b. Someones briefcase was left in my office.

   c. For old times sake, let's celebrate Louise's and Frank's anniversary with flowers.

   d. Its a good idea to check the company's letterhead for proper spelling, punctuation, and use of abbreviations such as ampersands (&'s).

   e. Her complaint was that there were too many ands in the students' essay and that there was a noticeable repetition of moreover's.

QUOTATION MARKS

Quotation marks are used to enclose words quoted (spoken or written), some titles, and words used in an unusual manner. Generally use a comma to set off a quotation.

13-16 Use quotation marks to enclose a direct quotation.

> Jim Goes said, "I expect attendance to be good at our next AMS meeting."
>
> "All correspondence should be answered," said the manager, "within two days."
>
> Was it Evelyn who said, "The meeting is now adjourned"?

Note: Place a question mark outside the quotation marks if the entire statement is a question. Place the question mark inside the quotation marks if only the quoted material is a question. Place commas and periods inside quotation marks.

> Gary asked, "Is it time to leave?"

13-17 Use single quotation marks to enclose a quotation within a quotation.

> In his speech to the graduating class, Dean Stanhope remarked, "I believe that, as John Kennedy said, 'It is time for a new generation of leadership . . . for there is a new world to be won.'"

13-9—13-15

a. C
b. someone's
c. times' sake
   Louise and
d. It's
e. and's
   student's

Chapter 13—Other Internal Punctuation Errors

13-18 Use quotation marks to enclose titles of book chapters, articles in magazines or newspapers, or other parts of complete works. (Use italics or underscore titles of books, magazines, newspapers, or other complete works.)

> One of the most popular columns in *The News and Observer* is "Under the Dome."

> The article "Microimage Methods" in the April issue of *Administrative Management* provides an analysis of film and electronic technologies.

13-19 Use quotation marks to enclose words or expressions that are used in a special manner or that may be unfamiliar to the reader. This technique should be used sparingly, or it will lose its effectiveness.

> Wohl stated that many companies have "Adidas networks" in which you run the diskette down the hall to your co-worker.

> "Computer phobia" is causing many managers to communicate poorly with the consultants.

UNDERSCORE

The underscore is used to give special emphasis to certain words or expressions. In typewritten copy, italics are indicated by underscoring. A printer sets all underscored words in italic type.

13-20 Use the underscore to set off titles of published works including books, magazines, newspapers, and videotape recordings. Also underline plays, movies, and musical compositions.

> We rented the videotape <u>Sound of Music</u> and thoroughly enjoyed watching it.

> Our library subscribes to <u>The Wall Street Journal</u> and numerous periodicals, including <u>Modern Office Technology</u> and <u>Personal Computing</u>.

13-21 Use the underscore to set off words being emphasized, defined, or used as examples. Foreign words should be underscored if they are likely to be unfamiliar to the reader.

Successful managers are <u>leaders</u>—not bosses.

They traveled <u>a pied</u> (on foot) to the Eiffel Tower.

<u>Glower</u> means "to look with sullen annoyance or anger."

For example, <u>imminent</u> should be included in the appendix with other confusing words.

▶ Use the underscore to refer to a word or letter.

I think we should delete <u>the</u> from the sentence.

He added an <u>s</u> to my name.

✓ Proofread the following sentences for errors in the use of quotation marks and the underscore. If a sentence is correct, write a C to the right of it.

a. Gwen said, "It was fairly easy to go from word processing to desktop publishing.

b. Facsimile systems were discussed in the article Facsimile Storage and Delivery, which appeared in the May issue of Office Systems.

c. Sally asked, "Did you go to the movie last night"?

d. The flight attendant asked, "Are you concerned about your safety on this flight?"

e. You are lying, "n'est-ce pas"?

DASH

The dash, an informal mark of punctuation, is used to indicate a sudden change in thought and to emphasize what follows. Use the dash sparingly so that it does not lose its impact. No space precedes or follows the dash.

13-22 Use a dash to indicate a sudden change in thought.

The best way—perhaps the only way—is to work overtime the next two weeks.

The political impact of his action—and that's what counts—cannot be measured.

13-16—13-21
a. publishing."
b. "Facsimile storage and Delivery,"
c. night?"
d. C
e. <u>n'est-ce pas?</u>

Chapter 13—Other Internal Punctuation Errors 187

13-23 Use a dash in place of commas to set off a nonessential element that needs special emphasis.

> That man is a thief—and I can prove it!

> Successful organizations have a common source of power—people.

▶ Use a dash in place of a semicolon for a stronger but less formal break between two independent clauses in a sentence.

> Frequently when people get upset, they don't expect you to provide answers—they just need to unleash their feelings.

▶ Use a dash in place of a colon to introduce explanatory words, phrases, or clauses when a stronger but less formal break is desired.

> Within two hours we had experienced a variety of weather—hail, rain, sunshine.

> To obtain the money, Jeff had to sell everything—his car, his house, and all of his furniture.

PARENTHESES

Parentheses are used to enclose nonessential, supplementary, or illustrative information. Unlike dashes, parentheses de-emphasize information.

13-24 Use parentheses to separate nonessential information from the rest of the sentence.

> To obtain your complimentary pass, stop at the second ticket booth (the one with the red flag on it).

13-25 Use parentheses to explain an abbreviation or to enclose periods of time.

> An immediate 10 percent salary increase will be given to any person with a CPS (Certified Professional Secretary) rating.

> The latter part of the twentieth century (1990-2000) will be a period of spectacular growth and change.

13-26 Use parentheses to enclose characters in a run-in enumeration.

> To enter the contest, you must (1) fill in the application form, (2) pay an entry fee, and (3) mail your entry.

✓ Proofread the following sentences for errors in the use of the dash and parentheses. If a sentence is correct, write a C to the right of it.

a. William Kilgore receives a good income (he clears more than $70,000 a year as a financial planner).

b. Two years ago, she began charging $90 an hour or $45 a half-hour for a wide range of financial advice and services.

c. The curriculum was presented at the OSRA (Office Systems Research Association) convention held in March.

d. Managing a company keeping it growing, profitable, and abreast of technology is a giant balancing act.

e. Please use the side entrance—the one on Arlington Boulevard.

SPELLING REVIEW

To improve your ability to detect spelling errors, master the words below. Watch for them in the exercises that follow and in succeeding chapters.

achievement	noticeable
analysis	parallel
bankruptcy	permissible
debtor	repetition
explanation	undoubtedly

PROOFREADING TIPS

Study these tips and apply them as you proofread:

1. Check each sentence to be sure a closing parenthesis, dash, or quotation mark has not been omitted.
2. Check to be sure that punctuation marks convey the proper meaning. Query the originator if necessary.
3. Check to be sure that substitutions have been entered where words have been crossed out.
4. Proofread each document twice—once for mechanical errors and once for content errors.

13-22—13-26
a. C
b. —or $45 a half-hour—
c. C
d. company—keeping technology—is
e. entrance (the one on Arlington Boulevard).

PROOFREADING APPLICATIONS

Proofread the following paragraphs and use the appropriate proofreading symbols to mark errors you find in punctuation and spelling. To aid you in proofreading, the number of errors is indicated in parentheses for Exercises P-1, P-2, and P-3.

P-1 This article deals with "The Anatomy of a Merger." This is the most noticeable fact, most mergers fail. Undoubtly, there are some false assumptions about mergers. Here is one: Top performers will remain with the organization. Actually, the explaination for most merger failures is people problems. People are often given the lowest priority during merger activity, therefore they often don't stay with the new organization. The result may lead to debtor problems or even bankruptcy. During a merger, its permissible to communicate information to employees so that uncertainty will be reduced. (5 errors)

P-2 Fifty percent of office time is spent communicating; talking, writing, or listening. It is the latter activity listening that constitutes the majority of communication time. Contrary to popular belief, listening is not a passive activity, and it involves more than just hearing. An active listener provides feedback to the speaker by nodding or saying, Yes or I see. You may be surprised at the difference listening can make in job achievement and in interaction with others. (5 errors)

P-1
1. fact: **M**ost
2. undoub**ted**ly
3. expl**an**ation
4. activity; therefore,
5. it's

Chapter 13—Other Internal Punctuation Errors

P-3 In my analysis of the book Presentations Plus, I learned that people gain 75 percent of what they know visually, 13 percent through hearing, and only 12 percent through other senses. A picture is three times more effective than words alone words and pictures together are six times more effective than words alone. In the current issue of The Secretary, published by Professional Secretaries International PSI, suggestions are provided for preparing effective visual presentations. Whether using nonprojected visuals (flip charts) or projected visuals transparencies or slides, the key to a successful presentation is planning. (5 errors)

P-4 People react to criticism in various unproductive ways, such as making excuses, arguing, counterattacking, or sulking. Its not easy to take criticism, but we will receive it as long as we interact with people. Realize that criticism isn't always negative, in fact it can be a catalyst for personal growth. Listen carefully when your critic is speaking then paraphrase what you heard. Ask pertinent questions, such as What do you want me to do differently? You may need to help the person define the real problem "Could you describe the problem as you see it?" Accepting criticism graciously and that's hard to do makes both you and your critic winners.

P-2
1. communicating:
2. activity—listening—
3. activity; and
4. "Yes"
5. "I see."

P-3
1. <u>Presentations Plus</u>
2. alone; words
3. <u>The Secretary</u>
4. International (PSI),
5. visuals (transparencies or slides),

P-4
1. It's
2. negative; in fact,
3. speaking; then
4. as "What . . . differently?"
5. problem:
6. graciously—and do—makes

PROGRESSIVE PROOFREADING

You work for the Department of Tourism for the State of Georgia, which publishes an annual travel guide. As secretary to the Associate Commissioner for Tourism, one of your responsibilities is to make sure there are no errors in the travel guide and related correspondence. Proofread the following documents for errors in spelling, grammatical construction, punctuation, number usage, and format. Your office uses block letter style with open punctuation.

Job 1 Proofread the advertisement below.

DISCOVER YOUR PLACE IN THE GARDENS

If you havent seen Colonial Gardens yet, your in for a treat. Discover the natural wonder of 10,000 acres of lakes, woodlands, gardens, and wildlife. Enjoy golf on our 18-hole, par-73 championship course. Take advantage of all the extras Colonial has to offer, tennis, swimming, nature trails, riverboat rides, and fishing.

All 210 of our rooms at the Colonial Inn has a waterfront or forest view, private balconies, and comfortable furnishings. If you're planning a meeting put us in your plans. We have more than 11000 square feet of meeting space. You can also enjoy our charming cottages or romantic villas.

Colonial. It's for families, couples, and friends. It's for people who appreicate natures beauty.

Call 1-800-555-5420 for reservations or information.

COLONIAL GARDENS

Job 2 Proofread the calendar of events by comparing it to the correct information on the registration cards shown on pages 194 and 195. Correct any mistakes you find. The information on the cards is correct.

State of Georgia Department of Tourism
7653 Peachtree Road, NE
Atlanta, GA 30308-9873

19-- CALENDAR OF EVENTS
SOUTHEAST GEORGIA

March
    10–17   St. Patricks Day Celebration
               Dublin
               Bobbie Whitehead   912/273-4260

    26–27   Harness Festival
               Hawkinsville
               Dale Morriw   912/429-3109

April
    14–28   Dogwood Festival
               Jessup
               Pam Barnes   912/290-3129

May
    10–24   Vidalia Onion Festival
               Vidalia
               Lewis Green   912/646-1293

June
    15–28   Blueberry Festival
               Alma
               Wanda Arnold   912/913-2175

July
    4   Fantastic Fireworks Extraavaganza
               Dublin
               Craig Southern   912/273-8261

October
    6   Great Pumpkin Festival
               Cochran
               Joann Keena   912/934-6112

    27   Georgia Sweet Potato Festival
               Ocila
               Gail Marshall   912/486-2681

19-- CALENDAR OF EVENTS
Registration Card

Date(s) May 10-24, 19--   City/County Vidalia
Event Title Vidalia Onion Festival
Location Vidalia
Contact Person Lewis Green   Phone 912/ 646-1293
                                    area code

19-- CALENDAR OF EVENTS
Registration Card

Date(s) October 6, 19--   City/County Cochran
Event Title Great Pumpkin Festival
Location Cochran
Contact Person Joanne Keena   Phone 912/ 934-6112
                                     area code

19-- CALENDAR OF EVENTS
Registration Card

Date(s) March 10-17, 19--   City/County Dublin
Event Title St. Patrick's Day Celebration
Location Dublin
Contact Person Bobbie Whitehead   Phone 912 / 273-4260
                                         area code

19-- CALENDAR OF EVENTS
Registration Card

Date(s) April 14-28   City/County Jesup
Event Title Dogwood Festival
Location Jesup
Contact Person Pam Barnes   Phone 912/ 290-3219
                                   area code

---

194   Chapter 13—Other Internal Punctuation Errors

19-- CALENDAR OF EVENTS
Registration Card

Date(s) _October 27, 19--_   City/County _Ocilla_
Event Title _Georgia Sweet Potato Festival_
Location _Ocilla_
Contact Person _Gail Marshall_   Phone _912_/_468-2681_
                                         area code

19-- CALENDAR OF EVENTS
Registration Card

Date(s) _July 4, 19--_   City/County _Dublin_
Event Title _Fantastic 4th Fireworks Extravaganza_
Location _Dublin_
Contact Person _Craig Southern_   Phone _912_/_273-8261_
                                         area code

19-- CALENDAR OF EVENTS
Registration Card

Date(s) _June 14-28, 19--_   City/County _Alma_
Event Title _Blueberry Festival_
Location _Alma_
Contact Person _Wanda Arnold_   Phone _912_/_913-2175_
                                         area code

19-- CALENDAR OF EVENTS
Registration Card

Date(s) _March 26-27, 19--_   City/County _Hawkinsville_
Event Title _Harness Festival_
Location _Hawkinsville_
Contact Person _Dale Morrow_   Phone _912_/_429-3109_
                                         area code

Chapter 13—Other Internal Punctuation Errors

Job 3 Proofread the following letter.

**State of Georgia
Department of Tourism**
7653 Peachtree Road, NE
Atlanta, GA 30308-9873

August 4, 19--

Ms. Gladys McCoy, Director
Macon Tourism and Trade
410 Riverside Drive
Macon, GA 31204-3798

Dear Ms. McCoy:

We;re getting ready to publish next years addition of Georgia--A Peach of a State and know you will want to provide updated copy for our article on central Georgia.

Please provide current information avoid repetition of last year's material) on planned activities, festivals, etc., on the enclosed card by September 30 so that we may incorporate your ideas into next year's publication and calender of events.

Will Macon paticipate as usual in "Georgia Days, which will be held at Cumberland Square in Atlanta on June 17-21 next year. Please send in your registration and exhibit needs on the enclosed form so that we may request appropriate space for you.

I understand you had a record attendance at the Cherry Jubilee Street Party last month. Congratulations on the excellent job you do in organizing and motivating your volunteers.

Sincerely

Charles B. Tamara
Associate Commissioner for Tourism
State of Georgia

sj

Enclosures

COMPUTERIZED PROOFREADING

Job 4 Proofread and Revise Travel Article
1. Load the file C13JOB4 from the template.
2. Proofread the article to be included in the travel guide and make any corrections.
3. Format the article as an unbound report.
4. Save the article under the name C13JOB4R.
5. Produce the article by following the standard procedures.

CHAPTER 14

CAPITALIZATION ERRORS

Objectives: *After completing this chapter, you should be able to*
- ▶ Recognize capitalization errors.
- ▶ Use the appropriate proofreading symbols to indicate changes in text.
- ▶ Spell correctly a list of commonly misspelled words.

FUNCTIONS OF CAPITALIZATION

Capitalization gives distinction, emphasis, and importance to words. Words may be capitalized in one instance and not in another, depending on the relative importance the writer wishes to attach to them. The current preference is not to overuse capitalization in business writing. Emphasis is lost when too many words are capitalized. If your workplace has special rules for the use of capitals, follow its style guide.

Use the following symbols to indicate changes in capitalization:

CAP or ≡   Use a capital letter.   Computer science 2112

lc or /   Use a lowercase letter.   Sincerely Yours

GENERAL GUIDELINES

The following are general principles for the capitalization of words. Your proofreading accuracy should improve as you review these rules.

14-1 Capitalize the first word of a sentence, a question, or a direct quotation. Do not capitalize the first word of an interrupted quotation.

> Exercise every day.
>
> When did the meeting adjourn?
>
> The memo read, "Revised guidelines are in effect immediately."
>
> "I am not aware," he said, "of any discrepancies."

▶ Capitalize a phrase or a single word that expresses a complete thought.

>Not now? Why?

14-2 Capitalize the first word of each item in a displayed list.

>Order the following supplies:
>Paper
>Envelopes
>Staples

▶ Capitalize the headings of an outline according to their level. First-level headings are in all capitals; second-level headings have main words capitalized; third and subsequent level topics have only the first word capitalized.

>I. FIRST-LEVEL HEADING
>   A. Second-Level Heading
>   B. Second-Level Heading
>   1. Third-level heading
>   2. Third-level heading
>II. FIRST-LEVEL HEADING

14-3 Capitalize the first word after a colon if that word begins a complete sentence.

>I had a surprise: My friends gave me a birthday party.

>She had one purpose in mind: to get the job.

✓ Proofread the following sentences for capitalization errors. If a sentence is correct, write a C to the right of it.

a. Eleanor pursues an interesting hobby: Stamp collecting.

b. Have you completed the survey of small businesses?

c. I. ADMISSION REQUIREMENTS
     A. Completion of 45 Semester Hours
     B. Overall Average of 2.5 on a 4.0 Scale
  II. Petition for Admissions

d. Todd said, "my employer gave me a raise."

e. The most important rule is this one: be brief.

14-4 Capitalize the first word and all important words in titles and headings. Do not capitalize articles (*a, an, the*), conjunctions (*and, but, nor, or*), and prepositions (*in, for, of, with*) unless they are the first or last words.

Book:	Information Processing for the Electronic Office
Magazine:	The Saturday Evening Post
Newspaper:	The Wilmington Morning Star
Article:	"How to Dress for Success"
Seminar:	"How to Give Effective Performance Appraisals"
Literary and artistic works:	Gone with the Wind Death of a Salesman

✓ Proofread the following sentences for capitalization errors. If a sentence is correct, write a *C* to the right of it.

a. Have you read the article, "Career Jobs for new College Grads"?

b. Betsy's latest book is *Information Processing for the 1990s*.

c. Did you see this month's issue of *The Journal of The Arts*?

d. The movie *Driving Miss Daisy* received many Oscar nominations.

e. I read about the Dogwood Festival in *The Knoxville News-Sentinel*.

PROPER NOUNS

As a general guideline, capitalize proper nouns or names of specific persons, places, and things. Following are some rules to help you in determining when a noun should be capitalized.

14-5 Capitalize proper nouns as well as the personal pronoun *I*. Do not capitalize common nouns that do not refer to a specific person, place, or thing.

Colorado River	*but* the river
University of Tennessee	*but* the university
Advanced Algebra 3076	*but* advanced algebra
Billings Chamber of Commerce	*but* chamber of commerce

14-1—14-3

a. ~~S~~^{lc}tamp
b. C
c. <u>Petition for Admissions</u>
d. <u>my</u>
e. <u>be</u>

14-4

a. **N**ew
b. C
c. of the Arts?
d. C
e. C

Chapter 14—Capitalization Errors 201

14-6 Capitalize well-known descriptive names or nicknames that are used to designate particular people, places, or things.

>the First Lady

>Babe Ruth (George Herman Ruth)

14-7 Capitalize words derived from proper names.

>Texan American

Note: Some derivatives change to common adjectives through frequent use.

>french fries   plaster of paris
>watt   china dishes

✓ Proofread the following sentences for capitalization errors. If a sentence is correct, write a C to the right of it.

a. The leaves have been eaten by japanese beetles.

b. Did you know that Tennessee is known as the Volunteer State?

c. The literary collection of the Columbia library is outstanding.

d. Most American businesses celebrate Independence Day.

e. The Snake river runs through the Grand Teton national park.

14-8 Capitalize organizational names when they refer to specific departments or groups within the originator's own organization. Do not use capitals when referring to a department or group in another organization.

>Send the report to Marcia in the Marketing Department.

>The Executive Board of our company is in the process of developing a new corporate strategy.

>Does he work in their advertising department?

14-5—14-7

a. **Japanese**
b. C
c. **Library**
d. C
e. **River National Park**

---

202   Chapter 14—Capitalization Errors

14-9 Capitalize specific brand names but not the product types.

Dove soap
Mercury automobile
Hershey candy
Jantzen swimsuits
MacIntosh computer

✓ Proofread the following sentences for capitalization errors. If a sentence is correct, write a C to the right of it.

a. Do you use a Ko-Rec-Type Ribbon for your printer?

b. Our human resources Department offers some special benefits.

c. Eileen traded her Buick Regal Automobile for a Dodge Caravan.

d. Doesn't everyone love Big mac hamburgers?

e. Did you know that Sheaffer Fountain Pens are making a comeback?

14-10 Capitalize both parts of a hyphenated word if they are proper nouns or proper adjectives. Do not capitalize prefixes to proper nouns.

ex-Governor Adams   Mayor-elect Cox
French-American cuisine   mid-Atlantic
North-South game   Spanish-speaking students

14-8, 14-9
a. ribbon
b. **Human Resources**
c. **automobile**
d. **M**ac
e. fountain **pens**

✓ Proofread the following sentences for capitalization errors. If a sentence is correct, write a C to the right of it.

a. It is Marvin's twenty-second anniversary with the organization.

b. The Marshall Plan was put into effect in the Post-World War II era.

c. Federal income tax returns are due in Memphis by mid-April.

d. A new japanese-American trade agreement has been signed.

e. Malcolm joined the local chapter of the English-Speaking Union.

Chapter 14—Capitalization Errors

14-11 Capitalize points of the compass when they refer to definite regions of the country or are used with other proper names. Do not capitalize these words when they indicate a direction.

>Rae lives east of the college.
>
>The Pelhams moved to the West Coast.
>
>ABC Moving is located on North Fifth Street.

▶ Capitalize words such as *northern* or *western* when they refer to the customs, cultural or political activities, or residents of the region.

>The Western states have supported their party's platform.
>
>*but* Flooding is rampant in several southern states.

✓ Proofread the following sentences for capitalization errors. If a sentence is correct, write a C to the right of it.

a. Plans are to develop the medical complex West of the city.

b. John moved to an apartment on Chicago's North Shore.

c. Connie is displaying true Southern hospitality.

d. To see large fields of tulips, drive East for eight miles.

e. Babbler & Sons has been purchased by Western Pacific Company.

14-12 Do not capitalize seasons of the year unless they are portrayed as persons.

>summer winds   fall conference   Old Man Winter

✓ Proofread the following sentences for capitalization errors. If a sentence is correct, write a C to the right of it.

a. Farmers' crops are in desperate need of spring rains.

b. To see New England in the Fall of the year is one of my dreams.

c. The poem reads, "And Summer with a nest of robins in her hair..."

d. No one has been able to predict the whims of mother nature this year.

e. Would you like to travel to Switzerland next winter for some skiing?

14-10
a. C
b. post
c. C
d. Japanese
e. C

14-11
a. west
b. C
c. C
d. east
e. C

204   Chapter 14—Capitalization Errors

ADDITIONAL CAPITALIZATION RULES

The following guidelines are presented to help you apply capitalization rules correctly in special situations. Rules for nouns followed by numbers, personal titles, and academic degrees are discussed.

14-13 Capitalize most nouns followed by numbers except for common nouns such as *sentence, page, paragraph, line,* and *size*.

Chapter 5	page 6
Route 95	paragraph 2
Flight 1034	sentence 1

✓ Proofread the following sentences for capitalization errors. If a sentence is correct, write a C to the right of it.

a. Did the secretary select Model No. 2166 or 2266?

b. The information found in table 3, page 10, should be very helpful.

c. While walking along highway 258, Eddie was stung by a bee.

d. Reserved seats for the concert are located in Section 5.

e. Martha has plans to leave for Ireland on Delta Airlines flight 471.

14-14 Capitalize a title that comes before a person's name.

The meeting was called to order by Chairman Richard Andruzzi.

▶ Capitalize a title in an address or signature line.

Mrs. Leslyn Winn, Vice President

Willis Chambers, Manager

▶ Do not capitalize a title when it follows the name in the sentence or is used in place of the name.

James Swanson, editor, received the Outstanding Journalist's Award.

The chairman of the group, Richard Andruzzi, called the meeting to order.

Note: If the official is referred to in formal minutes, rules, or bylaws, an exception is made and the title is always capitalized.

14-12
a. C
b. **f**all
c. C
d. **M**other **N**ature
e. C

14-13
a. C
b. **T**able
c. **H**ighway
d. C
e. **F**light 471

Chapter 14—Capitalization Errors 205

▶ Capitalize an official title that refers to a specific person and is a title of high distinction.

the President of the United States   the Prime Minister
the Governor of Arizona   the Secretary of State

✓ Proofread the following sentences for capitalization errors. If a sentence is correct, write a C to the right of it.

a. Will the secretary of state accompany President Bush to the summit conference?

b. Will Governor Roberts be the after-dinner speaker for the banquet?

c. Did you know that Prime Minister Thatcher was in this country last month?

d. Rod has been elected President of Office Systems Research Association.

e. The Editor of the local paper, Brooke Haines, won a Pulitzer Prize for her reporting about water contamination.

14-15 Capitalize the name of an academic degree immediately following a personal name whether it is abbreviated or written in full.

Carol Brooks, M.D.

Muriel Bloom, Doctor of Philosophy

▶ Capitalize the abbreviation of an academic degree.

B.S.   Ph.D.

▶ Do not capitalize an academic degree when used in general terms or with the word *degree*.

Margo just received her master's.

Does a bachelor of arts degree guarantee a good job?

14-16 Capitalize names of specific course titles but not areas of study (except for proper nouns or adjectives).

Keyboarding I   word processing
Information Processing 201   American history

14-14
a. **Secretary of State**
b. C
c. C
d. **president**
e. **e**ditor

✓ Proofread the following sentences for capitalization errors. If a sentence is correct, write a C to the right of it.

a. Phil has earned his B.S. Degree in chemistry.

b. I will be taking accounting, business law, programming, and English 201 this quarter.

c. The university awarded more than two thousand Bachelor's degrees at its commencement exercises.

d. Many companies require all managerial personnel to have b.a. degrees.

e. Inglis F. Duckett, Doctor of Education, is the author of many books.

SPELLING REVIEW

To improve your ability to detect spelling errors, master the words below. Watch for them in the exercises that follow and in succeeding chapters.

acknowledgment	fascinate
apologize	gratitude
embarrass	insistent
emphasize	miniature
equipped	perseverance

PROOFREADING TIPS

Study these tips and apply them as you proofread:

1. Unless you can apply a definite principle that calls for capitalization, do not capitalize.
2. Do not confuse proper nouns with the general uses of the same word.
3. If your workplace has special rules for the use of capitals, follow its style guide.

14-15—14-16

a. **degree**
b. C
c. **bachelor's**
d. **B.A.**
e. C

Chapter 14—Capitalization Errors

Proofreading Applications

Proofread the following documents and use the appropriate proofreading symbols to mark errors you find. To aid you in proofreading, the number of errors to be found is indicated in parentheses for the first two exercises. You must find the errors on your own in the third one.

P-1

Dear Mrs. McMurray:

You are invited to an autograph-signing party for David O'Toole. Mr. O'Toole, author of <u>Laughter Is The Best Medicine</u>, will be at the Village bookstore on Thursday, May 3, from 2 to 5 p.m. The store is located in South Hills Mall, which is one mile North of the downtown area.

Because of the popularity of the book, it has been printed for non-English-speaking people and in miniture copies for ease of carrying.

We at Twin Elms publishing company are happy to make it possible for you and your friends to meet Mr. O'Toole

Sincerely yours,

(5 errors)

P-2

Dear Charlotte,

Last Summer my friend Ruth and I had quite an experience in New York City. Shortly after arriving at our hotel, we went to the Villa Roma restaurant for dinner. Just after we had placed our orders, a frightening thing happened: the city experienced a complete blackout!

Next morning the electricity was still off, so we decided to take a sightseeing cruise around Manhattan Island. That was a good decision because the ship was equiped to serve us breakfast. We saw the Statue of Liberty, the Empire State building, and the World Trade Center, among other things.

Yours Truly,

(6 errors)

P-1

1. Laughter Is the Best
2. **Bookstore**
3. **n**orth of
4. miniature
5. **Publishing Company**

P-3

Dear Retired Teachers:

About 20 percent of our citizens are not equipped with the skills of literacy, and we are embarrased about it.

To erase illiteracy, the Literacy Volunteers Of Washington County need people with skills in reading, writing, and Mathematics to work as tutors. Refresher courses emphasizing these skills will be provided for tutors.

An informational meeting will be held on May 18 at the Eastern Middle School, located on Route 13, beginning at 8 p.m. in room 121. William Shannon, Ph.D., will lead the discussion.

We express our gratitude to all who are helping with this program. Through perseverance we can lick this problem of illiteracy.

                              Sincerely yours,

P-2

1. summer
2. Restaurant
3. The city
4. equipped
5. Building
6. Yours truly,

P-3

1. embarrassed
2. Volunteers of
3. mathematics
4. Room 121

PROGRESSIVE PROOFREADING

You are employed as an assistant to Dr. M. Ellen Schwartz, executive director of the American Business Education Association (ABEA). She is busy planning for the ABEA convention. Dr. Schwartz uses block letter style with open punctuation. Proofread the registration materials carefully for keyboarding, spelling, number expression, punctuation, grammar, abbreviation, and capitalization errors.

Chapter 14—Capitalization Errors

Job 1   Proofread the following news release.

AMERICAN BUSINESS EDUCATION ASSOCIATION
1111 South Wabash Street
Chicago, IL 60605-2912

abea NEWS RELEASE

February 28, 19--

More than two-thousand A.B.E.A. members are expected to converge on Miami, Florida, when the American business education association thirty-eighth annual convention convenes on March 13. This information comes from Doctor Sue D. Briley, President of the A.E.B.A. Dr. Briley, a Business Education instructor at Parks College, is serving the first year of a two-year term as President.

Using the theme "Get In Touch With The Future," Dr. Briley and her convention committee has planned a program featuring numerous leaders in the business education areas of Accounting, Computer Science, Keyboarding, and Economics.

Approximately fifty textbook publishers and equiptment salespeople are expected to exhibit their products.

The program committee has obtained two well-known persons to be speakers: Zig Ziglar at the luncheon and Diane Nichols at the banquet. The Florida ABEA members are sponsoring Florida Night, an evening of fun on the thirteenth of March in the Orange Bowl.

The convention will end with a business session on the 17th of March.

Dr. M. Ellen Schwartz

210   Chapter 14—Capitalization Errors

Job 2 Proofread the letter carefully.

AMERICAN BUSINESS EDUCATION ASSOCIATION
1111 South Wabash Street
Chicago, IL 60605-2912

January 13, 19--

Dr. Sandra Newton, professor
School of Business Education
Eastern University
1072 East 5th Street
Charleston, Ill.

Dear Mrs. Newton

Make your plans now to head South in late Winter to attend the American Business Education association's annual convention. The Palms hotel in Miami, FL, will be the sight for this 38th meeting, which beings on March 13 and ends on March 17.

"Get In Touch With The Future" is the theme of this year's convention. Several new, pertinent topics have been added, one of which is "Experiential Learning--The Educational Tool for the Future."

Send your hotel registration directly to the Palms Hotel, 2552 Third Avenue, SW, Miami, FL 33129-0615, no later than February 28 to ensure a room at the convention hotel. You may guarantee your reservation by including your Am. express card number.

To register for the convention, complete the registration form that is in the December issue of the ABEA journal. Mail it along along with your check to this office by Feb. 15.

Plan to attend the opening session followed by Florida Night in the Orange Bowl; a watch containing a minature TV will be given away as a door prize.

Please extend an invitation to students and emphasise the value of participating in a conference designed for professional growth.

Very Truly Yours

Dr. M. Ellen Schwartz

aa

Chapter 14—Capitalization Errors

Job 3 Proofread both the message and the copy of the budget. Check the accuracy of the figures by comparing them to the correct handwritten draft.

Center and format heading

Proposed Budget for ABEA Convention
Palms Hotel
Miami, Florida
March 13-17, 19--

> Amy:
> Will you proofread carefully the copy of the proposed convention budget, comparing it to the attached draft. Please return it by 2:30 as Dr. Briley is insistant that it be ready for the Executive Board meeting at 4.
> I apologize for the rush job.
> Morgan

Income
Registration Fees	$16,000
Meals (Luncheon, Banquet)	30,500
Sale of ABEA Materials	1,500
Total	$48,000

Disbursements
Hotel (Rooms and Meals)	$36,000
Registration Supplies, Printing	5,500
Refunds for Registrants	500
Convention Flowers & Decorations	700
Fruit Baskets	300
Favors (ABEA mugs)	3,500
Acknowledgments, Thank-You Gifts	250
Honoraria for Entertainment	600
Miscellaneous Expenses	650
Total	$48,000

```
              PROPOSED BUDGET FOR ABEA CONVENTION
                         Palms Hotel
                        Miami, Florida
                      March 13-17, 19--


     Income
           Registration Fees                         $16,000
           Meals (Luncheon, Banquet)                  30,000
           Sale of ABEA Materials                      1,500
           Total                                     $48,000

     Disbursments
           Hotel (rooms and meals)                   $36,000
           Registration Supplies, Printing             5,500
           Refunds for registrants                       500
           Convention Flower and Decorations             700
           Fruit Baskets                                 300
           Favors (ABEA Mugs)                          3,500
           Acknowledgments, Thank-You Gifts              250
           Honoria for Entertainment                     600
           Miscellenous Expenses                         550
           Total                                     $48,000
```

COMPUTERIZED PROOFREADING

Job 4 Proofread Travel Package Announcement

1. Load the file C14JOB4 from the template.
2. Proofread the announcement and format it with 1" margins.
3. Save the revised announcement as C14JOB4R.
4. Produce the document by following the standard procedures.

CHAPTER 15

EDITING FOR CONTENT

Objectives: *After completing this chapter, you should be able to*

- ▶ Identify errors caused by incorrect facts, inconsistencies, and missing information.
- ▶ Use the appropriate proofreading symbols to indicate changes in text.
- ▶ Spell correctly a list of commonly misspelled words.

PROOFREADING FOR EFFECTIVE COMMUNICATION

The real measure of a proofreader's skill lies in the ability to proofread written communication for meaning and accuracy and to edit and revise ineffective communication. While previous chapters have dealt primarily with mechanical or grammatical errors, this chapter addresses the need to proofread for content errors—errors that affect the correctness of the message.

Content errors include incorrect facts, inconsistencies, and missing information. The skillful proofreader must be able to identify these problems, make necessary changes, or bring questionable items to the originator's attention. You have already learned the appropriate symbols for making corrections to copy. If the correction is not obvious, use the following proofreading symbol to query the originator:

? Query the originator.   The new employee's social security number is 273-62-901 — ?

INCORRECT FACTS

When copy contains incorrect facts, confusion and frustration can result. It is not always easy to recognize such errors unless there is a rough draft or source document that can be used for comparison. Some items should always be checked for accuracy. If the copy makes reference to Wednesday, June 16, and June 16 is actually on Thursday, there is an obvious error.

You can sometimes recognize errors in figures by using reason and common sense. For example, the social security number on the previous page contained only eight digits. ZIP codes, invoice numbers, telephone numbers, social security numbers, and other items of special importance should always be checked.

Likewise, similar, unfamiliar, or foreign names (*Fugiwara*) should always be checked for accuracy. Notice the varied spelling of these names:

Andres, Andreas
Hansen, Hanson
Hernandes, Hernandez
Johnsen, Johnson, Johnston, Johnstone, Jonson
Schneider, Schneiter, Snider, Snyder
Schmid, Schmidt, Schmit, Schmitt

15-1 Eliminate incorrect facts by correcting inaccuracies in dates, figures, addresses, names, and numbers or by querying the originator. Note the incorrect facts in the following examples:

The Dow Jones Industrial Average rose from 1910 to 1942, a gain of ~~22~~ 32 points.

The play is scheduled for February 15-30. *15-28?*

✓ Proofread the following sentences for incorrect facts:

a. Former President Ronald Reagan attended a party for Regan campaign workers.

b. The deadline for registering to vote in the next election is Tuesday, April 31.

c. Send the proposal to ACS, 1144 Meade Street, Vienna, WV 2610.

d. At $2.39 apiece, 6 packages of pens will cost $15.34.

e. You may request a free copy by calling (800) 555-455.

INCONSISTENCIES

Whenever reference is made to specific information more than once in a document, be sure that the information appears consistently. For example, if there are two acceptable spellings for a word, the same spelling should be used throughout. If numbers are transferred from one document to another, be sure the numbers have been copied correctly. If block format is chosen for a letter, make certain that the format is used consistently in the letter.

15-2 Eliminate inconsistencies in copy by checking words, figures, and format for any discrepancies. Note the inconsistencies in the following examples:

> Mr. Dakas was elected mayor in 1986; Dacas has been an exemplary public official.

> This tape player can be purchased for only $189—where else can you find a unit like this for $199?

✓ Proofread the following sentences for inconsistencies:

a. Ruth Petersen has started her own company; it will be known as Peterson's Copying Service.

b. The sale is open to charge customers on Tuesday, July 3; it is open to the public on Thursday, July 6.

c. Suits priced at $340 were reduced 35 percent, a saving of $112.20.

d. The North Central Education Association (NCEA) sponsors an insurance program for NCAE members.

e. Only 23 of the 35 members attended the regional meeting, which is a record for this 36-member group.

MISSING INFORMATION

Because the meaning of a message may be affected when words, phrases, or even complete lines or sentences are omitted unintentionally, it is necessary to compare the final copy with the rough-draft copy to be sure nothing has been deleted. If the proofreader is not authorized to edit and make changes, errors that prevent the meaning from being clear must be called to the attention of the originator.

15-3 Eliminate confusion in copy by checking for missing information. Notice how missing information in the following example makes the meaning unclear:

> To get to the airport, turn right on this road.

Chapter 15—Editing for Content

15-1

a. Reagan campaign
b. April 31 - ?
c. WY 2610 - ?
d. $15.34
e. 555-455 - ?

15-2

a. Peters**e**n's
b. Thursday, July ?
c. **$119**
d. **NCEA** members
e. ?-member group

✓ Proofread the following sentences for missing information:

  a. It will be a dinner meeting and will be held in the Gold Room of the Plaza Hotel.

  b. To get there, go six blocks east and turn at the Willow Street intersection.

  c. The bids for the contract must be in no later than Wednesday, November.

  d. To delete the material from the computer screen, press the key.

  e. You will need an 8 x 10 mat for that job.

SPELLING REVIEW

To improve your ability to detect spelling errors, master the words below. Watch for them in the exercises that follow and in succeeding chapters.

analyst	independent
efficiency	insurance
fluctuating	productivity
implemented	programmer

PROOFREADING TIPS

Study these tips and apply them as you proofread:

1. Read the copy with a questioning mind by asking yourself these questions: Is the message perfectly clear? Are there any inconsistencies in the presentation of facts? Are there omissions?

2. Control the environment in which you proofread—noise and movement are distractions. Be sure there is sufficient light.

3. Verify the spelling of names.

4. When revising copy, cross out all unnecessary original copy.

15-3
a. will be held ? (when)
b. turn ?
c. November ?
d. the ? key
e. 8" x 10"

Proofreading Applications

Proofread the following exercises and use the appropriate proofreading symbols to mark errors you find in content, grammar, and spelling. To aid you in proofreading, the number of errors to be found is indicated in parentheses for Exercises P-1 and P-2.

P-1

DRIFTWOOD RESTAURANT OPENS NEW FACILITY

The Driftwood Restaurant, a popular eating place since opening in 1973, began serving breakfast at 6 a.m. Wednesday, April 28, 1992, at its new location, 4100 Trade Street. The restaurant now has more parking and greater seating capacity than the 18-year-old Banks Street location, according to Ken Adams, the owner.

The restaurant will be open daily from 6 a.m. to 11 a.m. From 4 p.m. to 5:30 p.m. the restaurant offers an Early Bird Special, serving a $10 meal for $7.50, which is a reduction of 20 percent. (3 errors)

P-2

Ms. Wendy Powell
429 Butler Street
Jacksonville, NC 2854-0429

Dear Ms. Powell:

Thank you for your interest in becoming an independent Dana dealer.

Because of the fluctuateing market, no new Dana dealerships are being opened at this time.

Mrs. Powell, we will your name on file so that we can notify you if a dealership does become available in your area.

Yours sincerely,

(4 errors)

P-1
1. **19**-year-old
2. 11 **p.**m.
3. **25** percent

Chapter 15—Editing for Content   219

P-3

TO: Electronic Publishing
FROM: Janie Dempsey
DATE: July 17, 19--
SUBJECT: System 40 Overview

A meeting has been scheduled for Thursday, July 26, from 2:30 to 4 p.m. to review the System 40 capabilities for the Electronic Publishing Department. Please plan to attend.

Sarah McKenzie will instruct us on the applications that will benefit us. I'm sure we will benefit tremendously from the insight Sara has gained from her previous experience as programmer and system anlyst.

P-2

1. 2854-0429 ?
2. fluctuating
3. **Ms.** Powell
4. will **keep** your

P-3

1. location not provided
2. Sara**h** has gained
3. analyst

PROGRESSIVE PROOFREADING

You are manager of TOPS (Temporary Office Personnel Services) in New Orleans, Louisiana. This business is one of three branches of a new business venture and is owned by Mary Dunstan, who resides in Baton Rouge, Louisiana. Your office provides two services to local business firms: It provides temporary office help, and it contracts to provide certain office jobs to be done in-house. At the present time, you are to proofread all work that has been done. The agency uses block letter format with open punctuation.

Job 1 Proofread the following letter for content and mechanical errors.

TOPS
(Temporary Office Personnel Services)
909 Linden Avenue
New Orleans, LA 70128-9400

August 15, 19--

Ms. Mary Dunstan
2001 King Alfred Drive
Baton Rogue, LA 71304-6421

Dear Ms. Dunstan

You asked me to make suggestions for improving the efficiency of TOPS. I believe I have an idea that will have a very positive affect on the productivity of this office, and I am eager to hear your reaction to it.

Recently I had the opportunity to examine a new publication from South-Western Publishing Company entitled "Programmed Proofreading." I recommend that we ask each temporary office employee to work through this book before beginning an actual assignment with us. If this recommendation is emplemented, the payoff in productivity and accuracy will, in my opinion be well worth the cost of the books.

Presently, I am spending too much time proofreading the documents produced by our employees. Many of the errors that I find are addressed in the book. Working through exercises that contain those errors will impress upon our employees the importance of accuracy. While I would continue to proofread the documents, I believe my proofreading time would be cut considerably.

There are 16 chapters in the third edition <u>Programed Proofreading</u>. I found Chapter on content errors to be especially helpful.

Sincerely

Charles Daniels

jp

Chapter 15—Editing for Content

221

Job 2 Verify the accuracy of the invoice by comparing it to the items ordered on the purchase order. Unit prices and extensions are entered automatically by the computer. However, TOPS telephoned and requested that the order for **5 1/4-inch diskettes** be changed to **3 1/2-inch diskettes** at **$68/box.**

Also, the price of print wheels has been raised to **$26.50**; this price has not been entered into the computer. Other information you will need to check is as follows.

Order No.: **LA19284**
Shipped By: **UPS**
Terms: **2/10, n/30**

B & B Supply Company

P.O. Box 5314
SHREVEPORT, LA 71102-3314

INVOICE

TOPS
909 Linden Avenue
New Orlean, LA 70128-9400

Date: August 21, 19--
Order No.: LA19284
Shipped By: UPS
Terms: 2/10, n/20

Quantity	Description	Unit Price	Total
1	Print wheel, Herald Elite 10/12	24.95	24.95
5 bxs	5 1/4" diskettes	41.95	209.75
6	T-III ribbons	8.79	52.74
12 rms	G-P dual-purpose paper, 20 lb	5.25	63.00
12 rms	G-P copier paper, 20 lb	6.65	79.80
12 rolls	Magic tape, 1/2 inch	1.89	22.68
1 doz	Tape dispenser	5.45	5.45
5 doz	Express pens, violet ink	9.12	45.60
			503.97

TOPS
(Temporary Office Personnel Services)
909 Linden Avenue
New Orleans, LA 70128-9400

PURCHASE ORDER

B & B Supply Company
P. O. Box 5314
Shreveport, LA 71102-3314

No.: LA19284

Date: August 15, 19--

Terms: 2/10, n/30

Shipped By: UPS

Quantity	Description	Unit Price	Total
12 rms	G-P dual-purpose paper, 20 lb	5.25	63.00
15 rms	G-P copier paper, 20 lb	6.65	99.75
8 bxs	No. 10 envelopes, 20 lb	14.35	114.80
5 bxs	5 1/4" diskettes	41.95	209.75
6	T-III ribbons	8.79	52.74
5 doz	Expresso pens, violet ink	9.12	45.60
1	Tape dispenser	5.45	5.45
12 rolls	Magic tape, 1/2 inch	1.89	22.68
1	Print wheel, Herald Elite 10/12	24.95	24.95
			638.72

By _____ Purchasing Agent

Chapter 15—Editing for Content

Job 3 Please check the accuracy of Rebecca D. Wollcott's Travel Expense Report by verifying its figures against the receipts and the handwritten list of expenses. Also verify the totals.

TRAVEL EXPENSE REPORT

Travel Authorization No.
239407

Employee Name
Rebecca D. Wolcot

I.D. Number
T6103

Destination
Jackson, Mississippi

Date(s)
8/25/-- to 8/27/--

Purpose of Trip
AMS meeting, meeting with manager of Meridian TOPS

Date From To	Transportation Miles	Amount	Air	Taxi	Meals	Lodging	Total
8/25 New Orleans/Jackson	179	46 54	--	--	22 50	60 00	129 04
8/26 Jackson/Meridian (round trip)	165	42 90	--	--	30 70	60 00	133 60
8/27 Jackson/New Orleans	179	46 45	--	--	11 55	--	58 00
TOTALS		135 89			64 75	120 00	320 64

Signature
_____

Date
8/29/--

Total Expenses $320.64
(Attach Receipts)

New Orleans — Jackson, Mississippi Trip

8/25 Drove to Jackson
179 miles at 26 cents per mile

A.M.S. dinner meeting at
The Jackson Inn $22.50

Room — The Jackson Inn

8/26 Breakfast $6.50

Drove to Meridian to meet
with local managers of TOPS
Round trip 165 miles

Lunch $8.75

Dinner at the Inn $16.45

Room at Jackson Inn

8/27 Breakfast $5.25

Lunch $6.30

Mileage from Jackson — New Orleans

Please prepare an expense report. Fill in anything I have left out. My receipts are attached.
RW

Chapter 15—Editing for Content

```
THE JACKSON INN
     ROUTE 20, EAST                                          (601) 555-2020
          JACKSON, MS   39205

ROOM    LAST NAME            FIRST              MIDDLE INITIAL
 329    WOLLCOTT,            REBECCA                 D.

ADDRESS    1805 ST. CHARLES AVENUE               ROOM RATE
           NEW ORLEANS, LA   70304-1805           $60.00

ARRIVAL         AUGUST 25, 19--                  NO. IN PARTY
DEPARTURE       AUGUST 27, 19--                       1

   DATE              DESCRIPTION                   AMOUNT
   8/25              RESTAURANT                     22.50
   8/25              ROOM, TAX INCLUDED             60.00
   8/26              RESTAURANT                      6.50
   8/26              RESTAURANT                     16.45
   8/26              ROOM, TAX INCLUDED             60.00
   8/27              RESTAURANT                      5.25

                              TOTAL              $170.70
                              PAID               $170.70
                              BALANCE            000.00
```

Guest Receipt	**SAM'S CAFE**	Guest Receipt	*Christy's*
Date 8/26 Amount $8.75		Date 8/27 Amount $6.30	

COMPUTERIZED PROOFREADING

Job 4 Edit report

1. Load the file C15JOB4 from the template.
2. Proofread the report very carefully for all kinds of mechanical errors and content errors.
3. Format the document as a two-page unbound report. Format the main and side headings in bold.
4. Save the report as C15JOB4R.
5. Produce the report following the standard procedures.

CHAPTER 16

EDITING FOR CONCISENESS

Objectives: *After completing this chapter, you should be able to*
- Identify clichés.
- Recognize obsolete expressions.
- Use active rather than passive voice.

The first draft of a written business communication usually needs to be edited for conciseness. Many people think that the more words they use the more effective their correspondence will be. Actually, the opposite is true. In business writing, the more concise your message is, the better chance you will have of communicating effectively.

Conciseness means using as few words as possible to convey the message completely. Conciseness does not mean being curt or abrupt, but it does mean eliminating unnecessary information and generally writing short sentences.

One of the proofreader's tasks may be to edit business documents for conciseness. When doing this, the proofreader should try to eliminate any unnecessary words or phrases. In particular, the proofreader should correct clichés, obsolete expressions, and passive voice.

CLICHÉS

Although you should use simple, familiar words in business writing, be careful that you don't fall into the habit of using overused words and expressions. These clichés have become trite and boring through overuse. Your business writing will be more precise and interesting if you avoid clichés.

16-1 Edit for clichés, which have lost their clear meanings through overuse.

Cliché: Our company has grown *by leaps and bounds* during the past year.

Concise: Our company has grown *by 5 percent* during the past year.

Cliché: Hal appears to be a *good* candidate for the position of branch manager.

Concise: Hal appears to be a *well-qualified* candidate for the position of branch manager.

Avoid these commonly used clichés:

rat race	dog-eat-dog
between a rock and a hard place	face the music
good	great
by leaps and bounds	sound out
manner of speaking	the bottom line
super	very
turn over a new leaf	awful
fish out of water	can of worms
water under the bridge	bite the bullet
take the bull by the horns	really
straight from the shoulder	track record

Proofread the following sentences for clichés. If a sentence is correct, write a C to the right of it.

a. She was caught between a rock and a hard place in making a decision about a new career.

b. Sam decided to bite the bullet and go ahead and work on the MBA degree.

c. I felt like a fish out of water when I was promoted to assistant manager.

d. With appropriate software packages, the computer can perform a variety of tasks.

e. Before you can gain control over stress, you need to identify its causes.

OBSOLETE EXPRESSIONS

Obsolete expressions are terms that are out of date and should not be used in today's business writing. Many writers mistakenly think that these dull, pompous terms make their written communication more effective. These same writers would never use these obsolete terms when talking with others. Most obsolete expressions are wordy and can be avoided by using more precise words or phrases.

16-2 Edit for obsolete expressions by choosing modern, more concise expressions.

Obsolete: We *are in receipt of* your manuscript.
Concise: We *have received* your manuscript.

Obsolete: *Enclosed please find* the booklet you requested.
Concise: *Enclosed is* the booklet you requested.

Obsolete: *Kindly advise* us of your decision as soon as possible.
Concise: *Please* let us know your decision as soon as possible.

The following obsolete words and phrases should be eliminated when editing, and the corresponding concise, present-day terminology should be used.

Obsolete Terms	Concise Terms
acknowledge receipt of	received
are in receipt of	received
as per your request	as you requested
at the present time	now
at this point in time	now
at your convenience	(state a date if possible)
at your earliest convenience	as soon as possible
attached herewith	attached
despite the fact that	although, despite
due to the fact that	because
enclosed please find	enclosed
hoping to hear from you soon	--------
. . . I remain—Sincerely yours	Sincerely yours
in closing	--------
in the event that	if
in the near future	soon
in view of the fact that	because
kindly advise	please tell
meet with your approval	approve
permit me to say	--------
please be advised that	--------
take the liberty	--------
thanking you in advance	thank you
trusting you will find	you will find
under separate cover	in another package [letter]
until such time as	until
we regret to inform you	unfortunately
we would ask that you	please
would like to recommend	recommend
would like to say	--------

16-1
a. She **found it difficult to make** a decision
b. [delete *bite the bullet and*]
c. felt **uncomfortable with my new responsibilities** when
d. C
e. C

Chapter 16—Editing for Conciseness 229

✓ Proofread the following sentences for obsolete terms. If a sentence is correct, write a C to the right of it.

a. Enclosed please find a certificate for $10 to apply toward your first purchase at King's Department Store.

b. Please let us know how you want your account listed with us.

c. Let us hear from you at your earliest convenience so that you will begin enjoying reading your Readers' Guild books.

d. Due to the fact that our conference is in Los Angeles, only 12 of our marketing representatives will be able to attend.

e. If you have any questions about your order, call us at 555-9302.

PASSIVE VOICE

Verbs should generally be written in active voice rather than passive voice. In active voice, the subject does the action. The subject comes before the verb, and the word being acted on (object) follows the verb [Cleo won the award]. In passive voice, the subject is deemphasized by being moved *after* the verb and is usually followed by the word *by* [The award was won by Cleo]. Notice that a form of the helping verb *to be* [*was*] is combined with the verb *won*.

Active voice creates a sharper, clearer picture in the mind of the reader than passive voice does. Generally passive voice verbs should be avoided except when the writer wants to avoid criticism or a negative statement. The passive voice is also used to emphasize the action rather than the person who performed the action.

16-3 Edit for passive voice by using active-voice verbs.

Passive: A survey on computer usage was conducted by Katherine.

Active: Katherine conducted a survey on computer usage.

Passive: A complete line of voice messaging equipment is offered by CompuCall.

Active: CompuCall offers a complete line of voice messaging equipment.

16-2
a. Enclosed **is** a certificate
b. C
c. you **as soon as possible** so
d. **Because** our conference
e. C

✓ Edit the following sentences by changing passive voice to active voice. If a sentence is correct, write a C to the right of it.

a. The average firm annually spends more than $1,000 for office products and services for each white-collar employee.

b. Telephone phobia can be overcome by companies but only with an organized approach to the problem.

c. Work that you enjoy commands all your energy and concentration.

d. The evidence suggests that executive time is expanding.

e. Beautiful copies can be delivered by Prestige copiers.

PROOFREADING TIPS

Study these tips and apply them as you proofread:
1. Avoid using overworked expressions (clichés).
2. Select updated rather than obsolete expressions.
3. Generally use active voice rather than passive voice.

16-3
a. C
b. **Companies can overcome telephone phobia** but
c. C
d. C
e. **Prestige copiers can deliver beautiful copies.**

Chapter 16—Editing for Conciseness

Proofreading Applications

Proofread the following paragraphs and use the appropriate proofreading symbols to mark errors in the use of clichés, obsolete expressions, and passive voice. To aid you in proofreading, the number of errors to be found is indicated in parentheses for Exercises P-1, P-2, and P-3.

P-1 To get out of the rat race, you have decided to go into business for yourself. You know what your product or service will be. At this point in time, you have made two of the most important business decisions you will ever make. Additional decisions will have to be made, however, to make sure your business gets started on the right foot. These decisions deal with how you organize your business, what goals you set, whom you'll work with, and how you attract your first customers or clients. (4 errors)

P-2 After deciding what type of business you want, seek help in starting your business. Basic business and legal questions can be answered by outside professionals, such as a lawyer and an accountant. If you're planning a business that is likely to grow by leaps and bounds, consider consulting with a banker, a compensation specialist, or even a marketing expert. After putting together the right outside team, make sure you hire the right people. (2 errors)

P-3 If you're planning a one-person business, consider a sole proprietorship. This organization enables a self-employed person to avoid the can of worms that comes with incorporation. In the event that your business will require hiring employees and selling products or services that could cause injury, you should consider incorporating. Your accountant and your attorney can help you determine the best type of organization. (2 errors)

P-1

1. [Delete *To get out of the rat race,*] You
2. [Delete *At this point in time,*] You have **now** made
3. **You will have to make additional decisions** to
4. started **right**.

P-2

1. **Outside professionals, such as . . ., can answer basic**
2. grow **rapidly and steadily,** consider

---

232   Chapter 16—Editing for Conciseness

P-4 After organizing your company, you must toot your own whistle. A new company has a definite advantage over more established businesses. Because there is no track record for others to refute, your only problem as a new business owner is to get your share of the marketplace. A variety of low-cost marketing tactics can be taken advantage of by a young company. You should beat the bushes giving talks and seminars that highlight your service or product. Just be sure to direct your presentations to the right audience—potential customers or individuals who can refer customers.

P-3
1. avoid the **problems** that **come**
2. **If** your business will require . . .

P-4
1. must **promote it**
2. no **established** record
3. **A young company can take advantage of** a variety of
4. You should **give** talks

PROGRESSIVE PROOFREADING

As secretary to the chair of the Administrative Services Department at Deerfield College, you are responsible for the correctness of all documents sent from the department. Proofread the following documents for errors, including use of clichés, obsolete expressions, and passive voice. The department uses block letter format, open punctuation, and simplified memorandum format.

Chapter 16—Editing for Conciseness

Job 1 Proofread the following letter for conciseness. Also check closely for any mechanical errors.

Deerfield College

January 8, 19--

Ms. Lee Spanner
5920 Old Dixie Road
Forest Park, GA 30050-3058

Dear Ms. Lee

Thank you for your interest in the Administrative Services programs at Deerfield College. As per your request, I am sending you under separate cover a copy of the college catalog.

You will see from the Administrative Services AAS degree program (page 91 of the catalog) that your electives may be concentrated in your area of interest--office management. Because you have work experience, you may also earn advanced placement credit for certain skills you already have, such as keyboarding and business machines.

Call me at 555-3482 if I can answer any questions or be of assistants. We look forward to your enrolling with us at Deerfield.

Sincerely,

Mrs. Jennifer Thomas, Coordinator
Administrative Services

lw

Job 2 Proofread the membership recruitment flyer for conciseness and mechanical errors.

SANTA IS CHECKING HIS LIST - - -

AND YOUR NAME IS NOT ON IT!

The list he's checking is the National Business Education Association (NBEA) membership roster.

Your renewal is needed by NBEA! Your membership dues are utilized to drum up enthusiasm for all phases of business education and to serve as a unifying agency among regional and other groups dedicated to business education.

Our NBEA staff and our national, regional, and state leaders are committed to shaping the future of business education and to increasing our strength so that the profession will continue to grow by leaps and bounds.

But we must have your dedication and commitment to the profession. And the first way you can show this committment is by joining NBEA. Because you have been a member in the past, I know that you appreciate the super benefits the organization provides: a publications program, national convention, legislative laision, research and development activities, and awards programs, to name a few.

Please give yourself an important holiday gift. Get your name back on the list by completing the enclosed application and sending your dues today.

                                        Jennifer Thomas
                                        Georgia Membership Director

Enclosure

P.S. If you have already joined NBEA this year, please forgive Santa; he's awfully rushed at this time of year and may have overlooked your name.

Chapter 16—Editing for Conciseness   235

Job 3 Proofread the announcement for content by comparing it to the class schedule on the next page. Check the message for conciseness as well.

```
              SUMMER STUDIES AT DEERFIELD
                         FOR
                ADMINISTRATIVE SERVICES
                      SUMMER 19--
```

Turn over a new leaf and come to summer school for only two days a week for eight weeks or two nights a week for four or eight weeks and get ahead in your program.

Have at least five weeks of fun in the sun--trips with your family or friends--or whatever!

```
1st Session     June 27 - July 24      ADMS 111/112           6-8:40 p.m. T/Th
                                       Keyboarding I, II

2nd Session     July 25 - August 23    ADMS 212/213           6-8:50 p.m. T/Th
                                       Word/Information Processing I, II

Full Session    June 27 - August 23    ADMS 250               9-11:40 a.m. M/W
                                       Business Communication

                                       ADMS 250               6-8:40 a.m. M/W
                                       Automated Accounting I

To Be Arranged                         ADMS 202    Business Machines
                                       ADMS 222    Occupational Internship
```

Deerfield College

SUMMER QUARTER 19-- SCHEDULE

Administrative Services Department

Course Name	Course No.	Cr.	Class Time	Day	Room
FIRST SESSION - JUNE 27 - JULY 24					
Keyboarding I	ADMS 111	3	6:00 pm - 8:40 pm	TT	T220
Keyboarding II	ADMS 112	3	6:00 pm - 8:40 pm	TT	T220
SECOND SESSION - JULY 26 - AUGUST 23					
Word/Inf. Proc. I	ADMS 212	5	6:00 pm - 8:40 pm	TT	T220
Word/Inf. Proc. II	ADMS 213	5	6:00 pm - 8:40 pm	TT	T220
FULL SESSION - JUNE 27 - AUGUST 23					
Business Machines	ADMS 202	5	To be arranged		
Business Commun.	ADMS 205	5	9:00 am - 11:40 am	MW	T222
Automated Acct. I	ADMS 250	5	6:00 pm - 8:40 pm	MW	T222
Occup. Internship	ADMS 222	5	To be arranged		

COMPUTERIZED PROOFREADING

Job 4 Edit and Format Memorandum

1. Load the file C16JOB4 from the template.

2. Proofread the memo and make all necessary corrections.

3. Format the document as a simplified memorandum. Use the current date and supply an appropriate subject. Send the memo to **Business Education Teachers** from the **Deerfield College Administrative Services Faculty**. Use your reference initials.

4. Save the document as C16JOB4R.

5. Produce the document by following the standard procedures.

CHAPTER 17

EDITING FOR CLARITY

Objectives: *After completing this chapter, you should be able to*
- Identify misplaced and dangling modifiers.
- Identify errors caused by lack of parallel construction.
- Use simple rather than complicated words.
- Spell correctly a list of commonly misspelled words.

Good ideas must be expressed clearly to be communicated effectively. Ideas not clearly worded may amuse the reader and embarrass the writer, but more importantly, the message may be misunderstood. The writer must convey the message so that the reader can clearly understand it. The proofreader's job is to be aware of the errors that interfere with clarity and to eliminate them.

Three common errors that cause the message to be unclear are misplaced and dangling modifiers, lack of parallel construction, and use of complex words rather than simple ones.

MISPLACED AND DANGLING MODIFIERS

A modifier is a word or group of words that describes. Modifiers must be positioned in the sentence so that the intended meaning is clear to the reader. If a modifier is misplaced, who or what performed the action of the sentence is unclear. If a modifier "dangles," it refers to the wrong word (or to none at all) in the sentence. Incorrect modifers destroy sentence clarity. To improve clarity, apply the following rules.

17-1 Place modifiers next to, or as close as possible to, the words they describe.

Incorrect: There should be no doubt about the intended message of the letter in the reader's mind.

Correct: There should be no doubt in the reader's mind about the intended message of the letter.

▶ Check the position of such words as *only*, *at least*, or *merely* to be sure the intended meaning is clear.

Incorrect: These discount cards are *only* given to full-time employees.

Correct: These discount cards are given *only* to full-time employees.

The correct sentences above make sense because the misplaced words were moved closer to the words they modify.

17-2 An introductory phrase or clause must be followed immediately by the word that it modifies. Correct dangling modifiers by inserting the noun or pronoun that the modifier describes or change the dangling phrase to a complete clause. The phrase or clause is *italicized* in the examples. The word being modified is in bold.

Incorrect: *While walking along the beach,* the sun sank from view.
(The *sun* was not *walking*.)

Correct: *While walking along the beach,* **Sharon** watched the sun sink from view.

Incorrect: *Proofreading hurriedly,* mistakes were made by the secretary frequently.
(*Mistakes* did not *proofread hurriedly* and *frequently* does not modify *secretary*.)

Correct: *Proofreading hurriedly,* the **secretary** frequently made mistakes.

Correct: *When the secretary was proofreading hurriedly,* mistakes were made frequently.

Note: A few introductory phrases are permitted to dangle. Examples include *Generally speaking, Taking all things into consideration,* and *Confidentially speaking.*

Taking all things into consideration, the decision was the best one.

✓ Proofread for misplaced and dangling modifiers. When you find an error, correct the sentence by rearranging the sentence or adding words to make the meaning clear. If a sentence is correct, write a C to the right of it.

a. After placing the order, my meal arrived promptly.

b. To open a savings account, a deposit of $100 is required.

c. At the beginning of the meeting, Jonathan questioned the budget increase.

d. Driving down the street, everything appeared to be in place to me.

e. Only Samantha works during summer vacation. (Hint: She never works at any other time.)

PARALLEL CONSTRUCTION

Words, phrases, or clauses should be expressed in similar grammatical form when they are within a sentence and are related in meaning. When similar elements are expressed in a similar structure, they are *parallel*. Parallel construction makes the sentence easy to read and to understand.

Parallel constructions are logically connected by the coordinating conjunctions *and*, *but*, and *or*. Care should be taken to see that the sentence elements connected by these conjunctions are of the same grammatical type. This principle applies not only to elements of a series but also to units in an outline and to headings. For example, if one heading (major or subheading) appears in complete-sentence form, the others should also.

17-3 Within each sentence, balance a noun with a noun, an adjective with an adjective, a phrase with a phrase, and a clause with a clause.

Incorrect: The manager's duties include *preparing the* payroll and *the depositing of the* money.

Correct: The manager's duties include *preparing the* payroll and *depositing the* money.

Incorrect: The information was *not verified, not accurate,* and *wasn't very convincing either.*

Correct: The information was *not verified, not accurate,* and *not convincing* either.

17-1, 17-2
a. I received my meal promptly.
b. you need a deposit . . .
c. C
d. I thought everything
e. Samantha only works

Chapter 17—Editing for Clarity 241

17-4 Conjunctions used in pairs (*both . . . and, either . . . or, neither . . . nor, not only . . . but also, whether . . . or*) should be followed by words in the same grammatical form.

> *Incorrect:* The college offers both *a degree in word processing* and *engineering*.
>
> *Correct:* The college offers a degree in both *word processing* and *engineering*.
>
> *Incorrect:* Freshmen not only *are insecure* but also *naive*.
>
> *Correct:* Freshmen are not only *insecure* but also *naive*.

✓ Proofread the following sentences and correct the structure where it is not parallel. If a sentence is correct, write a C to the right of it.

a. Dick's summer plans include painting the house, refinishing some furniture, and to play golf.

b. When using a word processor, I can correct errors faster, more conveniently, and is much easier than I can when using a typewriter.

c. Whether Steffi accepts the transfer or remains here will be her decision.

d. Jeff not only won a trip to South America but a car also.

e. Carrie is studying accounting, French, and how to keyboard.

SIMPLE WORDS

Business writers often use certain words and phrases because they *sound* right or businesslike. These words, which are usually longer and more complicated than needed, often sound dull and pompous to the receiver. Word length and word difficulty are often related, but not always. Many people know words such as *condominium* and *videocassette* but don't know words such as *pi* and *id*.

In general, short, simple, familiar words are more likely to be understood. Familiar words allow the reader to concentrate on the message; complicated and unusual words may call attention to the words themselves. When there is a shorter, less complicated word available, the writer should always choose it.

17-5 Edit for complex words by choosing short, simple words instead.

Confusing: Did you *utilize* our voice messaging system when you called?

Clear: Did you *use* our voice messaging system when you called?

Confusing: Please *ascertain* whether or not Jim is traveling to Turkey.

Clear: Please *find out* whether or not Jim is traveling to Turkey.

Following is a list of overused words with their shorter, simpler counterparts.

Difficult Words	**Simple Words**
ascertain	find out
cognizant	aware
commence	begin
communicate	write or call
compensate	pay
consummate	complete
encounter	meet
endeavor	try
expedite	rush, speed up
facilitate	help
perplexing	confusing, puzzling
procure	get
reciprocate	return
subsequent	following, later
sufficient	enough
terminate	end
transmit	send
utilize	use

17-3, 17-4

a. and **playing** golf.
b. and **easier** than
c. C
d. Jeff **won not only . . . but also** a car.
e. and **keyboarding**.

Chapter 17—Editing for Clarity

Edit the following sentences by substituting simple words for more difficult words. If a sentence is correct, write a C to the right of it.

   a. Cecil's lease on the building was terminated because he did not pay the rent.

   b. We expect 50 people to attend the rally on Fountain Square.

   c. Your interest in the news article indicates that you endeavor to keep up with current events.

   d. Please find out if other people are joining us on the tour.

   e. Subsequent to the passage of the education bill, Congress appropriated the necessary funds.

SPELLING REVIEW

To improve your ability to detect spelling errors, master this last set of words:

advantageous	realize
courteous	pursuing
develop	thoroughly
further	

PROOFREADING TIPS

1. Errors in misplaced modifiers and in parallelism usually disrupt the flow of the sentence. To detect such errors, listen carefully as you read the document to yourself.

2. Proofread to see that the words used are familiar to the reader.

3. Learn to recognize the problems that undermine clarity of writing and know their remedies.

17-5

a. was **ended** because
b. C
c. you **try** to
d. C
e. **After** the passage

Proofreading Applications

Proofread the following documents, checking particularly for errors in parallelism, misplaced and dangling modifiers, and complex words. The number of errors in the first two exercises is given.

P-1

November 30, 19--

Mrs. Harry R. Doesky
327 First Street
Great Bend, KS 67530-8247

Dear Mrs. Doesky

Yes, we can put your slides and photographs on videotape. For this service (1) purchase a video transfer kit, (2) you can bring your materials with a completed order form to our store, and (3) pick up in three weeks your new VCR tape and the original materials.

For futher information, call us at 555-1000.

Sincerely

(3 errors)

P-2

TO: Elizabeth
FROM: Donald
DATE: November 14, 19--
SUBJECT: Planning Meeting

Please plan to meet in my office at 3:15 p.m. tomorrow to plan a strategy for encouraging students to take vocational courses.

Although all graduates will not continue their education, all will find marketable skills advantageous. This idea is predicated on the knowledge that graduates who have had vocational courses will be coveted because employers are cognizant that they will have not only the marketable skills but also better attitudes, better human relations skills, and will have an appreciation for work.   (4 errors)

P-1
1. (2) bring your materials
2. pick up your . . . materials in three weeks
3. further

Chapter 17—Editing for Clarity

P-3

November 15, 19--

POWER ZOOM LENS
HAS AUTOFOCUS SYSTEM
DATE/TIME DISPLAY

are only three of the features that you will like about our best-selling SDB Camcorder. While recording, the power zoom lens can be used to film either close-up or distance shots. The autofocus system will focus on any subject that appears within a small circle on the lens automatically. Should you forget when you recorded your scenes, you will enjoy not only the date display but also the time display features.

To purchase your SDB Camcorder, come to our store the week of November 18-25.

P-2

1. idea is **based** on
2. will be **in demand**
3. employers are **aware**
4. and an appreciation

P-3

1. AUTOFOCUS SYSTEM
2. recording, **you can use the power zoom lens** to film
3. will focus **automatically**

PROGRESSIVE PROOFREADING

You are working as an assistant to Sylvia Gonzalez, owner-manager of Best Natural Products Co. One of your responsibilities is to proofread documents for mechanical errors and edit them for correctness, conciseness, and clarity.

Job 1 Edit the memo for clarity and conciseness. Also check for any mechanical errors.

BEST Natural Products Co.

INTEROFFICE COMMUNICATION

TO: All Personnel

FROM: Sylvia

DATE: October 24, 19--

SUBJECT: Good Telephone Techniques

Because our voices are the first contacts that many individuals have with us outside the company, we should strive to make a good first impression when we answer the telephone. Please review the following suggestions for developing better telephone techniques.

TELEPHONE TECHNIQUES

I. INCOMING CALLS

    A. Answer promptly.
    B. Greet the caller pleasantly.
    C. You should identify yourself and your company.
    D. Be helpful to the caller.
    E. Be curteous at all times.
    F. Screen calls as directed by your employer.
    G. Write messages accurately and so they are legible.
    H. Let the caller end the call.

II. MAKING OUTGOING CALLS

    A. Be sure of the number.
    B. Plan your call.
        1. Know what you are going to discuss.
        2. Have related materials at hand.
    C. Let the phone ring several times before hanging up.
    D. Identify yourself.
    E. Time zone differences.
    F. Be considerate.

Chapter 17—Editing for Clarity

Job 2 Proofread the two invoices against the telephone messages from which they were prepared. Use the price list to check the item numbers and prices. The terms are **2/10, n/30**; the sales tax is **6%**; shipment is via **UPS**; and the orders are numbered consecutively beginning with **BH090190**.

BEST Natural Products Co.

1402 Graham Road
Bryan, TX 77801-4128

PRICE LIST

Item No.	Product Description	Size	Price
AE-2349	Scouring Cleanser	9 oz	$ 4.75
LA-6180	Liquid Cleanser	16 oz	3.30
BD-7307	Automatic Dishwashing Concentrate	47 oz	8.95
BG-2294	Germicide	1 qt	11.85
BH-5568Q	Concentrated Cleaner	1 qt	6.40
BH-5561G		1 gal	22.35
BH-5565G		5 gal	97.20
NB-90010	Laundry Concentrate	10 lb	19.95
NB-90021		21 lb	39.95
LL-9751Q	Liquid Laundry Concentrate	1 qt	5.95
LL-9751G		1 gal	21.10
SS-73822	Dishwashing Liquid	22 oz	4.75
SS-6431G		1 gal	23.95
ST-8011Q	Concentrated Fabric Softener	1 qt	5.10
ST-8011G		1 gal	17.50

Chapter 17—Editing for Clarity

BEST Natural Products Co.

1402 Graham Road
Bryan, TX 77801-4128

INVOICE

Mrs. N. D. Rosenbloom
219 Ortiz Drive
Groves, TX 77619-3120

Date: October 25, 19--
Order No.: BH090190
Date Shipped: October 25, 19--
Shipped Via: UPS
Terms: 2/10, n/30

Quantity	No.	Description	Unit Price	Total
2	LA-6180	Liquid Cleanser	3.30	6.60
1	NB-90010	Laundry Concentrate, 10 lb	19.95	19.95
2 qt	ST-8011G	Concentrated Fabric Softener	5.10	10.20
		Total		36.75
		Sales Tax		2.21
		Total Amount		38.96

To _Sales Dept._
Time _9:20 a.m._ Date _10/25_

While You Were Out

M_rs. N. D. Rosenbloom_
of _219 Ortiz Drive, Groves TX 77619-3120_
Phone No. _479-2853_

☑ Telephoned ☐ Please call back
☐ Returned your call ☐ Will call again
☐ Left the following message:—

Send 2 liquid cleanser, 1 10-lb laundry conc, and 2 qt conc fab soft. Also info about water purification system.   By _js_

Chapter 17—Editing for Clarity

INVOICE

BEST Natural Products Co.
1402 Graham Road
Bryan, TX 77801-4128

Kwai San Restaurant
427 Center Street
Lufkin, TX 75901-1200

Date: October 25, 19--
Order No.: BH090191
Date Shipped: October 25, 19--
Shipped Via: UPS
Terms: 2/10, n/30

Quantity	No.	Description	Unit Price	Total
10	BD-7307	Automatic Dishwashing Concentrate, 47 oz	8.95	89.50
1	BH-5565G	Consentrated Cleaner, 5 gal	97.20	97.20
5 qt	BG-2249	Germicide	11.85	59.25
12	AE-2349	Scouring Cleanser	4.75	4.75
		Total		250.70
		Sales Tax		15.04
		Total Amount		265.74

To *Sales Dept.*
Time *1:45 p.m.* Date *10/25*

While You Were Out

M *Kwai San Restaurant*
of *427 Canter St., Lufkin TX 75901-1200*
Phone No. *(409) 210-0191*

- ☑ Telephoned
- ☐ Please call back
- ☐ Returned your call
- ☐ Will call again
- ☐ Left the following message:—

Send 10 47-oz. a.d.w. conc. 1 conc cleaner (5 gal), 5 qt germicide, 12 scouring cleansers

By *R*

Chapter 17—Editing for Clarity

Job 3 Edit the letter to Mrs. Rosenbloom for conciseness, clarity, and all types of mechanical errors. Best Natural Products prefers the modified block letter format and open punctuation.

BEST Natural Products Co.

1402 Graham Road
Bryan, TX 77801-4128
Telephone: (409) 555-7862

October 25, 19--

Mrs. N. D. Rosenbloom
219 Ortiz Drive
Groves, TX 77619-3120

Dear Mrs. Rosenbloom

Your telephone order of October 25 is being shipped by UPS today.

Thank you for your interest in our nonpolluting and biodegradable cleaning products and our water purification system.

Our cleaning products are not only throughly effective and safe for cleaning but also safe for the enviornment.

The quality of water is one of the most important choices we have to make today. Our company is working to develop a water purifying system that is economical, space-saving, and will be easy to operate. The system should be available in about six months. We will send you a brochure about the system as soon as the brochure becomes available.

Mrs. Rosenblooom, we do appreciate your business. Any time you have questions about our products, please call us using our toll-free number, 800-555-642.

Sincerely yours

Mrs. Carol A. Gary
Customer Service

kr

Chapter 17—Editing for Clarity

COMPUTERIZED PROOFREADING

Job 4 Proofread and Edit Letter

1. Load the file C17JOB4 from the template.
2. Use the following statement for verifying the correctness of the information in the letter. Edit the letter carefully for errors in conciseness and clarity. Also check for mechanical errors.
3. Save the revised document as C17JOB4R.
4. Produce the document by following the standard procedures.

BEST Natural Products Co.

1402 Graham Road
Bryan, TX 77801-4128
Telephone: (409) 555-7862

Account of   Henry Z. Loran
             1735 North 16 Street
             Lake Jackson, TX 77566-9800

Date	Charges	Credits	Balance
June 3	179.34		179.34
July 1		179.34	---
July 25	144.57		144.57
August 22	135.91		280.48

POSTTEST

Part A Proofread each of the following sentences for mechanical errors (spelling, abbreviation, word division, number expression, grammar, punctuation, capitalization), content errors, conciseness, and clarity. Use the appropriate proofreading symbols to indicate corrections. Sentences often contain more than one error. If a sentence is correct, write C after it. Solutions to the Posttest begin on page 278.

1. It was he who called.
2. Send letters to whomever is on the list.
3. No one can spell as well as her.
4. We believe that our's is the best cleaning product on the market.
5. One criterion for selecting the textbook is cost.
6. Our historian and reporter, Bob Lewis, has done a good job.
7. Here is the book and tape that you requested.
8. A number of children is enrolled in the Summer reading program.
9. Everyone has his or her own problems.
10. The employer promtoed Sam and I.
11. Many people drop the s from Dr. Daniels' name.
12. An error tolerance of 0.05 percent is permissable.
13. Yes, the team has all ready made their decision.
14. Will you please purchase 12 16-ounce tumblers?
15. Fantastic! We won the $10 million lottery!
16. Delta Flight 210 leaves from gate 7 at 8 a.m. on October 14.
17. S. America sells a lot of coffee to the United States.
18. To make this jacket you will need 3 yards of 54-inch material.
19. Ben Williams was transferred to the Loan department.
20. About two thousand people attended the Raleigh Summer Festival on July 29th.
21. More than three fourths of the stockholders voted on the 13 proposed changes.
22. Lynn Forrest, M.D., has opened an office in the Brody Building which is located at 5410 West Eighth Street, Topeka, Kansas.
23. Al is 6 feet 6 inches tall, and he has difficulty getting into his sports car.
24. The Goodwill Games, which were held in Seattle were telecast by WTBS-TV.

25. Ken paid $2.45 for the card and $6.25 for the booklet, making the total $8.60.
26. Per your request, nine of the 75 letters must be redone.
27. Did you read the article "An Open Letter to the President?"
28. Planning, as he drove to work, how he would handle the personnel problem.
29. They gave the papers to Earl and I for safekeeping.
30. Terry explained the proceedure, and then left us to carry it out.
31. To enroll more members is our first goal for this year.
32. Julie Koenig, an efficient hard-working employee, received a $1500 raise.
33. "I have a problem, said the treasurer about how to correct this error.
34. Her latest book, *How to Decrease Your Taxes*, is on the best-seller list.
35. When a manager buys disks, he must order the 3.5" size.
36. The spelling test was easy, that is why everyone past.
37. The check came today, therefore; I can pay my bills promptly.
38. Performers appearing on the telethon are: Casey, Dean, Jerry and John.
39. After paying six months rent, we were given a receipt.
40. Paula took the shelled the pecans and then stirred it into the cake.
41. The correct division for each of these words is omit-ted, gues-sing, sales-person, be-gin, and evacu-ate. (Note: Check word division.)
42. The three insurance plans affected 54 employees working in four branch locations.
43. My friends think I either have forgotten their addresses or the fact that I owe them letters.
44. Three honor students in art Kim, Karen, and Keith were recognized at the awards ceremony.
45. Underwood, Wooten, and Gaylord, Inc., will move its office to the Blount Building.
46. Mayor-elect Jenkins, as well as the city council members, is attending the Washington, DC, conference.
47. After I have completed the Business Communication course, I will be eligible for a job with *The Sun Times*.
48. As a rule, we provide maintenance service for all our products except the small appliances.
49. Our company's regional offices are located in Atlanta, Georgia; Austin, Texas, and Salem, Oregon.
50. Your responsibilities will include openin the office, sorting the mail, and to file the correspondents.

Part B Proofread the following letter for mechanical and content errors. The letter should be formatted in modified block style with mixed punctuation. Use the appropriate proofreading symbols to indicate changes.

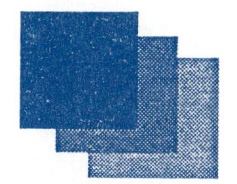

Boxberger Repair Shop

1266 East Windsor Road
Pontiac, MI 48054-1266

June 22, 19--

Reed Supply Company
666 S. Capitol Avenue
Lansing, Mich. 48933-0666

Dear Mr. Reed
    On June 15, I received the water hose I ordered from your company. When I connected the hose to the outlet at my shop it burst during the second day of usage. Your quarantee (copy enclosed) states that the hose is supposed to operate without defect for 90 days. Therefor, I am requesting a replacement for the defective hose.

Please let me know what I should do to return it.

                        Yours very truly,

                        Ray Boxberger, Manager

bdl

pc B. Perkins

SOLUTIONS

PRETEST

Proofread each of the following sentences for mechanical errors (spelling, abbreviation, word division, number expression, grammar, punctuation, capitalization), content errors, conciseness, and clarity. Write in your corrections. Sentences often contain more than one correction. Indicate a correct sentence by writing C after it. Each sentence is worth two points. Solutions to the Pretest are on page 257.

1. While waiting for the plane, my baggage was stolen.
2. Everyone except Barry Johnson and he joined the organization.
3. The governor of Georgia traveled to Europe to seek industry for the state.
4. 15 class members participated in the rally; that's more than one half of the class.
5. The clerk was insistant that those 3 sweaters I bought during the Fall sale could not be returned for any reason.
6. I would like to hire Susan Jackson, who all ready has had three years experience.
7. If you move to Washington, please give me a call.
8. The board voted it's approval of the preformance of the company's officers.
9. Neither Enjou nor Tai are enrolled in Accounting 411, a graduation requirement.
10. I plan to take a cruise before the cruise company's special expires; however, circumstances prevent my going at this time.
11. Janice assured me that the idea to go rafting was her's.
12. The administrative assistant, as well as the office manager, is attending the time management seminar.
13. The State of Florida is also known as the Sunshine State.
14. Frank and Doris's car cost $20,000, and they obtained a loan with 7.5% interest.
15. In Chapter 4, page 14, the following rule appears: Do not divide a word containing 5 or fewer letters.
16. A number of responses has been recieved from the Febuary 5th mailing.
17. The employment survey which traced thirty-three types of information in secretarial ads, revealed several key findings.
18. On June 1, 19-- I will travel to Hawaii to spend a three-week vacation.
19. You should select a paralegal program created, taught and graded by experienced attorneys.
20. Sam, Julie, and Bob has gone to the hardware store to get five gals. of paint.
21. Installing a computer in our records management department will increase its efficiency.
22. The sign read, "Keep the Place Neat," but children's toys were scattered everywhere.
23. Of all the communication books you sent me, there was only one I liked—*Improving Business Writing*.

257

24. Here is the brochure and the check that was omitted from your letter.
25. Ham and eggs is a traditional breakfast dish in the South.
26. Isn't this where your twin brother, Don, lives?
27. Molly, I found three quarters, one dime, and twelve pennies—a total of 92 cents.
28. A County prosecutor appeared in a case before the California supreme court.
29. The news bullentin reported that Gen Arnold's plane would arrive at Kennedy International Airport at 10:15 a.m.
30. There will, of course, be a charge for maintainance after the warranty expires.
31. She is a legal secretary in a Chicago law firm and wants to join a professional association.
32. If you enjoy running check with your local runner's association about referral services in other cities.
33. Andy exclaimed, "Stop/ The drawbridge is open!
34. The spelling test included these words: similar, accomodate, decision, and procedure.
35. The old, dilapidated house will be replaced by a lovely two-story house.
36. The word "telecommuting" has now become a part of the office worker's everyday vocabulary and should be a familar term to all involved in the business world.
37. Before the consultant arrives find out why she's coming.
38. Interior folders come in the same colors as hanging folders, but there just a bit shorter.
39. Today's manager has to juggle dozen's of tasks.
40. A Mid-August survey revealed that many Americans declared French fries to be they're favorite food.
41. The travel agent said, "Your final payment for the November 1 cruise is due on October 1, which is sixty days before departure."
42. In Math 465, 49 percent of the class failed the final exam.
43. Answering the telephone and filing is considered a routine office task.
44. Ms. Dorene Randal, a Yale alumnus, received her m.a. from Duke university and was recommmended for a doctoral fellowship by Dr. D. R. Brandon.
45. If your voice tends to drop as you utter the expression, then the expression is nonessential, if your voice tends to rise, the expression is essential.
46. Andy's job was to supervise a force of 6 salespeople in the southwest.
47. Scanning her schedule once more, Abilene decided to eat lunch at her desk.
48. We work for a small (ten employees), relatively new advertising agency.
49. My guess is that all of you—president and creative professionals alike/are younger than your counterparts at Franklin and Associates.
50. The immediate task for mangers is to get family issues on the company agenda.

Minneapolis Financial Corp.
928 Irving Avenue S
Minneapolis, MN 55403-7640
(612) 555-5521

January 16, 19--

Dear Friend and Insured Member

We heard quite a lot about "outpatient" surgery from members while attending the Kappa Phi regional meetings this summer. What we learned was that members want coverage for outpatient services just as much as, if not more than, for hospitalizations!

Outpatient Surgery Covered

So, here you are. A Surgical Plan that pays for outpatient surgery as well as for surgeries performed in the hospital. Simple procedures are covered as well as complicated ones. You need not undergo major surgery in order to realize benefits from this plan.

Pays Up to $2,000 for Each Surgical Procedure

After you've had surgery, you will receive a check for a specified amount--regardless of the actual cost of the operation! Easy, quick claim-payment procedures help keep costs down and premiums low.

The enclosed brochure provides information that will help you analyze the benefits of this plan. Please fill out and mail the Surgical Assistance Enrollment Form along with your check today. As soon as we receive your Enrollment Form and check, we will mail your Certificate, ID Card, and Claim Form by return mail.

Sincerely

Maurice Fulghum

fb

Enclosure

Chapter 2, Job 1

Blackwood, D. P. (Mr.)
100 Pope Street
Boykins, VA 23827-1460
322-45-6601
Mechanic
Esther Blackwood

Quinton, Elbert
306 Mill Road
Jacksonville, NC 28540-4010
246-81-6621
Attorney
Cletis Quinton

Butler, Ralph
154 Anderson Avenue NC
Merry Hill, NC 27957-3641
238-88-6624
Teacher
Kay Tice

Sheppard, Paige (Ms.)
209 Gum Road
Raleigh, NC 27605-9142
233-44-2212
Computer Programmer
Mary Sheppard

Cox, James
116 Catawba Road
Nashville, NC 27856-1468
266-88-8811
Former
None

Wallace, Michael
201 Berkeley Street 3
Suffolk, VA 23404-2100
201-33-4444 4
Veterinarian
Susan Wallace

Chapter 2, Job 2

INTEROFFICE MEMORANDUM

TO: Judy Forrest, Medical Group Manager
FROM: Leo Thomas, Regional Sales Manager
DATE: January 16, 19--
SUBJECT: Kappa Phi Outpatient Surgery Campaign

Congratulations on a job well done in organizing the Outpatient Surgery Campaign for the Kappa Phi educational group. As you know, sales have exceeded our goal by 21 percent.

The consensus among the members of Kappa Phi was that this insurance plan met the needs of the group, made up primarily of women. Many of the members were not familiar with our organization before you introduced this plan. Now we find that they are interested in other types of insurance, including life and automobile.

I look forward to recognizing individual members of your team at the annual awards banquet. Their efforts have been an integral part of our success.

fb

Chapter 2, Job 3

June 15, 19-- (line 14)

Mr. Lucas Abernathy
911 St. Andrews Drive
Fredericksburg, VA 22401-9110

Dear Mr. Abernathy

Thank you for your inquiry about our homeowner's policies. You may choose from either a basic or a comprehensive policy. Should you desire further coverage, we can also tailor a policy to fit your specific needs.

Briefly, our basic policy covers losses from the following:

1. Fire or lightning
2. Windstorm or hail
3. Explosions
4. Riots, civil commotion, or vandalism
5. Breakage of glass
6. Smoke
7. Theft of personal property

Our comprehensive policy covers the above losses in addition to:

8. Damage from ice, snow, or sleet
9. Collapse of building
10. Overflow of water
11. Freezing of plumbing
12. Injury from artificially generated current

Each of our policies may be purchased without a deductible or with either a $100 or a $250 deductible.

Enclosed is a brochure which gives a concise description of each of these policies and defines each of the above losses. After you have had a chance to analyze it, I will call you for an appointment.

Sincerely yours

Thomas A. Foley, Agent

jb

Enclosure

Chapter 2, Job 4

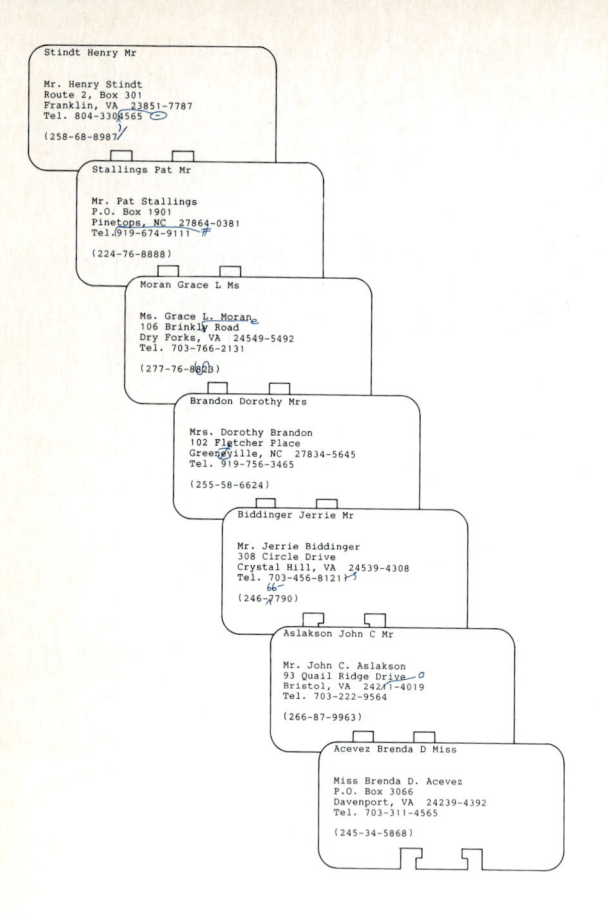

Chapter 3, Job 1

```
Stindt Henry Mr
  Mr. Henry Stindt
  Route 2, Box 301
  Franklin, VA  23851-7787
  Tel. 804-330-6565
    (258-68-8987)
```
```
Stallings Pat Mr
  Mr. Pat Stallings
  P.O. Box 1901
  Pinetops, NC  27864-0381
  Tel. 919-674-9111
    (224-76-8888)
```
```
Moran Grace L Ms
  Ms. Grace L. Moran
  106 Brinkly Road
  Dry Forks, VA  24549-5492
  Tel. 703-766-2131
    (277-76-8888)
```
```
Brandon Dorothy Mrs
  Mrs. Dorothy Brandon
  102 Fletcher Place
  Greenville, NC  27834-5645
  Tel. 919-756-3465
    (255-58-6624)
```
```
Biddinger Jerrie Mr
  Mr. Jerrie Biddinger
  308 Circle Drive
  Crystal Hill, VA  24539-4308
  Tel. 703-456-8121
    (246-66-7790)
```
```
Aslakson John C Mr
  Mr. John C. Aslakson
  93 Quail Ridge Drive
  Bristol, VA  24211-4019
  Tel. 703-222-9564
    (266-87-9963)
```
```
Acevez Brenda D Miss
  Miss Brenda D. Acevez
  P.O. Box 3066
  Davenport, VA  24239-4392
  Tel. 703-311-4565
    (245-34-5868)
```

Chapter 3, Job 2

April 1, 19--

Mrs. Abbie Nelson
16 Sandcastle Drive
Tallahassee, FL 32308-9000

Dear Mrs. Nelson:

Have you overlooked your February payment on your account, Mrs. Nelson? Your last payment of $75 for the computer that you purchased was made over a month ago. Please put a check in the mail to us by April 15. We believe you want to continue to be eligible for credit.

If you have any questions about your account, please call Rosa at 919-331-4211.

Sincerely,

April 1, 19--

Dr. Lawrence Mayo
673 Andersen Drive
Rochester, NY 14626-8765

Dear Dr. Mayo:

Have you overlooked your February payment on your account, Dr. Mayo? Your last payment of $92 for the printer that you purchased was made over a month ago. Please put a check in the mail to us by April 15. We believe you want to continue to be eligible for credit with us.

If you have any questions about your account, please call Mary at 919-321-4211.

Sincerely,

April 1, 19--

Mr. James Holden
200 Tenth Street
Jacksonville, FL 32333-4182

Dear Mr. Holden:

Have you overlooked your February payment on your account, Mr. Holden? Your last payment of $75 for the software that you purchased was made over a month ago. Please put a check in the mail to us by April 15. We believe you want to continue to be eligible for credit.

If you have any questions about your account, please call Mary at 919-331-4211.

Sincerely,

Chapter 3, Job 3

RIVERSIDE PAINT COMPANY

Balance Sheet
March 1, 19--

ASSETS

Cash			$10,250.20
Petty Cash			520.00
Accounts Receivable		895.55	
Less Allowance for Bad Debts		100.00	795.55
Merchandise Inventory			50,225.00
Supplies - Office			3,250.00
Supplies - Store			2,500.00
Total Current Assets			67,540.75
Plant Assets:			
Office Equipment	5,000.00		
Less Accumulated Depreciation . . .	1,200.00	3,800.00	
Store Equipment	9,000.00		
Less Accumulated Depreciation . . .	2,000.00	7,000.00	
Total Plant Assets			10,800.00
Total Assets			$89,140.75

LIABILITIES AND OWNERS' EQUITY

Accounts Payable	13,775.60	
OWNERS' EQUITY	75,365.15	
TOTAL OWNERS' EQUITY AND LIABILTIES		$89,140.75

Chapter 3, Job 4

MINUTES OF THE BOARD OF DIRECTORS
ADAMS CONSTRUCTION COMPANY

January 15, 19--

Call to Order and Attendance. The Board of Directors of Adams Construction Company met on Monday, January 15, 19--, at 7 p.m. in the Jones Conference Room. Chairperson Baker presided. All members were present except for Susan Pilgreen.

Approval of Minutes. The minutes of the December 3, 19--, meeting were read and approved with one addition. Mr. Baker noted that because many of the concerns about the environment had been addressed, these concerns should be integrated into the minutes.

Treasurer's Report. The treasurer's report was submitted and approved. It included no major discrepancies from the projected budget.

Committee Reports. The Maintenance Committee chairperson, Anthony Bumgardner, submitted three estimates for repairs to the building. Anthony reported that the representative from Klingensmith Company (which has been awarded the contract) indicated that he would guarantee satisfaction and would definitely follow up to find out if we are satisfied.

Clarence Farlow noted that approximately ninety new customers were added to our mailing list during the past month, many of whom are good prospects.

Adjournment. The meeting was adjourned at 8:30 p.m.

Respectfully submitted,

Clarence Farlow

WALLACE COMPUTER SOLUTIONS

MANAGING INFORMATION WITH COMPUTERS

Seminar co-sponsored by Wallace Computer Solutions and
the College of Businesss, Montana State University
Friday, January 27, 19--
Bus. Admin. Bldg. Room 1311

Consultants

Prof. Paul Uhr Senior, MBA, School of Business, Mont. St. U.
Ms. Lillie Taylor, CPS, Office Manager, Quadrangle Products, Inc.
Dr. William R. Joyner, Chairperson, Information Sciences Dept.
Montana State Univ.

Program

Registration	8:30 a.m. – 8:55 am
Morning Session	9:00 a.m. – 12:15 p.m.
Lunch	12:30 p.m. – 1:45 p.m.
Afternoon Session	2:00 p.m. – 4:30 p.m.

Registrants limited to 25
Seminar fee: $99 per person
Enrollment deadline: January 20
Send check to Business Education Services, P.O. Box 2136, Bozeman, Montana 59717-4368

Chapter 4, Job 1

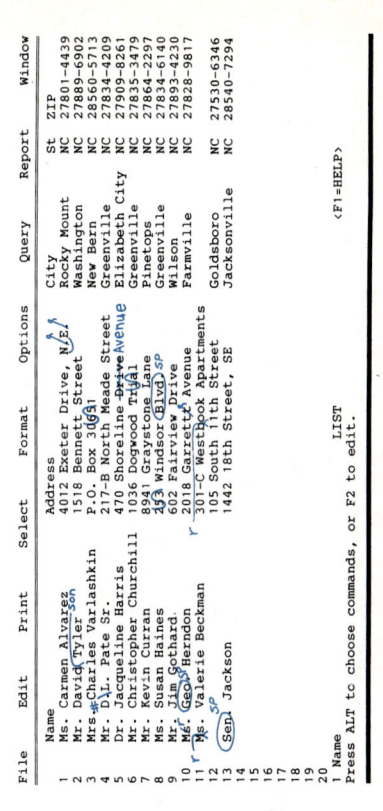

Chapter 4, Job 2

SPECIAL NOTICE

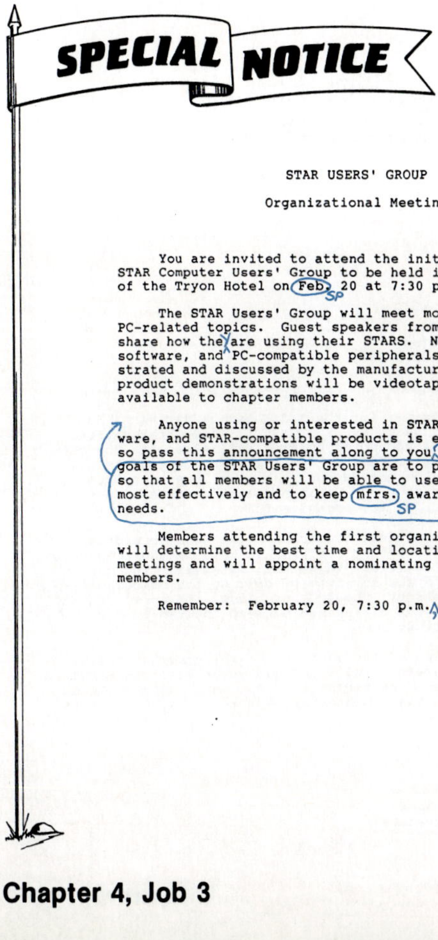

STAR USERS' GROUP
Organizational Meeting

You are invited to attend the initial meeting of the STAR Computer Users' Group to be held in the Prince Room of the Tryon Hotel on Feb. 20 at 7:30 p.m.

The STAR Users' Group will meet monthly to discuss PC-related topics. Guest speakers from industry will share how they are using their STARS. New products, software, and PC-compatible peripherals will be demonstrated and discussed by the manufacturers. These product demonstrations will be videotaped and made available to chapter members.

Anyone using or interested in STAR Computers, software, and STAR-compatible products is eligible to join, so pass this announcement along to you friends. The goals of the STAR Users' Group are to provide a network so that all members will be able to use their computers most effectively and to keep mfrs. aware of consumers needs.

Members attending the first organizational meeting will determine the best time and location of the monthly meetings and will appoint a nominating committee for board members.

Remember: February 20, 7:30 p.m. Tryon Hotel

Chapter 4, Job 3

WALLACE COMPUTER SOLUTIONS

INTEROFFICE MEMORANDUM

To: Department Managers and Supervisors

From: Garry Morrison, General Manager

Date: January 20, 19--

Subject: Expense Reduction

Please analyze your tentative budget carefully; then let me have your strategies for reducing our costs as soon as possible but no later than February 1.

As you review the budget, you will see that our utilities expense is almost double what it was four years ago. Advertising expense has increased about 30 percent. Taxes are up more than 20 percent. The cost of insurance rises every year. If we are to remain competitive in the business environment, we must reduce our expenses.

My goal is to incorporate your ideas into the management plan for the February 15 annual meeting.

dw

Chapter 4, Job 4

261

FORM PARAGRAPHS:

A. You have been an enthusiastic and dependable supporter of Partners, Inc., for five years.

B. You have been one of Partners' most enthusiastic backers, and we appreciate the support you have given us.

C. Because you have so generously contributed your time or other resources to Partners, the Advisory Board members invite you to be our guest at our annual gala dinner on March 30 at the City Center at 6:30 p.m. You may bring a guest.

D. We are already at the height of planning the annual Partners' Auction. This year the auction will be held on February 15. As in the past, all proceeds will go to help the youth of our community. May we count on your continued support? If your answer is YES, and we hope it will be, please notify us by January 20.

E. As we prepare for this year's auction scheduled for February 15, may we once again count on your support? If your answer is YES, and we hope it will be, please let us know the items or service that you will provide for the auction by January 20.

F. If you will be able to attend, please return the enclosed reservation form by March 16 so that we can reserve a place for you.

G. Enclosure

Chapter 5, Job 1

Partners, Inc.
1110 Logan Street
Denver, CO 80203-9176 (303) 555-6478

January 10, 19--

Ms. Jane Daniels, Mgr.
WEXZ Newstalk 1530
517 North Ninth Street
Denver, CO 80204-7825

Dear Ms. Daniels

PUBLIC ANNOUNCEMENT

For the past four years, your station has very generously advertised the Partners' Auction as a public service announcement. The Partners' Auction is held annually to raise money to support projects for the youth in our community. Can we count on your continued support this year?

If your response is YES, and we hope it will be, would you read the enclosed news release on your Community Calendar program beginning January 20 and running through February 5.

Sincerely yours

Joseph A. Ramirez
Executive Secretary

gg

Enclosure

Chapter 5, Job 2

Partners, Inc.
1110 Logan Street
Denver, CO 80203-9176
(303) 555-6478

NEWS RELEASE

January 10, 19--
To release January 29, 19--

FIFTH ANNUAL PARTNERS' AUCTION

The Fifth Annual Partners' Auction will be telecast on WRAL-TV from noon to midnight on Saturday, February 5. Local merchants have generously donated approximately fifteen hundred gifts. Viewers can bid on any of them by calling one of the numbers that will be listed on the television screen. The retail value of each item will be given, and each item will be sold to the highest bidder.

All persons working with the auction donate their time; thus, every nickel goes directly to Partners to aid the youth of the community. Show your support for youth projects by supporting Partners' Auction.

#

Chapter 5, Job 3

Partners, Inc.
1110 Logan Street
Denver, CO 80203-9176 (303) 555-6478

January 15, 19--

Mr. E. C. Troiano
AMS Electronics
5245 Trade Street
Denver, CO 80213-8275

Dear Mr. Troiano

Mark your calendar for the Fifth Annual Partners' Auction to be held on Saturday, February 5, in Scott Pavilion. The auction is sponsored by area businesses for the benefit of Partners, Inc., an organization devoted to helping the youth of the community. As a loyal supporter of Partners, you know how vital the auction is as a means of raising funds for the organization.

WRAL-TV will telecast the auction from noon to midnight. As each item is put up for bid, it will be shown on television, and its retail value will be given. You can place your bid for any item by calling the numbers listed on the screen. Should your bid be for more than the retail value, the difference between the two is deductible on your taxes.

Persons working at the auction are volunteering their services; therefore, all proceeds go directly to Partners. We hope you will participate in Partners' biggest fundraiser of the year. When Partners benefits, the entire community benefits.

Sincerely yours

Joseph A. Ramirez
Executive Secretary

re

Chapter 5, Job 4

March 1, 19--

Mr. Peter Wallace, Manager
General TV and Appliance, Inc.
1927 Greeley Boulevard
Denver, CO 80208-1927

Dear Mr. Wallace

You have been an enthusiastic and dependable supporter of Partners, Inc., for five years.

Because you have so generously contributed your time or other resources to Partners, the Advisory Board members invite you to be our guest at our annual gala dinner on March 30 at the City Center at 6:30 p.m. You may bring a guest.

If you will be able to attend, please return the enclosed reservation form by March 16 so that we can reserve a place for you.

Sincerely

Gary McDougald

xx

Enclosure

Chapter 5, Job 5

Phelps Real Estate Agency
1125 Umstead Drive Indianapolis, IN 46204-6154 (317) 555-3222

January 20, 19--

Ms. Patricia Strum
1 Kildaire Farm Road
Indianapolis, IN 46205-9241

Dear Ms. Strum

Good news! The house you are interested in on Thirty-third Street has been reduced $5,000. The price is now within the range you mentioned to me on the 4th. May I urge you to act quickly.

Because of the favorable mortgage rates that are now available, you can own this 2,200-square-foot house and still have mortgage payments of less than $900.00 per month. For a limited time, the Indianapolis Federal Savings and Loan Association will approve your application for an adjustable rate loan within thirty days. If it is not approved, you will not be charged the 1% discount rate.

Please call me at 555-3222 to set up an appointment. My office hours are from 9:00 to 5 p.m. Mon-Sat.

Sincerely

Terry B. Andrus
Agent

df

Chapter 6, Job 1

GREENWOOD SUBDIVISION. Spaciouus and convenient ranch for economy-consious owner. While its main features are three bedrooms, a living room with fireplace, and and a den that could be a forth bedroom, it also has a semi-wooded backyard, a 12- by 27-foot deck, and a twelve- by twelve-foot area with a hot tub. A detached garage provides space for a car and cabinet storage. For more details, call Chris at 555-42000.

Chapter 6, Job 2

DAR
Delhi Association of Realtors
325 Alabama Street
Indianapolis, IN 46204-6154
(317) 555-7355

MINUTES OF MEETING
DELHI ASSOCIATION OF REALTORS

Place of Meeting
The Delhi Assoc of Realtors held its monthly meeting on Tuesday, January 18, 19--, at The Heritage Restaurant. The social hour began at 6:00 o'clock, and dinner was served at 7. Seventy-eight of the 85 members were present in addition to four guests.

Call to Order
Immediately following dinner, J.R. Hawkins, president, called the meeting to order and welcomed the members and guests. She noted that the January attendance was 10% above the December attendance.

Approval of Minutes
The minutes were presented by Secretary Tom Phelps. Jim Miller noted that the state convention would be held on the ninth of March instead of on April 10 as stated in the minutes. The correction was made, and the minutes were approved.

Treasurer's Report
In the absence of Susan Peoples, Tom Phelps gave the treasurer's report. The Association has a balance of $1,210 in the treasury, and bills amounting to $76.10 ($35.10 to Rouse Printing Company and $41 to The Heritage Restaurant) are outstanding. An extension of 10 days has been granted to members who haven't paid their dues.

Chapter 6, Job 3

263

Market Review	Robert Blankenship was called on to give a summary of the developments that have taken place in the local real estate market. Phelps Real Estate Company has been selected as exclusive marketing agent for Breckenridge subdivision on Leesville Rd. The 79-lot single-family subdivision is a Drexter development. Northwoods Village, a 228-unit luxury apartment community developed by Dallas C. Pickford & Associates, will open on the 1st of August. The community is located at Ten Northwoods Village Drive, one-half mile south of Interstate 40.
Speaker	Following the business session, the president introduced Mrs. Sarah Dunbarton, president of Dunbarton Associates, as speaker for the meeting. Mrs. Dunbarton discussed the potential effects of recent tax legislation on the real estate market. She predicted that the prime rate will drop another half point before it hits bottom. In the local area, there will probably be an increase of 12-15 apartment buildings on the market within the next 6 months.
Adjournment	Following the presentation, the treasurer drew the lucky number to determine who would win the centerpiece. 320 was the lucky number, and the winner was Joann Durham. The lucky number was 320. The meeting was adjourned at 9:15 p.m. Members were reminded that the next meeting would be on the third Tuesday of February.

Respectfully submitted,

Tom Phelps, Secretary

Chapter 6, Job 3 (Continued)

SHOULD YOU USE A REAL ESTATE AGENT?

Do you need a real estate agent when you buy or sell a house? Your immediate response might be that enlisting the help of a professional would be unnecessary. However, unless you have plenty of time and lots of experience, you could be taking a large risk if you do not seek the help of a professional realtor.

An agent can provide buyers with pertinent information to help them meet their location needs. The requirements of a family with a ten-year-old child will be different from those of a couple with grown children. The proximity of a good school and recreational facilities is important to parents with young children.

A professional agent can also advise a buyer on an affordable price range based on yearly income. For example, should a buyer with an income of $35,000 be looking at homes in the $90,000 range? An experienced agent would advise the buyer to spend no more than 2 1/2 times gross income. Debt factors, however, must also be considered.

Once the buyer has found a suitable house, the agent can guide the buyer through the transaction by helping to negotiate a price and by putting the buyer in touch with mortgage lenders, contractors, appraisers, inspectors, and insurance agents.

Chapter 6, Job 4

A professional realtor can also save a seller time, money, and frustration. Too often a homeowner seeks the help of a professional only after having incurred problems. One seller spent $350 on advertising, $300 on travel showing the house, $78.25 on phone calls, and $800 on maintenance while the house was on the market (a total of $1,528.25). Additionally, the client suffered a great deal of frustration before engaging a professional realtor.

When enlisting the help of a real estate agent, keep the following points in mind:

1. Ask for references from clients who have bought property recently.
2. Investigate the community in which you are interested.
3. Deal with a professional agent who has a good reputation.
4. Find out if the company which the realtor represents belongs to the local real estate board.

By taking advantage of an agent's experience, access to properties, and information about the local real estate market, people can avoid the pitfalls inherent in purchasing or marketing their homes.

Chapter 6, Job 4 (Continued)

Yes

a. Ms. Katrina Ann Dewar
8577 Estate Drive South
West Palm Beach, FL 33411-9753

Sales Promotion

Dear Ms. Dewar

b. Please let me know when we can get together to discuss the property.

Very Sincerely Yours,

Ms. Donna Raynor

Enclosure

ah

c. Carson Real Estate Enterprises
1860 Memorial Drive
Greenville, SC 29605-8642

Ladies and Gentlemen

d. Mr. M. C. Alexander
1620 Quantico Court
San Jose, CA 95230-1009

Dear Mr. Alexander

e. Ms. Ilo Carlson
8090 Pinetree Street
Little Rock, AR 72201-0057

Dear Ms. Carlson

f. Sincerely,

Brian Davis, Manager

dt

c Carolyn Walston

7-3

WALSH PAPERS
2250 Harris Road
Huntsville, AL 35810-2250
(509) 555-5892

June 16, 19--

Ms. Jennifer Elaine-Carson
Route 2, Box 507B
Huntsville, AL 35807-8615

PURCHASE ORDER 471

Dear Ms. Carson

Thank you for your order for six boxes of stationery, Stock No. 331. The quality of the stationery you have selected will let your customers know that they are important to you.

Because of the recent shipping strike, there has been a delay in our receiving the merchandise from the factory. We have been informed that the shipment has been sent, however, and we should receive it within a week. Your order will be on its way to you as soon as we receive the shipment. We hope this delay will not inconvenience you too much.

We appreciate the business you have given us in the past, and we look forward to serving you in the future.

Sincerely

Audrey D. Leapley, Manager
Shipping Department

ec
c R. P. Michaels

7-4 Letter A

Martindale Publishing — Internal Memorandum

TO: Associate Editors
FROM: Danny Bright, Executive Editor
DATE: Production Meetings
SUBJECT: April 10, 19--

On Monday, April 25, all associate editors should plan to meet in Conference Room C, third floor, at 10 a.m. The purpose of this meeting is to identify topics that are of concern to you as a supervisor.

You are a vital member of our editorial team, and your input is essential to keeping production running smoothly during this very heavy copyright year. Based on your input, we will establish an agenda for future meetings.

re

7-5

PERIN OFFICE SYSTEMS
3903 Spaulding Drive, Atlanta, GA 30338-3903
(404)555-1719

March 17, 19--

Ms. Cleo Mendoza
Phillips and Solomon
431 N. Main Street
Champlain, NY 12919-4300

Dear Ms. Mendoza

Thank you for the opportunity to demonstrate our new DataPhone telephone system for you at the TeleCom Exhibition last week. As you make your decision on a new system, keep in mind the following features that DataPhone offers:

1. **Speed dialing.** This feature can bring as many as 20 often-called numbers together in one place on the desktop console. By pressing a preprogrammed button, you can place a call in less than 3 seconds. Speed dialing eliminates searching for phone numbers.

2. **Call pickup.** This feature helps to eliminate unanswered calls by allowing anyone to answer a ringing phone.

3. **Conferencing.** This feature provides an easy, convenient way to bring people together without having to travel or even to leave their desks.

4. **Call forwarding.** This feature is particularly useful since it allows a person away from his or her desk to automatically forward calls to another extension.

5. **Speaker.** An optional feature, this is an extremely convenient way to talk with your hands free to take notes or operate the computer keyboard.

Perin Office Systems provides installation and employee training free of charge to companies that purchase the DataPhone system. Call us today to discuss your phone needs.

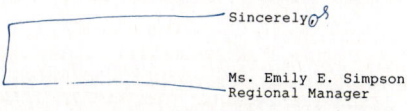

Sincerely

Ms. Emily E. Simpson
Regional Manager

ri

Chapter 7, Job 1

PERIN OFFICE SYSTEMS
3903 Spaulding Drive, Atlanta, GA 30338-3903
(404)555-1719

March 17, 19--

Mr. Roger Moe
Eastman Brothers, Inc.
7861 Monroe Street
Tallahassee, FL 32301-7654

Dear Mr. Moe
~~Ladies and Gentlemen~~

Enclosed is a short report reviewing the preliminary design factors that your project committee must consider when planning the 15,000-square-foot addition to your existing facilities.

We will provide complete documentation for these recommendations at our initial planning session on April 7. In the meantime, good luck with your planning.

Sincerely yours

Ms. Emily E. Simpson
Regional Manager

jp

Enclosure

Chapter 7, Job 2

265

OFFICE DESIGN FACTORS
Eastman Brothers, Inc.

Because office design does affect job performance and job satisfaction, several factors should be considered in the preliminary stages of planning the construction or renovation of any facility. This report discusses these factors and gives recommendations that may increase employees' productivity by as much as 30% and decrease absenteeism.

Work Space

The area where workers spend most of their time is their work space. The factors to be considered when work space is designed are discussed below.

Enclosures. The open office plan with enclosures gives workers the privacy they need, supports communication, and improves productivity more than either the fully open or fully closed office plan. To be effective, the partitions surrounding each work area should be higher than standing height on 3 sides.

Floor area. The amount of usable floor space a worker can call his or her own is based on job need and status. According to Quible (1989), the minimum requirements for various employees are as follows:

Top-level executives	425 square feet
Middle-level executives	5-300 square feet
Supervisors	200 square feet
Office employees	75-100 square feet

Layout. The physical arrangement (layout) of furniture and walls greatly affects job performance, comfort, status, and ease of communication. Workers should have two good work surfaces and a single front entrance. The layout should be designed so that others are not seated directly in front of the employee.

Lighting

Proper lighting is determined by the quality and quantity of light. Approximately 150 footcandles are recommended for computer usage. Most lighting problems are caused by too much light, resulting in in glare on documents or reflections on monitors. Although most workers prefer to be near a window, windows do cause glare.

Ambient light fixtures (which illuminate the entire office area) combined with task lighting (which lights specific work surfaces) create the most effective lighting system.

Noise

Office conversations, ringing telephones, and outside noise account for most office noise. Sound-absorbent materials used throughout the building, acoustical enclosures on printers, and layout are effective means of reducing office noise. Office noise should be less than 65 decibels (Casady 1989).

Energy

Energy needs include lines for power, phones, and data. To determine these needs, these questions need to be answered: Do you expect high growth in computer usage? Do you expect to rearrange workstations frequently? If so, how often?

Access floors raised of the structural slab provide an excellent solution for distributing heat, air conditioning, and wiring for data and telephone services. These floors have unlimited capacity and may be accessed at any point by service units without calling an electrician. Additionally, quality and speed of transmission will not be affected as your transmission needs grow.

PERIN OFFICE SYSTEMS
3903 Spaulding Drive, Atlanta, GA 303
(404)555-1719

Please check to be sure that I haven't missed any errors. Mr. Holms prefers the modified block letter style with mixed punctuation. Thanks tr

March 17, 19--

Ms. Jessica Shimer
2905 Sandcastle Dr.
Tallahassee, FL 32308-9625

Dear Ms. Shimer:

Thank you for your interest in the Perin Laser Copier, Model 212. Enclosed is a brochure detailing its unique features, its specifications, and its cost.

The Perin Laser Copier is the most technologically sophisticated copier on the market today. This laser-driven copier uses a scanner to digitize originals. Text (including columns) can be manipulated before printing begins. Because it is digital, the laser copier can transmit images to other printers and produce high-resolution copies in seconds.

After you have had a chance to review this brochure, I will give you a call to provide you with additional product or price information or to set up a demonstration. In the meantime, please call me at the number listed above if you have any questions.

Sincerely yours,

Robert C. Holms
Sales Representative

tr
Enclosure

Current date

All Product Managers
COMPUTER MAINTENANCE

As more and more managers are using computers, it becomes increasingly important that everyone practice good procedures for operating and maintaining computers and peripherals. Please review these procedures to keep your equipment in good working order.

1. Keep your equipment away from direct sunlight, heat vents, and open windows. Extreme temperatures can damage chips and other components.

2. Keep food and beverages away from equipment and diskettes.

3. Eliminate smoking near equipment. Tobacco smoke contains dust and tars that can damage or clog equipment.

4. Keep paper clips that have been stored in a magnetic container away from diskettes. Keep diskettes away from magnets or any electronic equipment. These items contain magnetic fields that can cause portions of text to be erased.

5. Use antistatic mats under your computer. Static electricity can cause memory loss.

6. Never oil your printer or any part of your system. Oil will clog the machine.

7. Check power requirements to be sure your power is sufficient.

8. Do not take anything apart, even if in your judgment, you can fix it. Call Helen Mathys (Ext. 278), and she will contact our service representative.

xx

Chapter 7, Job 5

Louisville
Chamber of Commerce
Civic Plaza Building
701 West Jefferson Street
Louisville, KY 40202-4161

WELCOME, ROSE SOCIETY MEMBERS

A gracious welcome awaits you and the other 2,500 Rose Society members and guests who will be attending the Society's convention in Louisville. This meeting is the second Society meeting to be held here, the first one having been held 23 years ago. Both the organization and the city were a bit younger and smaller then.

Louisville, a fun-filled vacation city, is located right on the northern edge of southern hospitality. You'll find it has lots of new things going for it--things like River City Mall in the heart of downtown, turn-of-the-century neighborhoods offering boutiques and restaurants, and Churchill Downs, home of the Kentucky Derby. Louisville is also located near many other Ky. attractions.

Maps and brochures highlighting points of interest are included in your registration packet. We hope that your stay in Louisville will be enjoyable and that you will visit our city again.

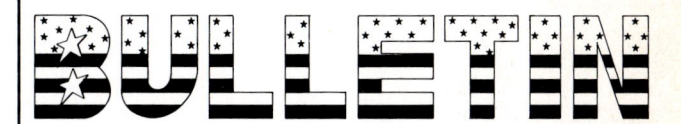

BULLETIN

Chapter 8, Job 1

Louisville
Chamber of Commerce
Civic Plaza Building
701 West Jefferson Street
Louisville, KY 40202-4161

May 29, 19--

Ms. June Davidson
3162 North Tenth Street
Wichita, KS 67203-9149

Dear Ms. Davidson:

We are delighted to send you the information you requested about Queen's Park.

From the map on the enclosed brochure, you can see that the park is divided into 5 areas. Each of the areas includes games and rides, exhibits, live entertainment, concession stands, a restaurant, and a zoo. Something is available for every member of the family to enjoy.

On the enclosed list of rates, you will note that persons under 6 and those over 70 are admitted free. Note, too, there are always group rates available.

The park operates on a daily schedule in the summer but is open only on weekends during the spring and fall. The staff post announcements on the bulletin board at the entrance to the park.

The enclosed pamphlet contains a coupon good for a $5 discount on one adult admission ticket. We hope you will be able to use it soon.

Yours very truly,

Alexis J. McQuillan
Department of Tourism

rl
Enclosure

Chapter 8, Job 2

Louisville
Chamber of Commerce
Civic Plaza Building
701 West Jefferson Street
Louisville, KY 40202-4161

February 10, 19--

Ms. Alita Guitterez, President
National Sales Company, Inc.
3910 Trade Street
Louisville, KY 66044-5133

Dear Ms. Guitterez:

Welcome to Louisville! We are delighted that your company chose to locate in our city.

As a member of the business community, you are eligible for membership in the Louisville Chamber of Commerce. On the first Tuesday of each month, we have a breakfast meeting to which each new businessman and businesswoman are invited. This meeting provides an opportunity for us to get to know each other. Each third Tuesday, we have a dinner and a business meeting at the Arbor Inn.

We hope your schedule will permit you to attend the next meeting, which will be at Tom's Restaurant on the 6th at 7:30 a.m. The Hospitality Committee are in charge of this function. If you can attend, please call 555-2361.

To welcome you as a new member of the business community, we plan to feature a story about your company in the next issue of our newsletter. Will you submit an article of about 500 words about your company? To meet our deadline, we will need the material by the 25th.

Again, welcome to our city!

Very truly yours,

Ms. Cynthia Shepherd, Director
Public Relations

tr

Chapter 8, Job 3

267

Chapter 8, Job 4

Current date

Ms. Ruth Niemer, Director
Convention Housing Bureau
United States Chamber of Commerce
P.O. Box 54321
Des Moines, IA 50318-4126

Dear Ms. Niemer:

Don Jenkins, our president, and I `are` planning to attend the United States Chamber of Commerce Convention in your city, August 20-25.

Since the number of rooms reserved for this convention `is` limited, we want to make our reservations now. Both of us `want` single rooms. Although it is not necessary, we would like to have adjoining rooms.

We would prefer to stay at the convention hotel; however, `if` it is not available, either the Plaza or the Palmer Hotel `is` `all right`.

There are a number of `Chamber` members planning to attend. They or their secretaries `have` the housing information; you should be hearing from them soon.

Sincerely yours,

Alexis J. McQuillan
Director of Tourism

xx

Chapter 9, Job 1

School of Technology
City College
989 Johnstown Road
Chesapeake, VA 23310-4961

January 10, 19--

Mr. Greg West
4572 East Ninth Street
Chesapeake, VA 23310-4572

Dear Mr. West:

Your request for readmission to City College has been reviewed by members of the Admissions Committee and *me* at our January 8 meeting.

After the *third* semester, a student must have earned 36 hours, and *he or she* must have a grade-point average (g.p.a.) of 1.80 in order to stay in school. You *were* enrolled for three semesters. During that time you earned 27 hours with a *g.p.a.* of 1.67. Consequently, admission is not possible at this time.

We recommend that you attend summer school. If you do so, you must take 2 3-hour courses that are relevant to your major area of study. With a grade of C or better in each of these courses, the committee and I will be happy to reconsider your petition for admission.

Sincerely yours

Joseph W. Wrenn
Associate Dean

rv

Chapter 9, Job 2

School of Technology
City College   MEMO

TO: All Staff
FROM: Brian Layman, Dean
DATE: January 10, 19--
SUBJECT: Establishment of Task Force

At the suggestion of numerous staff members, the College is pursuing the idea of purchasing a new computer system. Members of the staff with whom I have talked have shown enthusiasm for this idea.

A task force of interested staff members *is* being formed to conduct a more thorough study of the needs of the staff. Based on its findings, the task force will then make recommendations for the purchase of a computer system and software. I need to know who among the staff *is* interested in serving on the task force.

Responsibilities of the task force include the following: (1) assessing the staff's needs, (2) gathering information about computer systems, (3) evaluating the available software, and (4) making recommendations to the purchasing agent and *me*.

If you *are* interested in actively researching this topic and meeting this challenge, please send me a memo indicating your interest.

rv

Chapter 9, Job 3

School of Technology
City College   MEMO

TO: Department Chairpersons
FROM: Brian Layman, Dean
DATE: January 10, 19--
SUBJECT: Parking Regulations

In an effort to improve staff parking conditions, the Campus Traffic Committee *has* developed the following parking regulations. Will you please see that all members of your department receive this information regarding the new regulations.

1. All current campus parking permits expire on September 14. Beginning September 15, new permits are required.

2. Parking is prohibited in areas other than those designated for staff members.

3. Permanent permits must be displayed in the rear window of all vehicles.

4. Any staff member in possession of more than 5 unpaid parking tickets will forfeit *his or her* right to park on the campus.

Because Chief Security Officer Calder has been aware of the numerous problems in parking, he was very receptive to the recommendations made by the staff. In fact, it was *he* who suggested that such a committee be formed.

rv

January 10, 19--

Dr. Rosemary Scott
6170 Eighth Avenue, W
Chesapeake, VA 23320-8574

Dear Dr. Scott

You may attend the Phi Beta Lambda regional conference to be held in Lynchburg March 25-27.

Kristen Gray, the organization's president, spoke for all the Phi Beta Lambda members when she requested you be permitted to attend this meeting. The members, many of whom are preparing for the state contests, have the enthusiasm but not the resources for attending the meeting.

Please bring back information that will be relevant to the contests. You will likely get a lot of additional miscellaneous materials that will be beneficial to both you and the members.

While I recognize that the meeting comes at a very busy time in the semester, I hope you will regard this experience as an opportunity for professional growth.

Please let me know whether you will be able to attend. Incidentally, you will be reimbursed for your expenses. Just be sure to report them to the secretary.

Sincerely yours

Brian Layman, Dean

xx

Chapter 9, Job 4

RIDGE HILLS REAL ESTATE
3168 NORTHWOOD DRIVE
RUSTON, LA 71270-6653
318-555-8700

July 12, 19--

Mrs. Elizabeth Harris
Claims Representative
United Insurance Company
32940 South 3d Street
Ruston, LA 71272-8977

Dear Mrs. Harris:

On June 23 Todd Roberts suffered personal injuries from an accident in a car driven by Carol Shultz. Both are agents for our company and were on company business at the time of the accident.

Mr. Roberts was a passenger in Mrs. Shultz's car when she past another vehicle and entered into the path of an oncoming car. The site of the accident was on Highway 37 about 5 miles from Bloomington. Mrs. Shultz has been cited for negligent operation of a motor vehicle.

Brett Arnold, council for our company, advised Mr. Roberts not to proceed with a suit. Mr. Roberts agreed.

Should there be further developments in this situation, I will notify you.

Yours very truly

Walter T. Hartsell
Gen. Mgr.

xx

Chapter 10, Job 1

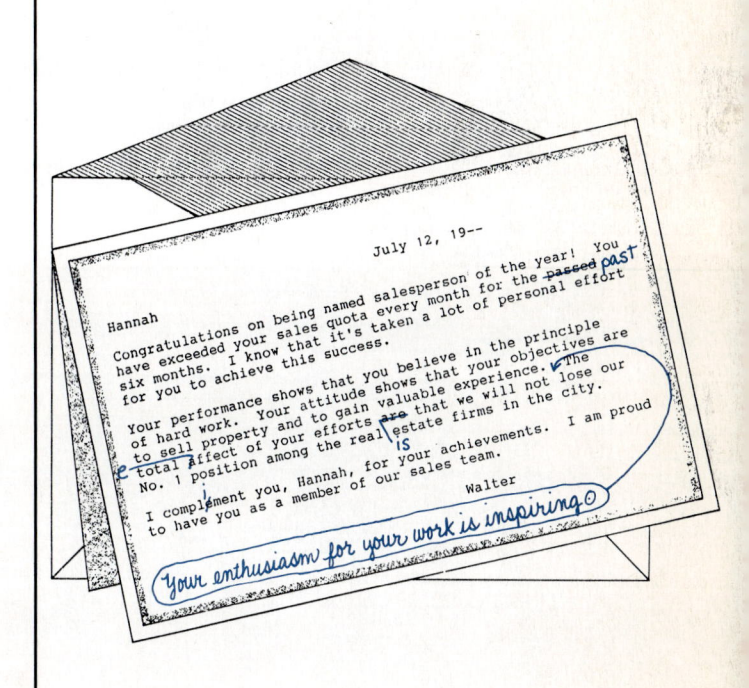

RIDGE HILLS REAL ESTATE
3168 NORTHWOOD DRIVE
RUSTON, LA 71270-6653
318-555-8700

July 19, 19--

Mr. Bryant Whitehurst
Plant Manager
Toggs Manufacturing Co.
P. O. Box 7022
Indianapolis, IN 46208-9865

Dear Mr. Whitehurst:

The one hundred-acre sight on Five-Mile Rd. you wanted for your new plant is available. Even though the owners have already had a lot of inquiries about the property, I believe they're prepared to accept your proposed offer.

If you are serious about obtaining this property, I suggest that you submit an offer immediately. Real estate prices are not likely to decrease further this year. In fact, it is likely to increase.

Because the owners insist on a cash transaction, you may want to get your counsel's advise about the best way to finance the principal loan. Please call me to discuss your plans about this matter.

Sincerely yours,

Walter T. Hartsell
General Manager

yri

Chapter 10, Job 2

July 12, 19--

Hannah

Congratulations on being named salesperson of the year! You have exceeded your sales quota every month for the past six months. I know that it's taken a lot of personal effort for you to achieve this success.

Your performance shows that you believe in the principle of hard work. Your attitude shows that your objectives are to sell property and to gain valuable experience. The total affect of your efforts are that we will not lose our No. 1 position among the real estate firms in the city.

I complement you, Hannah, for your achievements. I am proud to have you as a member of our sales team.

Walter

Your enthusiasm for your work is inspiring

Chapter 10, Job 3

269

To: Jill Carmichael, Advertising Manager
From: Walter Hartsell, General Manager
Date: July 12, 19--
Subject: Review of Advertising Costs from 1990 to 1992

The attached table shows a comparison of our advertising costs for the past three years. Will you look at the costs to see where we can reduce our expenses without affecting our business. I am all ready to shave the budget wherever possible.

Should we drop any of these methods in order to allot more funds to other areas? If so, specify which ones need to be omitted and which, if any, need to be increased. All accounts except Television and Newspapers appear to have increased 50 percent or more during this time.

Let me have your comments by July 17.

xx

Attachment

ADVERTISING COSTS

	1990	1991	1992
Television	$14,795.72	$15,947.50	$19,588.52
Radio	870.08	1,180.12	1,409.61
Newspapers	11,096.79	12,785.63	14,589.70
Homebuyer's Guide	2,292.18	2,933.88	3,885.12
Circulars	3,597.28	4,672.30	5,047.90
Miscellaneous	641.20	769.44	961.80
Total	$33,293.25	$38,288.87	$45,482.65

Chapter 10, Job 4

McDowell Travel Agency
4500 West Kennedy Blvd.
Tampa, FL 33609-3421

November 5, 19--

Ms. Mary McCarthy
1166 Norwood St.
Cleveland, OH 44197-8032

Dear Ms. McCarthy

Thank you for your letter requesting brochures, price lists, and information sheets about cruises leaving from Miami, FL. Your inquiry comes at a time when a number of interesting, exotic cruises are available at fabulously low prices.

You should receive up-to-date information within the next few days from three cruise lines about their winter cruises. Consider each line's total cost, the cost of air travel to the point of departure, and the itinerary when you are making a choice. You will note that prices for a seven-day cruise range from $795 to $2,150 per person.

The enclosed brochure will provide helpful decision information about choosing a cruise. After you make your decision about the cruise, fill out and return the data sheet. You can then leave everything in our hands and rest assured that satisfactory arrangements will be made.

We look forward to serving as your liaison with the cruise line of your choice and assisting you in any way possible.

Sincerely

Mrs. Laura E. Spellman
Marketing Manager

dp
Enclosures

Chapter 11, Job 1

PARADISE ISLAND
"Your Bahamas Getaway Vacation"

Ask about our
• Golf and tennis clinics
• Honymoon packages
• Island dance lessons

From $299
★ 3 days/3 nights including air
(3 nights from $339 including air)

1 800 555 2435

McDowell Travel Agency

Please rush FREE brochures and information to:
NAME _____
STREET _____
CITY _____ STATE _____ ZIP _____

Chapter 11, Job 2

270

CHOOSING THE RIGHT CRUISE FOR YOU

As the winter cruise season approaches, discounts on ship fares are plentiful in the travel industry, and smart consumers are taking advantage of the special bargains. Now is the time to consider taking a leisurely cruise if it is one of those things that will fulfill a lifetime dream for you. If you have never pictured yourself as a passenger on a cruise ship, consider the following facts.

Passenger Profile

Once cruises were a pastime for the rich and the retired. Today cruises are taken by individuals from all walks of life and all income levels. Forty-eight percent of cruise passengers now earn less than $30,000 a year. Nearly half are under 45 years of age, and 10 percent are under 25.

It is estimated that more than a million and a half people will take cruises on about one hundred cruise ships this year, and cruise lines are competitively vying for this business. Two qualities of the cruise experience are being stressed: value and convenience. Now is a great time to participate in what some refer to as the "cruise revolution."

Cost and Convenience

Consider the price of the average cruise. The price that you pay includes accommodations, baggage handling, meals, entertainment (including first-run movies and live performances), room service, daily activities ranging from computer lessons to disco dancing, travel to any number of ports, and reduced air fare from home.

Convenience is another factor that you must consider as you contemplate taking a cruise. In what other way can you travel from one country to another without having to unpack and repack your bags? Where else can you spend days or weeks without having to open your wallet or purse constantly? You don't even have to worry about arranging travel schedules, making plane reservations, or waiting long hours in airports.

Activities on Board

To be sure that your cruise proves to be all that you expect it to be, you should take the time to find out what the various cruise lines offer and to whom they cater. For example, some cruise lines cater to children and make special provisions for them. Other lines cater only to adults. Some provide for academic pursuits while others primarily provide entertainment and recreation.

Chapter 11, Job 3

You should give some thought to the types of activities that you might enjoy. Do you want entertainment? Do you want some physical fitness programs? Do you want to learn something? At least one cruise ship doubles on a regular basis as a floating university. There is no pressure to participate in any of the activities provided by the cruise line. If you wish, you can relax on the deck with a book or watch television in your own cabin. You can choose your own recreation.

Cruise Itinerary

Another important criterion that will effect your selection of a cruise is the planned itinerary of the ship. Consider the number of stops you would be making and the ports you would be visiting. Is there particular cities you have always wanted to tour? Your travel agent can provide you with a detailed list of port choices and itinerary options to help you decide on the best cruise.

How to Get Started

After you have made some of the major decisions regarding your preferences in a cruise, see your travel agent. The agent can help determine which cruise suits your needs and provide answers to any other questions that you might have. In other words, your travel agent is the liason between you and the cruise line. Contact your travel agent today and take the worry out of traveling.

Chapter 11, Job 3 (Continued)

CELEBRATE THE FOURTH OF JULY AT SAHARA RESORT--
WE'LL GIVE YOU THE WORKS!

A picnic in the park, a swim in the lake, rousing music topped off by fireworks, and laser shows that light up an almost perfect starry night. What better way to show your spirit than with a Fourth of July celebration bursting with color and excitement at Sahara Resort.

After a satisfying day of family fun, lie back and enjoy music by "The Deltas" and a performance by the "Flying High Circus" while we bring the celebration to a blazing close with a laser show and fireworks display rated to be among "the Best in Florida." For a real All-American Fourth of July celebration, the place to be is Sahara Resort.

For more information or reservations, contact the McDowell Travel Agency toll free.

1-800-555-2435

Chapter 11, Job 4

PERFECT-PAGE SOFTWARE: THE ANSWER TO YOUR IN-HOUSE PUBLISHING NEEDS.

For more information on our cost-effective plan for producing professional-quality reports, brochures, and forms right in your office, fill out and return the attached card today. Upon receipt of your inquiry we will send you information about PERFECT-PAGE desktop publishing software.

Name _____ Position _____
Company _____
Address _____
City _____ State _____ Zip _____

Mail today to: The Upjohn Software Company
1010 Rives Street
Baltimore, MD 21226-2318

Chapter 12, Job 1

The Jackson Herald
News Release

April 22, 19--
RELEASE: IMMEDIATELY
CONTACT: Savella Marino

JACKSON COLLEGE HOSTS DESKTOP PUBLISHING SEMINAR

JACKSON, Ohio. More than fifty local companies are expected to attend the second annual Desktop Publishing Seminar at Jackson College on May 5, 19--. This year the seminar will integrate new graphics software packages with desktop publishing applications.

According to Dr. Sharon Hilltop, seminar coordinator, this seminar is particularly designed for companies that want to produce cost-effective, high-quality documents. The utilization of desktop publishing is especially appropriate in producing company brochures, advertising flyers, reports and proposals, newsletters, and business forms.

The conference will begin at 9 a.m. and conclude at 4 p.m. Included in the $50 registration fee will be a luncheon and seminar materials. To register for the seminar, call 614/555-2208.

###

Chapter 12, Job 2

271

DESKTOP PUBLISHING

A New Concept in Document Production

What is desktop publishing? Why is it capturing the attention of so many people? Will it become the standard way to produce ads and brochures? to produce all corporate communications?

Although some of these questions may remain unanswered for some time, the occurrence of one thing is sure: Desktop publishing is definitely changing the communication process for a number of organizations.

What is Desktop Publishing?

Desktop publishing describes the process by which a professional-quality document is produced using a microcomputer system and a special software.

> "Desktop publishing may replace word processing software for final output."

Software

WYSIWYG, which stands for "What you see is what you get," characterizes much of the composition software. WYSIWYG (pronounced "wisywig") means that what you see on the screen is exactly what you'll get when the copy is printed.

Printer

The utilization of laser printers facilitates the use of multiple type sizes and styles on the same page. Graphics (letterheads, logos, and freehand drawings done with a mouse) and scanned images (photographs or drawings) may be integrated into the copy with ease.

Is There a Market?

Until recently, professional-quality printing was strictly limited to the domain of graphic arts professionals: typesetters, pasteup artists, and printers. Desktop publishing enables typeset-quality pages to be produced in-house. With a little practice and some good design ideas, managers, office workers, or students can create their own layouts complete with borders, rules, columns of type, and other graphic elements.

> "Now companies can produce cost-effective, near-typeset quality documents in-house."

How Is It Used?

A questionaire sent to more than ninety users revealed that people are using desktop systems for an array of different purposes: ads, brochures, business forms, manuals, proposals, newsletters, resumes, and transparency masters.

Katherine Smith, vice president of a publishing consulting firm, predicts that desktop publishing will replace word processing software for final output. One consultant commented, "Now companies can produce cost-effective, near-typeset quality documents in-house."

This handout on desktop publishing was prepared by Kim Stephens. For more information on desktop publishing systems call her at extension 212.

Chapter 12, Job 3

REGISTRATION LIST
DESKTOP PUBLISHING SEMINAR
May 5, 19--

Name	Company	ZIP Code	Work Phone
Burns, Jerry	The Tripp Company	45692-6441	562-8461
Finlay, Jean	Hammermill, Inc.	45640-8462	543-8942
Fredericks, Laurie	Stevens Industries, Inc.	45640-8902	543-1431
Konica, Michelle	Gaylord and Mortensen	45640-8148	543-9112
Pascarella, Lou	Cullen Business Systems	45640-4416	543-2949
Radwan, Lee	UMI Lighting	45640-2316	543-9444

Chapter 12, Job 4

DISCOVER YOUR PLACE IN THE GARDENS

If you haven't seen Colonial Gardens yet, you're in for a treat. Discover the natural wonder of 10,000 acres of lakes, woodlands, gardens, and wildlife. Enjoy golf on our 18-hole, par-73 championship course. Take advantage of all the extras Colonial has to offer: tennis, swimming, nature trails, riverboat rides, and fishing.

All 210 of our rooms at the Colonial Inn have a waterfront or forest view, private balconies, and comfortable furnishings. If you're planning a meeting put us in your plans. We have more than 11,000 square feet of meeting space. You can also enjoy our charming cottages or romantic villas.

COLONIAL GARDENS

Colonial. It's for families, couples, and friends. It's for people who appreciate natures beauty.

Call 1-800-555-5420 for reservations or information.

COLONIAL GARDENS

272   **Chapter 13, Job 1**

**State of Georgia
Department of Tourism**
7653 Peachtree Road, NE
Atlanta, GA 30308-9873

19-- CALENDAR OF EVENTS
SOUTHEAST GEORGIA

March
- 10-17 — St. Patrick's Day Celebration, Dublin, Bobbie Whitehead — 912/273-4260
- 26-27 — Harness Festival, Hawkinsville, Dale Morrow — 912/429-3109

April
- 14-28 — Dogwood Festival, Jesup, Pam Barnes — 912/290-3129

May
- 10-24 — Vidalia Onion Festival, Vidalia, Lewis Green — 912/646-1293

June
- 14-28 — Blueberry Festival, Alma, Wanda Arnold — 912/913-2175

July
- 4 — Fantastic Fireworks Extravaganza, Dublin, Craig Southern — 912/273-8261

October
- 6 — Great Pumpkin Festival, Cochran, Joanne Keena — 912/934-6112
- 27 — Georgia Sweet Potato Festival, Ocilla, Gail Marshall — 912/486-2681

Chapter 13, Job 2

**State of Georgia
Department of Tourism**
7653 Peachtree Road, NE
Atlanta, GA 30308-9873

August 4, 19--

Ms. Gladys McCoy, Director
Macon Tourism and Trade
410 Riverside Drive
Macon, GA 31204-3798

Dear Ms. McCoy:

We're getting ready to publish next year's edition of Georgia--A Peach of a State and know you will want to provide updated copy for our article on central Georgia.

Please provide current information (avoid repetition of last year's material) on planned activities, festivals, etc., on the enclosed card by September 30 so that we may incorporate your ideas into next year's publication and calendar of events.

Will Macon participate as usual in "Georgia Days," which will be held at Cumberland Square in Atlanta on June 17-21 next year? Please send in your registration and exhibit needs on the enclosed form so that we may request appropriate space for you.

I understand you had a record attendance at the Cherry Jubilee Street Party last month. Congratulations on the excellent job you do in organizing and motivating your volunteers.

Sincerely

Charles B. Tamara
Associate Commissioner for Tourism
State of Georgia

sj

Enclosures

Chapter 13, Job 3

The coastal area of the state holds charms that will entice the visitor to return. Savannah, with its combination of European architecture, historic sights, meandering streets, and lush foliage, is the beginning of this 100 miles of coastline. A busy port city on the Savannah River, Savannah was founded 257 years ago as England's last colony in the New World.

About an hour's drive south is the parallel port city of Brunswick and the more southern resort islands. First laid out in 1771, Brunswick is now a modern port handling sea tonnage from the world over. Fascinating Victorian architecture is represented in all its glories here. Roads from Brunswick lead to four islands known as "golden" for their sunny skies and warm sands nearly year-round.

St. Simons Island has lush resorts, vacation condos, horse stables, marinas, tennis courts, golf courses, boutiques, art galleries, and interesting restaurants. The small-town village boasts a community park and fishing pier. The view of Jekyll Island and the Atlantic Ocean is well worth the climb up the 1872 lighthouse.

Sea Island lies across a thin strip of marsh; its fame is rooted in the easy affluence and elegance of the Gilded Age. A focal point is The Cloister, one of the country's enduring grand resort hotels.

Jekyll Island, formerly the vacation spot for some of America's wealthiest families, evokes the quiet feeling that time has stopped

Chapter 13, Job 4

2

and history has been preserved. Leisure-time pursuits include biking and jogging, pier and deep-sea fishing, tennis, and water skiing.

Cumberland Island, 16 miles long, is one of the world's largest barrier islands. With outstanding scenic qualities, Cumberland offers natural wildlife, backpacking, and camping.

Chapter 13, Job 4 (Continued)

---

abea NEWS RELEASE

AMERICAN BUSINESS EDUCATION ASSOCIATION
1111 South Wabash Street
Chicago, IL 60605-2912

February 28, 19--

More than two thousand ABEA members are expected to converge on Miami, Florida, when the American Business Education Association's thirty-eighth annual convention convenes on March 13. This information comes from Dr. Sue D. Briley, President of the ABEA. Dr. Briley, a Business Education instructor at Parks College, is serving the first year of a two-year term as President.

Using the theme "Get In Touch With The Future," Dr. Briley and her convention committee have planned a program featuring numerous leaders in the business education areas of Accounting, Computer Science, Keyboarding, and Economics.

Approximately fifty textbook publishers and equipment salespeople are expected to exhibit their products.

The Program Committee has obtained two well-known persons to be speakers: Zig Ziglar at the luncheon and Diane Nichols at the banquet. The Florida ABEA members are sponsoring Florida Night, an evening of fun on the 13th of March in the Orange Bowl.

The convention will end with a business session on the 17th of March.

Dr. M. Ellen Schwartz

###

Chapter 14, Job 1

273

American Business Education Association
1111 South Wabash Street
Chicago, IL 60605-2912

January 13, 19--

Dr. Sandra Newton, professor
School of Business Education
Eastern University
1072 East 6th Street
Charleston, Ill. IL

Dear Mrs. Newton

Make your plans now to head south in late winter to attend the American Business Education association's annual convention. The Palms hotel in Miami, FL, will be the sight for this 38th meeting, which beings on March 13 and ends on March 17.

"Get In Touch With The Future" is the theme of this year's convention. Several new, pertinent topics have been added, one of which is "Experiential Learning--The Educational Tool for the Future."

Send your hotel registration directly to the Palms Hotel, 2552 Third Avenue, SW, Miami, FL 33129-0615, no later than February 28 to ensure a room at the convention hotel. You may guarantee your reservation by including your Am express card number.

To register for the convention, complete the registration form that is in the December issue of the ABEA journal. Mail it along with your check to this office by Feb. 15.

Plan to attend the opening session followed by Florida Night in the Orange Bowl; a watch containing a miniature TV will be given away as a door prize.

Please extend an invitation to students and emphasize the value of participating in a conference designed for professional growth.

Very truly yours

Dr. M. Ellen Schwartz

aa

Chapter 14, Job 2

Amy:
Will you proofread carefully the copy of the proposed convention budget, comparing it to the attached draft. Please return it by 2:30 as Dr. Criley is insistant that it be ready for the Executive Board meeting at 4. I apologize for the rush job.
Morgan

PROPOSED BUDGET FOR ABEA CONVENTION
Palms Hotel
Miami, Florida
March 13-17, 19--

Income
　　Registration Fees　　　　　　　　　　$16,000
　　Meals (Luncheon, Banquet)　　　　　　30,000
　　Sale of ABEA Materials　　　　　　　　1,500
　　Total　　　　　　　　　　　　　　　　$48,000
Disbursements
　　Hotel (rooms and meals)　　　　　　　$36,000
　　Registration Supplies, Printing　　　　5,500
　　Refunds for registrants　　　　　　　　　500
　　Convention Flowers and Decorations　　　700
　　Fruit Baskets　　　　　　　　　　　　　　300
　　Favors (ABEA Mugs)　　　　　　　　　　3,500
　　Acknowledgments, Thank-You Gifts　　　　250
　　Honoria for Entertainment　　　　　　　600
　　Miscellenous Expenses　　　　　　　　6,650
　　Total　　　　　　　　　　　　　　　　$48,000

Chapter 14, Job 3

ABEA MEMBERS

Let us tell you about a package plan that ABEA and Scottish Airlines have put together for those of you who are going to the convention in Miami. The plan consists of three parts:

1. Discounted Plane Fares. You don't have to be rich and famous to afford our fares. Just by being a member of ABEA, your flight rates alone will be discounted by 25 percent.

2. Rental Cars. Rental cars are included for those who want to travel in the area; north to Fort Lauderdale, which is located on Highway 1, or south to Key West, among other places. In addition to our special rate, you can get 500 bonus miles on your Frequent Flyer Bonus Program just by showing your boarding pass when you pick up your car.

3. Activities Information. Miami has some fascinating activities scheduled for mid-March. Selected ones include the ballet, Lady of the Camellias; the play, A Man for All Seasons; and the Dade County Council of Arts Folk Festival. We can get the ballet and play tickets for you at a discount if you will let us know how many of each you will need. More information can be obtained from This Week in Miami, the weekly magazine published by the Miami Chamber of Commerce.

Other attractions include historic buildings, several fine malls, and a four-block shopping extravaganza called the Miracle Mile. Bus tours and harbor cruises are also available.

To take advantage of this offer, fill in this form and mail it to the address given. After receiving it, we will make the arrangements for you.

- -

Name_____ School_____
City_____ State_____ ZIP_____
Departure date_____ Return date_____
Number of ballet tickets_____ Play tickets_____

Mail to: ABEA, 1111 South Wabash Avenue, Chicago, IL 60605-2912.

Chapter 14, Job 4

TOPS TOPS
(Temporary Office Personnel Services)
909 Linden Avenue
New Orleans, LA 70128-9400

August 15, 19--

Ms. Mary Dunstan
2001 King Alfred Drive
Baton Rogue, LA 71304-6421

Dear Ms. Dunstan

You asked me to make suggestions for improving the efficiency of TOPS. I believe I have an idea that will have a very positive effect on the productivity of this office, and I am eager to hear your reaction to it.

Recently I had the opportunity to examine a new publication from South-Western Publishing Company entitled Programmed Proofreading. I recommend that we ask each temporary office employee to work through this book before beginning an actual assignment with us. If this recommendation is implemented, the payoff in productivity and accuracy will, in my opinion, be well worth the cost of the books.

Presently, I am spending too much time proofreading the documents produced by our employees. Many of the errors that I find are addressed in the book. Working through exercises that contain those errors will impress upon our employees the importance of accuracy. While I would continue to proofread the documents, I believe my proofreading time would be cut considerably.

There are 16 chapters in the third edition of Programed Proofreading. I found Chapter on content errors to be especially helpful.

Sincerely

Charles Daniels

jp

Chapter 15, Job 1

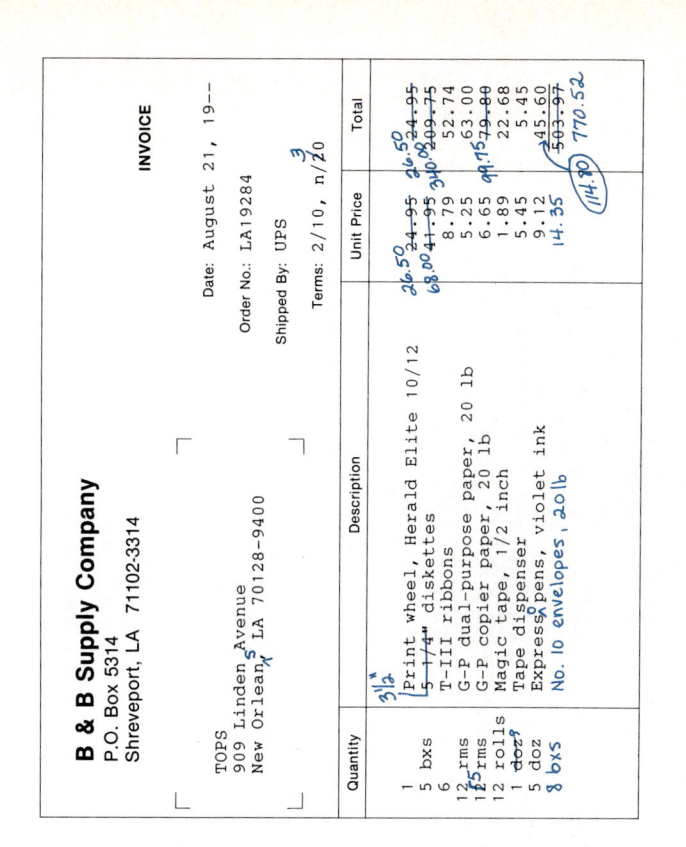

Chapter 15, Job 2

B & B Supply Company
P.O. Box 5314
Shreveport, LA 71102-3314

INVOICE

Date: August 21, 19--
Order No.: LA19284
Shipped By: UPS
Terms: 2/10, n/20

TOPS
909 Linden Avenue
New Orleans, LA 70128-9400

Quantity	Description	Unit Price	Total
1 bxs	Print wheel, Herald Elite 10/12 [3½"]	26.50	26.50
6 ~~5~~ bxs	5-1/4" diskettes	24.95	~~24.95~~ 149.70
12 rms	T-III ribbons	~~68.00~~ 41.95	~~340.00~~ 209.75
12 ~~25~~ rms	G-P dual-purpose paper, 20 lb	8.79	52.74
25 rms	G-P copier paper, 20 lb	5.25	63.00
12 rolls	Magic tape, 1/2 inch	6.65	~~90.75~~ 79.80
1 doz ?	Tape dispenser	1.89	22.68
5 doz	Express pens, violet ink	5.45	~~45.60~~ 503.97
8 bxs	No. 10 envelopes, 20 lb	~~9.12~~ 14.35	~~(114.80)~~ 770.52

Chapter 15, Job 3

TRAVEL EXPENSE REPORT

Travel Authorization No.: 239407
Employee Name: Rebecca D. Wolcot̲t̲
I.D. Number: T6103
Destination: Jackson, Mississippi
Date(s): 8/25/-- to 8/27/--
Purpose of Trip: AMS meeting, meeting with manager of Meridian TOPS

Date	From	To	Miles	Amount	Air	Taxi	Meals	Lodging	Total
8/25	New Orleans/Jackson		179	46 54	--	--	22 50	60 00	129 04
8/26	Jackson/Meridian (round trip)		165	42 90	--	--	3̶0̶ 70	60 00	13̶3̶ 4 60
8/27	Jackson/New Orleans		179	46 (45)	--	--	11 55	--	58 0̶0̶ 09
TOTALS			135 98 ~~89~~				65 ~~64~~ 75	120 00	321 73 ~~320 64~~

Signature _____
Date: 8/29/--
Total Expenses (Attach Receipts): $~~320.64~~ 321.73

Chapter 15, Job 4

IS FLEXPLACE IN YOUR VOCABULARY?

Some years ago, many organizations adopted flextime, making it possible for employees to juggle work schedules and home responsibilities. Now there is "flexplace" (sometimes referred to as "telecommute").

What Is "Flexplace"?

The flexplace arrangement enables employees to do all or part of their work away from the corporate office. Various forms of decentralized workplaces are possible: satellite offices or branch offices that are linked electronically to main offices, neighborhood offices that are shared by employees of different companies, and employees' homes.

For Whom Is Flexplace Designed?

Flexplace is best implemented in information-intensive firms that have computers, networks, and databases installed: banks, insurance companies, and financial institutions. Managers and professionals who work independently, as well as computer specialists, secretaries, and data entry specialists, are best suited for flexplace. Consider these cases:

--Disabled from a severe accident, Leslie Longhill works at home as a program analyst; her computer is linked by phone lines to clients' computers and to her company's computer.

--Rod and Frances Brewer operate a consulting business for a large corporation. Frances also works part-time as a programmer for a large corporation.

Chapter 15, Job 4 (Continued)

--A composition firm employs Janet Gabor to meet its fluctuating needs. At the same time, Janet, mother of three young children, also fulfills her family responsibilities.

Advantages of Flexplace

Some employers consider flexplace as a means for reducing costs, attracting personnel who would not otherwise be available for employment, and increasing productivity. A large insurance company estimated that 16 home-based persons produced 50 percent more than persons working at the office. Another computer company reported a 35 percent increase in productivity.

Today when people are seeking an alternative to the high costs and frustrations of commuting to work, many persons consider that the freedom of workplace may be an important benefit. Flexplace enables persons who are self-motivated and who manage their time well to work independently. However, caution must be exercised that working at home doesn't create additional stress by making it impossible to escape the demands of the office.

Conclusion

Is flexplace for you? Everybody must analyze his or her own situation to determine what is best. Research and experimentation by organizations that are willing to establish flexible arrangements will reveal whether they are viable.

275

Deerfield College

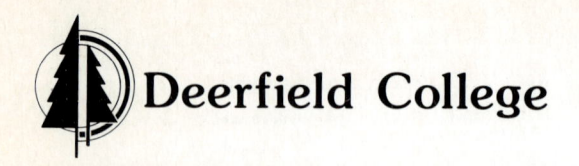

January 8, 19--

Ms. Lee Spanner
5920 Old Dixie Road
Forest Park, GA 30050-3058

Dear Ms. ~~Lee~~ Spanner

Thank you for your interest in the Administrative Services programs at Deerfield College. As per your request, I am sending you ~~under separate cover~~ a copy of the college catalog.

You will see from the Administrative Services AAS degree program (page 91 of the catalog) that your electives may be concentrated in your area of interest--office management. Because you have work experience, you may also earn advanced placement credit for certain skills you already have, such as keyboarding and business machines.

Call me at 555-3482 if I can answer any questions or be of assistance. We look forward to your enrolling with us at Deerfield.

Sincerely,

Mrs. Jennifer Thomas, Coordinator
Administrative Services

lw

Chapter 16, Job 1

SANTA IS CHECKING HIS LIST - - -

AND YOUR NAME IS NOT ON IT!

The list he's checking is the National Business Education Association (NBEA) membership roster. NBEA needs your renewal ~~is needed by NBEA~~. Your membership dues are used ~~utilized~~ to ~~drum up~~ enthusiasm for all phases of business education and to serve as a unifying agency among regional and other groups dedicated to business education.

Our NBEA staff and our national, regional, and state leaders are committed to shaping the future of business education and to increasing our strength so that the profession will continue to grow ~~by leaps and bounds~~.

But we must have your dedication and commitment to the profession. And the first way you can show this commitment is by joining NBEA. Because you have been a member in the past, I know that you appreciate the ~~super~~ benefits the organization provides: a publications program, national convention, legislative liaison, research and development activities, and awards programs, to name a few.

Please give yourself an important holiday gift. Get your name back on the list by completing the enclosed application and sending your dues today.

Jennifer Thomas
Georgia Membership Director

Enclosure

P.S. If you have already joined NBEA this year, please forgive Santa; he's awfully rushed at this time of year and may have overlooked your name.

Chapter 16, Job 2

SUMMER STUDIES AT DEERFIELD
FOR
ADMINISTRATIVE SERVICES
SUMMER 19--

~~Turn over a new leaf and~~ come to summer school for only two days a week for eight weeks or two nights a week for four or eight weeks and get ahead in your program.

Have at least five weeks of fun in the sun--trips with your family or friends--or whatever!

1st Session	June 27 - July 24	ADMS 111/112	6-8:40 p.m. T/Th
		Keyboarding I, II	
2nd Session	July 26 - August 23	ADMS 212/213	6-8:40 p.m. T/Th
		Word/Information Processing I, II	
Full Session	June 27 - August 23	ADMS 260	9-11:40 a.m. M/W
		Business Communication	
		ADMS 250	6-8:40 a.m. M/W
		Automated Accounting I	
To Be Arranged		ADMS 202 Business Machines	
		ADMS 222 Occupational Internship	

276

Chapter 16, Job 3

Current Date

Business Education Teachers

SPEAKERS FOR CLASSES AND MEETINGS

Are you looking for speakers for your classes or student organization meetings? [OMIT COPY] The Administrative Services faculty at Deerfield College are starting a Speakers Bureau. We are available to speak to your students on one of the following topics:

1. Office Jobs Available and the Skills Needed to Succeed

2. Current Trends in Office Automation

3. Professional Organizations: How Can They Help Me?

Also available before or after the presentation is a seven-minute slide program about Administrative Services at Deerfield College. This presentation describes the types of programs and courses our department offers.

Please complete the attached form and return it to us within two weeks. We would like to meet with you and your students.

Deerfield College Administrative Services Faculty

xx

Attachment

Chapter 16, Job 4

Chapter 17, Job 1

BEST Natural Products Co.

INTEROFFICE COMMUNICATION

TO: All Personnel
FROM: Sylvia
DATE: October 24, 19--
SUBJECT: Good Telephone Techniques

Because our voices are the first contacts that many individuals have with us outside the company, we should strive to make a good first impression when we answer the telephone. Please review the following suggestions for developing better telephone techniques.

TELEPHONE TECHNIQUES

I. INCOMING CALLS

    A. Answer promptly.
    B. Greet the caller pleasantly.
    C. ~~You should~~ identify yourself and your company.
    D. Be helpful to the caller.
    E. Be courteous at all times.
    F. Screen calls as directed by your employer.
    G. Write messages accurately and ~~so they are~~ legibly.
    H. Let the caller end the call.

II. ~~MAKING~~ OUTGOING CALLS

    A. Be sure of the number.
    B. Plan your call.
        1. Know what you are going to discuss.
        2. Have related materials at hand.
    C. Let the phone ring several times before hanging up.
    D. Identify yourself.
    E. (Remember) Time zone differences.
    F. Be considerate.

Chapter 17, Job 2

BEST Natural Products Co.
1402 Graham Road
Bryan, TX 77801-4128

INVOICE

Mrs. N. D. Rosenbloom
219 Ortiz Drive
Groves, TX 77619-3120

Date: October 25, 19--
Order No.: BH090190
Date Shipped: October 25, 19--
Shipped Via: UPS
Terms: 2/10, n/30

Quantity	No.	Description	Unit Price	Total
2	LA-6180	Liquid Cleanser	3.30	6.60
1	NB-90010	Laundry Concentrate, 10 lb	19.95	19.95
2 qt	ST-8011G	Concentrated Fabric Softener	5.10	10.20
		Total		36.75
		Sales Tax		2.21
		Total Amount		38.96

BEST Natural Products Co.
1402 Graham Road
Bryan, TX 77801-4128

INVOICE

Kwai San Restaurant
427 Center Street
Lufkin, TX 75901-1200

Date: October 25, 19--
Order No.: BH090191
Date Shipped: October 25, 19--
Shipped Via: UPS
Terms: 2/10, n/30

Quantity	No.	Description	Unit Price	Total
10	BD-7307	Automatic Dishwashing Concentrate, 47 oz	8.95	89.50
1	BH-5565G	Concentrated Cleaner, 5 gal	97.20	97.20
5 qt	BG-2249	Germicide	11.85	59.25
12	AE-2349	Scouring Cleanser	4.75	57.00 ~~4.75~~
		Total		302.95 ~~250.70~~
		Sales Tax		18.18 ~~15.04~~
		Total Amount		321.13 ~~265.74~~

Chapter 17, Job 3

BEST Natural Products Co.
1402 Graham Road
Bryan, TX 77801-4128
Telephone: (409) 555-7862

October 25, 19--

Mrs. N. D. Rosenbloom
219 Ortiz Drive
Groves, TX 77619-3120

Dear Mrs. Rosenbloom

Your telephone order of October 25 is being shipped by UPS today.

Thank you for your interest in our nonpolluting and biodegradable cleaning products and our water purification system.

Our cleaning products are not only throughly effective and safe for cleaning but also safe for the enviornment.

The quality of water is one of the most important choices we have to make today. Our company is working to develop a water purifying system that is economical, space-saving, and ~~will be~~ easy to operate. The system should be available in about six months. We will send you a brochure about the system as soon as the brochure becomes available.

Mrs. Rosenblooom, we do appreciate your business. Any time you have questions about our products, please call us using our toll-free number, 800-555-642-?

Sincerely yours

Mrs. Carol A. Gary
Customer Service

kr

Chapter 17, Job 4

October 25, 19--

Mr. Henry Z. Loran
1735 North 16 Street
Lake Jackson, TX 77566-9800

Dear Mr. Loran

You are both my friend and my valued customer. That is why I find it embarrassing to have to write to you about your overdue account.

When you applied for credit, I extended it to you on the basis of your credit record. Until recently your account has been classified as "prompt pay." Now it is in jeopardy of being placed in the "slow pay" category.

Why you have not paid is puzzling to me. You must have a good reason, and I want to find out what that reason is. Please use this opportunity to explain and to let me help you work something out. Otherwise, your "prompt pay" rating will be in danger.

To retain your good credit reputation, you must send a check today for $280.48, the amount that is now more than 60 days overdue.

Cordially

Carl Barr
Credit Manager

xx

277

POSTTEST

Part A Proofread each of the following sentences for mechanical errors (spelling, abbreviation, word division, number expression, grammar, punctuation, capitalization), content errors, conciseness, and clarity. Use the appropriate proofreading symbols to indicate corrections. Sentences often contain more than one error. If a sentence is correct, write C after it. Solutions to the Posttest begin on page 278.

1. It was he who called. *C*
2. Send letters to whomever is on the list.
3. No one can spell as well as her. [she]
4. We believe that our's is the best cleaning product on the market.
5. One criterion for selecting the textbook is cost. *C*
6. Our historian and reporter, Bob Lewis, has done a good job. *C*
7. Here is the book and tape that you requested. [are]
8. A number of children is enrolled in the Summer reading program. [are]
9. Everyone has his or her own problems. *C*
10. The employer promiced Sam and I. [me]
11. Many people drop the s from Dr. Daniels' name. *C*
12. An error tolerance of 0.05 percent is permissable. [i]
13. Yes, the team has all ready made their decision. [its]
14. Will you please purchase 12 16-ounce tumblers? [sp]
15. Fantastic! We won the $10 million lottery! *C*
16. Delta Flight 210 leaves from gate 7 at 8 a.m. on October 14.
17. S. America sells a lot of coffee to the United States. [sp]
18. To make this jacket you will need 3 yards of 54-inch material.
19. Ben Williams was transferred to the Loan department.
20. About two thousand people attended the Raleigh Summer Festival on July 29th.
21. More than three fourths of the stockholders voted on the 13 proposed changes. *C*
22. Lynn Forrest, M.D., has opened an office in the Brody Building which is located at 5410 West Eighth Street, Topeka, Kansas.
23. Al is 6 feet 6 inches tall, and he has difficulty getting into his sports car. *C*
24. The Goodwill Games, which were held in Seattle were telecast by WTBS-TV.

25. Ken paid $2.45 for the card and $6.25 for the booklet, making the total $8.60.
26. ~~Per~~ As your request**ed** ~~nine~~ 9 of the 75 letters must be redone.
27. Did you read the article "An Open Letter to the President"?
28. Planning, as he drove to work, how he would handle the personnel problem. — Fragment
29. They gave the papers to Earl and ~~I~~ me for safekeeping.
30. Terry explained the procedure; and then left us to carry it out.
31. To enroll more members is our first goal for this year. C
32. Julie Koenig, an efficient, hard-working employee, received a $1,500 raise.
33. "I have a problem," said the treasurer, "about how to correct this error."
34. Her latest book, *How to Decrease Your Taxes*, is on the best-seller list. C
35. When a manager buys disks, he or she must order the 3.5" size.
36. The spelling test was easy; that is why everyone ~~past~~ passed.
37. The check came today; therefore, I can pay my bills promptly.
38. Performers appearing on the telethon are: Casey, Dean, Jerry, and John.
39. After paying six months' rent, we were given a receipt.
40. Paula took the shelled ~~the~~ pecans and then stirred ~~it~~ them into the cake.
41. The correct division for each of these words is omit-ted, guess-ing, sales-person, be-gin, and evacu-ate. (Note: Check word division.)
42. The three insurance plans affected 54 employees working in four branch locations. C
43. My friends think I (either) have forgotten their addresses or the fact that I owe them letters.
44. Three honor students in art—Kim, Karen, and Keith—were recognized at the awards ceremony.
45. Underwood, Wooten, and Gaylord, Inc., will move its office to the Blount Building. C
46. Mayor-elect Jenkins, as well as the city council members, is attending the Washington, D.C., conference.
47. After I have completed the Business Communication course, I will be eligible for a job with *The Sun Times*.
48. As a rule, we provide maintenance service for all our products except the small appliances. C
49. Our company's regional offices are located in Atlanta, Georgia; Austin, Texas; and Salem, Oregon.
50. Your responsibilities will include opening the office, sorting the mail, and ~~to file~~ filing the ~~correspondents~~ correspondence.

Posttest Solution   279

Part B Proofread the following letter for mechanical and content errors. The letter should be formatted in modified block style with mixed punctuation. Use the appropriate proofreading symbols to indicate changes.

Boxberger Repair Shop
1266 East Windsor Road
Pontiac, MI 48054-1266

June 22, 19--

Reed /cap Supply Company
666 (S.) Capitol Avenue
Lansing, ~~Mich.~~ MI 48933-0666

DS

~~Dear Mr. Reed~~ Ladies and Gentlemen :

DS

[Indent paragraph] On June 15, I received the water hose I ordered from your company. When I connected the hose to the outlet at my shop, it burst during the second day of usage. Your guarantee (copy enclosed) states that the hose is supposed to operate without defect for 90 days. Therefore, I am requesting a replacement for the defective hose.

Please let me know what I should do to return it.

DS

Yours very truly,

Ray Boxberger, Manager

bdl
Enclosure
pc B. Perkins

APPENDIX

FREQUENTLY MISSPELLED WORDS

absence	congratulations	February	nickel	recognize
accidentally	conscientious	fluctuating	ninety	recommend
accommodate	conscious	foreign	ninth	reference
accumulate	consensus	fourth	noticeable	regard
achievement	convenience	fulfill	occasionally	relevant
acknowledgment	copyright	further	occurrence	repetition
advantageous	courteous	grammar	omitted	representative
amateur	criticism	gratitude	opportunity	responsible
analysis	debtor	guarantee	pamphlet	restaurant
analyst	decision	height	parallel	schedule
analyze	definitely	immediately	particularly	separate
announcement	description	implemented	permanent	similar
annual	develop	incidentally	permissible	sponsored
apologize	development	independent	perseverance	strictly
appropriate	efficiency	insistent	persuade	sufficient
approximately	eligible	insurance	possession	surprise
bankruptcy	eliminate	integral	precede	therefore
beginning	embarrass	integrate	prerequisite	thoroughly
believe	emergency	itinerary	privilege	transferred
brochure	emphasize	judgment	procedure	unanimous
bulletin	enthusiasm	knowledgeable	productivity	undoubtedly
calendar	environment	leisure	profited	usable
category	equipped	liaison	programmer	utilization
changeable	exaggerate	license	psychology	valuable
column	experience	maintenance	pursuing	volume
commitment	explanation	merchandise	quantity	waive
committee	extension	miniature	questionnaire	writing
compatible	facilitate	miscellaneous	realize	
competitive	familiar	mortgage	receipt	
concession	fascinate	necessary	receiving	

COMMONLY MISSPELLED U.S. CITIES

Abilene, TX
Albuquerque, NM
Amarillo, TX
Anaheim, CA
Anchorage, AK
Baltimore, MD
Baton Rouge, LA
Berkeley, CA
Birmingham, AL or MI
Bismarck, ND
Boise, ID
Butte, MT
Charlotte, NC
Chattanooga, TN
Chesapeake, VA
Cheyenne, WY
Chicago, IL
Cincinnati, OH

Des Moines, IA
Detroit, MI
Dubuque, IA
Durham, NC
El Paso, TX
Erie, ...
Fay...
A...
For...
Fre...
Gai...
Ho...
Ho...
Ind...
Kal...
Lar...
Las...
Lin...
Lo...

Louisville, KY
Memphis, TN
Miami, FL
Milwaukee, WI
Minneapolis, MN

Roanoke, VA
Sacramento, CA
St. Louis, MO
San Antonio, TX
San Bernardino, CA
San Diego, CA
San Francisco, CA
San Jose, CA
Santa Fe, NM
Savannah, GA
Schenectady, NY
Shreveport, LA
Sioux City, IA
Syracuse, NY
Tallahassee, FL
Tucson, AZ
Wichita, KS
Worcester, MA

STATE, DISTRICT, AND ...

Alabama, AL
Alaska, AK
Arizona, AZ
Arkansas, AR
American Samoa, AS
California, CA
Colorado, CO
Connecticut, CT
Delaware, DE
District of Columbia, DC
Florida, FL
Georgia, GA
Guam, GU
Hawaii, HI
Idaho, ID
Illinois, IL
Indiana, IN
Iowa, IA
Kansas, KS

New Jersey, NJ
New Mexico, NM
New York, NY
North Carolina, NC
North Dakota, ND
No. Mariana Islands, CM

..., OK
..., OR
..., PA
..., PR
..., RI
..., SC
..., SD
..., TN
Territories, TT
..., VT
Virginia, VA
Virgin Islands, VI
Washington, WA
West Virginia, WV
Wisconsin, WI
Wyoming, WY

282   Appendix